Mison 美森教育

丛书主编◎孙乐

剑桥领思备考
强化系列

Linguaskill

Linguaskill

50天攻克

剑桥领思 通用英语

阅读篇:16天
READING

编著◎郭佳佳

大连理工大学出版社
Dalian University of Technology Press

图书在版编目（CIP）数据

50天攻克剑桥领思通用英语. 阅读篇. 16天 / 郭佳佳编著. -- 大连：大连理工大学出版社, 2023.12
（剑桥领思备考强化系列丛书 / 孙乐主编）
ISBN 978-7-5685-4656-0

Ⅰ. ①5… Ⅱ. ①郭… Ⅲ. ①英语水平考试—阅读教学—自学参考资料 Ⅳ. ①H310.41

中国国家版本馆CIP数据核字（2023）第197425号

大连理工大学出版社出版
地址:大连市软件园路80号　邮政编码:116023
发行:0411-84708842　邮购:0411-84708943　传真:0411-84701466
E-mail:dutp@dutp.cn　　　URL:https://www.dutp.cn/

辽宁星海彩色印刷有限公司印刷　　　　大连理工大学出版社发行

幅面尺寸：185mm×260mm　　印张：16.5　　　字数：318千字
2023年12月第1版　　　　　　　　2023年12月第1次印刷

责任编辑：李玉霞　　　　　　　　　　责任校对：孙　扬
封面设计：美森教育

ISBN 978-7-5685-4656-0　　　　　　　　定　价：60.00元

本书如有印装质量问题，请与我社发行部联系更换。

前　言

一、剑桥领思考试简介

　　剑桥领思（Linguaskill）是由英国剑桥大学英语考评部研发的一项在线英语测评，它借助人工智能技术来测试应试者的英语水平。剑桥领思以模块的形式，全面测试听、说、读、写四项英语技能。剑桥领思的特点是快速便捷，由于是在线考试，考生可以随时随地参加。同时，相比于传统考试，剑桥领思可以快速提供成绩，一般在考试完成后72小时内考生就可以获得成绩报告。考试成绩对标欧洲语言共同参考框架（CEFR），该框架是描述学习者语言能力的国际标准。由于其高效、准确、权威，目前剑桥领思已获得数千家国际组织机构的认可，在中国，认可剑桥领思成绩的组织机构包括但不限于中国石油天然气集团、中建国际建设、中国五矿集团、美的集团、中山华利集团、中国教育国际交流协会、山东省人民政府外事办公室、西交利物浦大学、宁波诺丁汉大学、昆山杜克大学等。

　　根据考生自身目标和想测试的英语种类，剑桥领思考试分为剑桥领思通用英语测评和剑桥领思职场英语测评两种。其中，剑桥领思通用英语测评更侧重日常生活与学习等英语应用语境，测试的是日常生活英语。

二、本套书编写目的

　　目前市面上针对剑桥领思通用英语的备考书籍几乎处于空白，想要参加这一考试的考生急需相关的学习材料。美森教育图书编撰委员会的教师为了满足广大考生的这一需求，编写了本套图书。希望本套图书能成为众多考生领思通用英语备考路上的得力助手，帮助大家获得高分。

三、本套书核心特色

1. 以题型为主线，循序渐进提升

　　本套书包含听力篇、阅读篇、写作篇和口语篇4个分册，每个分册都是以考试题型为主线来编排的，考生在学习时可以逐个题型一一突破，稳扎稳打。在内容上，本套书

非常注重知识的循序渐进，每个题型的学习都按照"基础篇—提分篇—实战篇"来设置，考生先通过"基础篇"掌握每种题型考查的内容和基本的答题策略，然后通过"提分篇"来深入学习重点、难点，最后通过"实战篇"来做题巩固。这一结构安排可以让考生将每种题型吃透，对知识的掌握也会更牢固。

2. 精选高质量的实战习题，充分练习

本书编写团队的教师均是剑桥领思中国运营中心的合作教师，且一线教学经验丰富。本套书中的所有实战习题也都是在总结大量领思通用英语考试试题后编写而成的，与真实考试的考点、难度高度一致，对于考生来说是非常宝贵的练习材料，考生一定要充分练习，多进行总结，实现稳步提升。

3. 提供详细解析，厘清解题思路

无论任何考试，相信考生都清楚一点：做题重要，总结更重要。因此，本套书中的所有习题均提供了详细的解析，为考生梳理解题思路。考生在做完题后要仔细研读解析，总结每道题的考点、自己理解有误之处以及未掌握的知识点，有针对性地查缺补漏。

4. 全真模拟题，考前冲刺提升

本套书每个分册的最后一章都提供了全真模拟题，让考生在考前进行模拟练习，做最后的冲刺提升。每套全真模拟题都力求还原真实考试，考生可以检验自己的学习成果，之后对于不足再次进行强化训练。

5. 英籍外教原声音频，扫码即听

本套书听力分册的音频由英籍外教录音，发音纯正，语音、语调、停顿等细节也充分还原真实考试。书中提供了二维码，扫码即可获取音频，方便考生随时随地听音。

在筹备及编写本套书的过程中，美森教育图书编撰委员会以下资深教师委员也参与了工作，他们分别是：孙乐、孙旭、李建荣、姚宝娇、杨李健、陈雪、孙晓丹、于京圣、姚宝丹、邢思毅、隋良东、景作鹏、皮姗姗、邢汝国、景文学、隋秀丽、景文菊、陈威、刘庆杰、孙连军、宋海蛟、周翼、潘宇、尹辉、张清川、孙成伟、辛连厚、吴馨玲、邵淑梅、侯殿东、朱汉民、王守斌、韩琦、崔林杰、杨丹、王海军等，在此一并表示感谢。

希望本套书能够切实地帮助到广大的领思考生，同时也真诚期待热心的读者对本书提出宝贵的意见和建议。

美森教育

www.mison.cn

关注"剑桥领思考试"微信公众号

随时随地获取领思学习干货

致读者

亲爱的本书读者：

在您正式开始学习本书之前，请务必扫描下面的二维码观看本书的使用讲解视频，同时获取读者专享免费课程。

视频是本书作者团队的代表教师特意录制的，为大家介绍了本书的特点和结构，并精讲了高效使用本书的具体方法。

读者专享免费课程是给大家额外附赠的领思通用英语备考课（价值599元），该课程适用于所有备考领思通用英语的考生，为大家详细讲解备考重点，提供考试指导。

相信大家在看过视频和课程之后，能够有效提高学习效率，最终获得领思高分。

目　录

Part 3　完形填空

Part 4　开放式完形填空

Part 5 拓展阅读

考前冲刺——全真模拟题

参考答案与解析

带你认识剑桥领思阅读考试

一、剑桥领思通用英语测评概述

1. 剑桥领思通用英语测评简介

剑桥领思（Linguaskill）是一项由剑桥英语考评部（Cambridge English Assessment）于2020年推出的，权威、快速、便捷的在线英语水平考试，学校可以通过测试了解应试者的英语听、说、读、写水平。

该测试具有以下几个特点：

（1）便捷。考生可以在熟悉的场地，在方便的时间安排考试，并通过电脑与手机联网在远程监考环境下参加测试。

（2）模块化考试。考生可以根据需要评估的能力，自由选择测试模块。目前共分为三个主要模块，分别是听力与阅读（Listening and Reading）、写作（Writing）和口语（Speaking）。

（3）自适应性测试。阅读和听力模块以人工智能为支撑，采用最先进的自适应性理论，试题的难易程度会依据应试者的前一题回答情况而调整。

（4）出分快。考生通常可以在考试后72小时内获得成绩报告，节约了等待的时间。

模块构成：

听力与阅读（二合一）	约60~85分钟
写作	45分钟
口语	约15分钟

根据考生自身目标和想测试的英语种类，考试分为剑桥领思通用英语测评和剑桥领思职场英语测评两种。剑桥领思通用英语测评更侧重日常生活与学习等英语应用语境，测试的是日常生活英语。考试话题包括学习和工作、未来计划、购物、旅行和科技等等。

领思考试通用英语测评的特点在于它是一项侧重应用能力并且涉及广泛主题的考试，考试的材料多与日常生活学习相关，因此，对日常生活各项主题与词汇的把握是考生获得高分的一个重要因素。领思考试通用英语测评的用词一般相对日常化，单词含义也往往较为简单，但涉及的话题较为宽泛，需要考生多加积累相关常识与词汇。

2. 剑桥领思通用考试流程

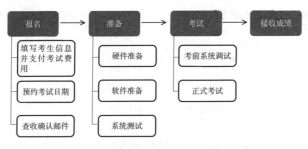

二、阅读考试概述

剑桥领思通用考试的阅读和听力考试属于计算机自适应性测试，能根据考生的答题情况自动调整题目难度，因此题目数量和顺序以及答题时间不是固定的。在阅读和听力考试中，考生每回答一个问题，计算机就能更加了解其英语水平。当考生回答的题目达到一定数量，计算机能准确判断其英语水平后，测试就会结束。

在自适性测试的过程中，每道题都会由计算机根据考生前一道题的回答结果来进行选择。一般来说：

➤ 如果考生答对一道题，计算机接下来会选择难度更高的一道题

➤ 如果考生答错一道题，计算机接下来会选择难度更低的一道题

下图简单地展示了自适性测试的过程：

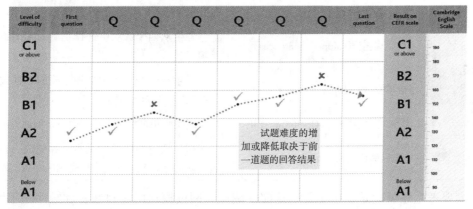

剑桥领思通用阅读考试主要考查考生的日常英语阅读能力，试题包含短句与文章两种类型。考试测评生活场景中的语言运用，语言的基本功底，以及对长篇阅读的理解，可全方位检测考生的语言运用能力，信息理解、检索、整合能力等。阅读和听力部分为一场考试，阅读部分在听力部分之后进行。

阅读考试开始界面

Now click on the **right arrow** to begin the Reading part of the test.

三、阅读考试题型介绍

阅读模块（Reading）由5种题型构成，具体如下：

考试模块	题型	考查重点
阅读	阅读并选择（Read and Select）	考生阅读包含简短文字的通知、标识、备忘录或者信件，然后从三个选项中选择最符合短文意思的句子或短语。
	句子填空（Gapped Sentences）	考生从四个选项中选择正确的单词给句子填空。
	完形填空（Multiple-choice Gap-fill）	考生从四个选项中选择正确的单词或短语给短文中的句子填空。
	开放式完形填空（Open Gap-fill）	考生将单词填写在短文中空格的地方。
	拓展阅读（Extended Reading）	考生读一篇较长的文本，并完成一系列选择题。题目顺序与文中信息顺序一致。

需要考生注意的是，由于是自适应性测试，阅读模块的题目数量和顺序是不固定的，以上5种题型在考试中并非完全按上述顺序出现，完形填空和开放式完形填空这两种题型有时可能只出现一种，题型的顺序和数量取决于考生答题时的具体表现。

四、阅读考试评分标准与成绩解读

考生通常会在考试结束后72小时内收到成绩报告单。有别于传统的纸质成绩单，剑桥领思的成绩将以电子邮件的方式发送至考生邮箱，考生也可通过剑桥考评官网在线查询。

剑桥领思通过使用CEFR欧标来评测考生的真实英文能力，采用分段方式（82~180+）来报告成绩，同时提供从"A1及以下"到"C1及以上"多个级别来反映考生的英语水平，成绩报告单样式如下：

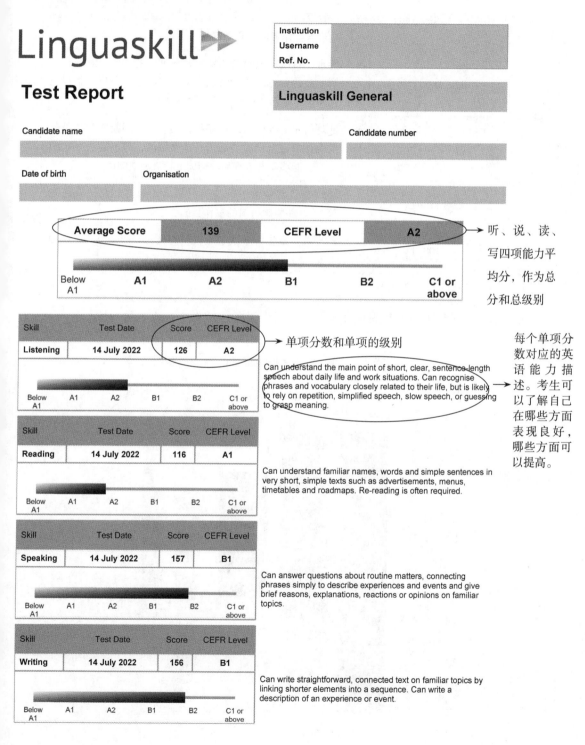

Linguaskill ▸▸

Institution
Username
Ref. No.

Test Report

Linguaskill General

Candidate name

Candidate number

Date of birth

Organisation

Average Score	139	CEFR Level	A2

Below A1 | A1 | A2 | B1 | B2 | C1 or above

听、说、读、写四项能力平均分，作为总分和总级别

Skill	Test Date	Score	CEFR Level
Listening	14 July 2022	126	A2

Below A1 | A1 | A2 | B1 | B2 | C1 or above

单项分数和单项的级别

Can understand the main point of short, clear, sentence-length speech about daily life and work situations. Can recognise phrases and vocabulary closely related to their life, but is likely to rely on repetition, simplified speech, slow speech, or guessing to grasp meaning.

每个单项分数对应的英语能力描述。考生可以了解自己在哪些方面表现良好，哪些方面可以提高。

Skill	Test Date	Score	CEFR Level
Reading	14 July 2022	116	A1

Below A1 | A1 | A2 | B1 | B2 | C1 or above

Can understand familiar names, words and simple sentences in very short, simple texts such as advertisements, menus, timetables and roadmaps. Re-reading is often required.

Skill	Test Date	Score	CEFR Level
Speaking	14 July 2022	157	B1

Below A1 | A1 | A2 | B1 | B2 | C1 or above

Can answer questions about routine matters, connecting phrases simply to describe experiences and events and give brief reasons, explanations, reactions or opinions on familiar topics.

Skill	Test Date	Score	CEFR Level
Writing	14 July 2022	156	B1

Below A1 | A1 | A2 | B1 | B2 | C1 or above

Can write straightforward, connected text on familiar topics by linking shorter elements into a sequence. Can write a description of an experience or event.

阅读模块的分段分数及对应的英语能力描述如下表所示：

阅读水平	领思阅读考试成绩	英语能力描述
熟练自如	C1及以上（180+）	• 能充分理解各种领域中高难度、长篇幅的文章，不仅能读懂文章，还能总结文章的主旨及核心要义，通过文字内容发掘作者的观点与态度。
独立运用	B2（160~179）	• 能理解自己所熟悉的领域的较高难度的文章，能判断文章的表达重点。阅读时能基本不使用参考资料，做到独立阅读，并且能适应阅读不同领域的文章。
独立运用	B1（140~159）	• 能理解与个人经历或兴趣相关的文章，判断文章各段落的表达重点。同时能阅读其他领域语言风格较为平实的文章，能够在参考资料的辅助下较流利地阅读。
基础能力	A2（120~139）	• 能理解日常生活中的文字材料（如信件、便条、通知等），并能明确材料的写作目的。
基础能力	A1（100~119）	• 能理解日常生活中文字量较小的材料（如标识、方位图等）。
/	A1及以下（82~99）	/

考生也可以通过下表对领思成绩与其他剑桥考试的成绩做一个直观的对比。

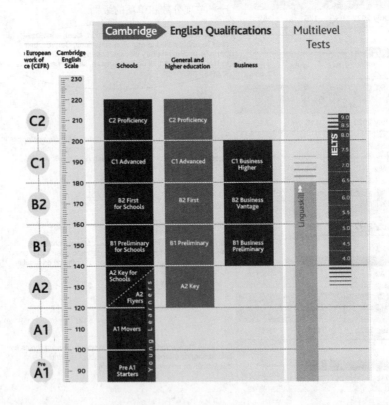

Part 1　阅读并选择

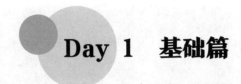

Day 1 基础篇

一、题型介绍

　　阅读考试的第一类题型是阅读并选择。命题方式为单选题，考生需要阅读一段简短的材料，然后从三个选项中选出最符合短文描述的内容。给出的短文材料通常为通知、广告、标识、信件等。材料的篇幅较短，通常不会超过70个词。三个选项一般是对短文中细节的叙述或是对短文整体内容的概括，所以这一题型主要考查的是考生对短篇材料细节的理解和对短篇阅读材料概括的能力。

二、考试界面

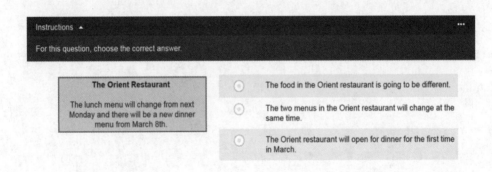

✓　界面最上方是本部分的答题说明

✓　界面左侧是阅读材料

✓　右侧是选项，通过点击每个选项前面的○进行选择

✓　点击右下角箭头可以切换到下一题（注意答完的题目不能再切换回来进行检查）

三、考查技能

本题型在整个阅读考试中难度相对偏低，主要考查考生以下技能：

- ✓　通知、邮件、广告、标识等生活中常见材料的阅读与理解
- ✓　对细节的理解和对内容的概括
- ✓　对单词、短语、句子的改写

接下来，我们来了解这种题型常见的命题方式

1. 细节题

这类题目在该题型中出现的频率最高，问题往往围绕材料中的某一要素展开，主要考查考生准确提取材料中细节信息的能力。这类题目中，正确选项往往是对原文的同义改写。如材料中出现"There is no parking area available.", 选项中可能会出现"There is no vacant parking space.", 选项中的"vacant parking space"就是"parking area available"的同义转换，二者均表示"空余的停车位"的含义，句意同为"那里没有空余的停车位"。

这种题目的错误选项往往会通过以下方式迷惑考生：

一是张冠李戴，即将材料中的信息与所指的对象进行错误匹配，这种形式的选项在考试中十分常见。如材料中说到"Children under 5 is free, and under 10 is half price.", 而选项中将年龄和所享受的优惠匹配错误。

二是偷换概念，即将材料句子中的某一要素替换为其他表达。如材料中表述为："The park will open on alternate days.", 而选项中出现"The park will open every two days.", 注意"alternate days"为隔日，而"every two days"为每两日，二者表达的含义不同。

三是忽视条件，即选项将材料中的某一表述提取出来后，改变了其中的条件。如材料中出现"Weather permitting, we are going to play football tomorrow.", 而选项中可能会将"Weather permitting"去掉，显然这是错误的。

2. 归纳题

这种题目往往着眼于宏观层面，即从材料整体出发进行设问，要求考生能够将细节信息整合，并进行归纳。这类题目往往会按照下面的方式设问：

一是根据材料中的信息，总结一般的规律，但选项中会出现具体场景。如材料中说到"Please change your ticket 48 hours before departure.", 选项中可能会出现"某人想改签某月某日的票，他必须在某月某日前操作"的表述。

二是根据材料中的已知信息进行合理的猜想。如材料中说到"If you place an order, you will get more information.", 选项中说到 "The recipient hasn't placed an order yet."。可知该选项正确，如果收件人还未下过订单，就不会收到这样的信息。

四、答题策略

这一类型的题目所涉及材料的典型特点是贴近生活，基本上涵盖了生活中常见的短篇材料，如通知，广告、信件、标识等。与考试中的其他题型相比，这类题型难度并不大，阅读这类文章时需要注意以下几个要素：

✓ Who：材料的发送者是谁，受众是谁或哪一群体
✓ When：材料所述的事件是在什么时间发生或以怎样的顺序发生
✓ Where：材料中的事物会出现在什么地点或材料中所述事件在什么地点发生
✓ What：材料中提到了什么或读者需要注意什么

注意：不是所有材料都包含以上所有要素。

针对本题型，建议采用以下答题思路：

1. 通读短文，充分理解

这一步骤中，首先要明确材料是何种类型，阅读选项，并根据选项判断试题通过什么方式进行设问。这样在阅读材料时能有的放矢，并且能带着问题阅读，提高信息抓取的效率。

通读短文，根据四大要素（4W）充分理解材料的内容。尤其要注意容易成为命题依据的内容，如材料中涉及的人物、地点、时间、因果、条件句等。如果遇到不认识的单词，可以根据前后内容来推断其意思。

2. 细读选项，对比分析

仔细阅读三个选项，对比分析它们所表达的真实含义，并根据不同的设问方式采取不同的分析方法。

对于细节类题目，我们可以采取以下方法：

（1）充分与材料结合，明确选项中的叙述内容与材料中的哪一部分相对应，弄清材料中的叙述对象是谁，并分析材料与选项中相关叙述的对象是否相同，识别出"张冠李戴"的错误。

（2）分析选项中的内容与材料相关内容的叙述是否一致，各成分的表述是否一致。由于该题型中的正确答案往往是材料内容的同义改写，所以考生经常会将某些易混淆的概念视为同义改写，不进一步辨别，从而导致错误。

（3）重视原文中的限定性成分，观察选项中的内容在材料中是否有条件要求或适用范围限制。考试中考生经常因为将注意力集中于主干成分，而忽视限定性成分，造成不

必要的错误。

　　对于归纳类题目，可以采取以下方法：

　　找出材料中的相关表达，这一步骤并不是只限于含义相同或相近的表达，因为归纳类题目往往无法从字面含义上寻找到依据。如果材料中的语句可以成为得出选项内容的依据，那么该选项即为正确答案。因此，考生需发掘出材料语句和选项语句的本质含义。

3. 回到原文，确认答案

　　这一步骤经常被考生忽略，但却很重要。这一步骤的目的在于验证所选择的答案是否正确。在对比选项与材料内容时，我们往往将目光集中于材料中的某一个句子，而忽视了其他语句是否也含有与选项相关的内容。我们着重从这一方面，对比选项和材料内容，验证答案，并且这也可以判断一些难以确认的选项。

五、典型例题及详解

CAR PARK

Parking charges apply to all parking spots, including those constructed for VIP drivers.

A. Free parking spaces won't be provided for the VIP drivers.

B. All these spaces are constructed for the need of VIP drivers.

C. Drivers who are not VIP will be punished if they park here.

➢　策略指导

通读短文，掌握短文内的四大要素（4W）

Who：司机

When：不涉及

Where：停车场

What：停车费适用于所有停车位，包括为贵宾司机建造的停车位。

➢　试题详解

【答案】A

【材料类型】通知

【题目翻译】

A 不会给贵宾司机提供免费停车位。

B 所有停车位都是为满足贵宾司机的需求而建。

C 非贵宾司机在此停车会受到处罚。

【解析】本材料为一则通知，文字量较小。材料中说到"停车费适用于所有停车位，包括那些为贵宾司机建造的停车位"，所以可知在这里的任何停车位上停车都要收费，即使贵宾也不例外。所以A选项正确。

材料说的是停车收费的问题，并没有提到停车位为谁而建，所以B选项错误。C选项说的是非贵宾司机在此停车会受罚，材料中没有涉及与之相关的内容，所以C选项错误。

六、同义改写练习

在下面横线上填入不同的词或短语来表达原句意思。

1. The neighbourhood committee will construct a large activity center soon.

The neighbourhood committee will construct a _____ activity center soon.

The neighbourhood committee _____ a large activity center soon.

A large activity center _____.

2. He won the prize thanks to the diligence and good luck.

He won the prize _____ the diligence and good luck.

_____, he won the prize.

He didn't win the prize _____.

3. The exhibition is going to open at 12 noon on Saturday.

The _____ is going to open at 12 noon on Saturday.

The exhibition _____ at 12 noon on Saturday.

The exhibition _____ 12 noon on Saturday.

4. Many students are good at dealing with the urgent task.

_____ students are good at dealing with the urgent task.

Many students are _____ dealing with the urgent task.

_____ is the strength of many students.

5. The ability to express is particularly important for the graduates.

The _____ to express is particularly important for the graduates.

The ability to express is _____ important for the graduates.

The ability to express is of _____ for the graduates.

6. The suggestion of the masses promotes the implement of the project.

The _____ of the masses promotes the implement of the project.

The suggestion of the masses _____ the implement of the project.

The suggestion is _____.

7. The class teacher is not only responsible for teaching，but also the management.

The class teacher is responsible for teaching，_____ the management.

The class teacher _____ not only teaching，but also the management.

Both_____ are _____.

8. It is necessary to obtain permission before entering this area.

It is _____ to obtain permission before entering this area.

Entering this area _____ obtaining permission.

Obtaining permission is _____.

9. We don't know how to avoid this problem.

We don't know _____ avoid this problem.

We _____ how to avoid this problem.

How to avoid this problem_____.

10. His testimony is unbelievable though he is the witness of the accident.

His testimony is _____ though he is the witness of the accident.

We_____though he is the witness of the accident.

Day 2　提分篇

一、通知

1. 短文特点

通知是日常生活中较为常见的文体类型，应用范围较为广泛。很多场合下都能够看到这种文体。这类文体的语言较为简洁凝练，依据通知的事项，风格可正式，也可随意。通知一般都采取开门见山的方式，所以考生读取这类文体的信息并不困难，而且语言风格较为平实，符合大多数人的阅读习惯。

通知中呈现出的信息可以概括为三个层面：一是主题，即为了什么而进行通知；二是相关人群，即谁或哪一群体应关注通知；三是通知的具体内容，即想让有关人员了解什么信息。

2. 例题及详解

> The toilet is planned to be overhauled, which will be carried out over the next two weeks. To meet the needs of citizens, it will be open on alternate days.

A. The notice informs citizens of a two-week toilet closure.

B. The notice advises citizens that there will be a modification of the toilet opening.

C. The notice asks for citizens' assistance during the repair work.

➤ 策略指导

通读短文，掌握短文内的四大要素（4W）

Who：厕所使用者

When：检修为期两周

Where：厕所

What：厕所计划进行检修，检修将持续两周，检修期间厕所隔天开放

➤ 试题详解

【答案】B

【材料类型】通知

【题目翻译】

A　通知提示市民厕所将关闭两周。

B　通知告知市民厕所的开放时间将有变化。

C　通知要求市民在检修时提供帮助。

【解析】根据通知最后一句话"为了满足市民需求，厕所将隔天开放"可知厕所的开放时间有变化。所以，B选项正确。

本题很容易误选A选项，根据通知第一句"厕所计划检修，为期两周"，容易误认为厕所关闭的时长与检修时长相同，都是两周，但最后一句话提到厕所隔天开放，可知这两周中，厕所并非每天都关闭，所以A选项错误。这则通知目的在于通知厕所开放时间的变化，并未提到寻求市民帮助的内容，所以C选项错误。

二、广告

1. 短文特点

广告是一种目的性很强的文本类型，其目的在于宣传产品或服务，从而提高消费者对其的认知度，激发消费者的消费欲望。广告的语言风格较为平易近人，多用结构简单的句子。而且行文方式较为多变，有些广告中会刻意安排一些语句来吸引人们的关注。

总体上看，广告的内容可大致分为三个层次，一是主题信息，即广告宣传的对象；二是产品或服务的特色所在；三是购买产品或服务的注意事项。

2. 例题及详解

Wonderful home appliance repair service
Are you still worried about the broken appliance? We pick up, repair and return items as soon as possible. Customers can place an order by call, email or contacting the after-sales service. After repair, customers should take away the appliance in 48 hours, otherwise, storage fee is required.

A. All the broken home appliance will be repaired in 48 hours.

B. Customers have to deliver the broken home appliance by themselves.

C. If you pick up the home appliance in good repair after 3 days, you will cost more.

➢　策略指导

通读短文，掌握短文内的四大要素（4W）

Who：因家电损坏而困扰的人

When：不涉及

Where：家电维修所

What：家电维修服务

➤ 试题详解

【答案】C

【材料类型】广告

【题目翻译】

A 所有损坏的家电都将在48小时内维修。

B 顾客必须自己运送损坏的家电。

C 如果你在家电修好3天后取走，会花费更多。

【解析】广告中的最后一句说到"维修过后，需要在48小时内将家电取走，否则会收取保管费"。由此可知，48小时内取走家电是不收取保管费的。所以C选项正确，因为3天后，即72小时后取走会收取保管费。

广告中第二句说到"我们会尽快取货、维修、返还"，此处并未说明多久后会进行维修；广告中提到的48小时说的是顾客应该在家电修好后的48小时内取走，所以A选项错误。由材料的第二句还可以得知，维修所可以把损坏的家电取走，消费者不需要自己运送，所以B选项错误。

三、邮件

1. 邮件特点

邮件是一种实用性较强的文体，日常生活中，邮件的应用范围较为广泛，可通过邮件进行咨询、解答、请求、致歉等。日常生活中的邮件话题往往较为轻松，一般都是围绕个人事务展开，场景是我们较为熟悉的，所以解读起来难度并不大。

从内容上看，邮件的核心信息包括两部分，一是发送邮件的意图，即邮件主题。二是对与主题相关的事件进行解释。此外邮件中还包含一些非核心成分，如问候语等。

2. 例题及详解

> From: Sam
>
> To: Ben
>
> Thanks for consulting about the travel package. An outline of the package is attached. If you reserve one of the packages now, you will receive further details, including advice on hotel accommodation.

A. The email may be sent by an employee from a bank.

B. Ben has asked for information about the package.

C. Ben has booked hotel accommodation for the travel.

➤　**策略指导**

通读短文，掌握短文内的四大要素（4W）

Who：山姆、本

When：不涉及

Where：不涉及

What：对于旅行套餐咨询的回复

➤　**试题详解**

【答案】B

【材料类型】邮件

【题目翻译】

A 这封邮件可能由银行的员工发送。

B 本曾经询问过套餐信息。

C 本已经订好了旅行时居住的酒店。

【解析】由于发件人对咨询旅行套餐进行感谢，所以可推测出本已经咨询过旅行套餐，所以 B 选项正确。

材料的第一句话说到"感谢咨询旅行套餐"，可知这封邮件与旅行相关，且邮件的发送者应该在旅行社工作，所以 A 选项错误。邮件中的最后一句说到"如果现在预订其中一个套餐，可获取更多详细的信息，包括酒店住宿建议"。这里虽然提到了酒店，但并不能判断出本是否已经订好了酒店，所以 C 选项错误。

四、标识

1. 标识特点

标识与生活息息相关，标识反映的是生活场景下某一事物对人们的提示。从功能上看，该文本类型与通知相似，都起到提示告知的作用。但与通知相比，标识的实用性更强，带有一种引导指示的意味。

从语言特点上看，标识的语句往往更为精炼，而且祈使句出现的频率更高。与其他题材相比，标识中还会出现一些非语言成分，如插图、箭头等，用来进行辅助说明。

2. 例题及详解

> If the yellow light flashes, check the machine for residual congestion. If no congestion is found, pull the plug and restart it. If the oil mass is low, the yellow light will flash on and off.

A. If there is a residual jam, the yellow light will be on.

B. If the yellow light flashes, the machine must be broken.

C. If the oil mass is insufficient, the yellow light will flicker for a long time.

➤ 策略指导

通读短文，掌握短文内的四大要素（4W）

Who：该产品的使用者

When：不涉及

Where：不涉及

What：机器的使用说明

➤ 试题详解

【答案】A

【材料类型】标识

【题目翻译】

A 如果有残渣堵塞，黄灯会亮。

B 如果黄灯闪烁，机器一定是出故障了。

C 如果油量不足，黄灯会长时间闪烁。

【解析】标识中的第一句说到"如果黄灯闪烁，检查机器是否出现残渣堵塞"，A选项与这一表述相符，所以A选项正确。

根据标识中的第二句可知"如果没有发现堵塞的情况，拔掉插头重启"，这句话的言外之意在于，黄灯闪烁有可能是故障造成的，也有可能不是故障所致，重启就可以解决问题，所以B选项错误。标识的最后一句说到"如果油量低，黄灯会忽明忽暗"，C选项与这一表述不符，所以C选项错误。

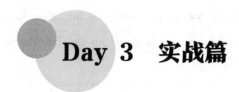

Day 3 实战篇

1.

> From: Jeffery
> To: Lily
>
> Sorry I was absent from your birthday party yesterday. I couldn't identify the restaurant and got lost!
> I arrived at the restaurant indeed eventually, but your party had already finished.

Jeffery is emailing to _____

A. complain that Lily's address to the restaurant was wrong.

B. apologize for his being late for Lily's birthday party.

C. ask whether the restaurant for Lily's birthday party was changed.

2.

> Recycling
>
> Put recyclable materials in the green bin, unrecyclable materials in the yellow bin, and poisonous waste in the black bin.

A. Batteries should go in the black bin.

B. Plastic bottles can be thrown in the random bin.

C. Paper should be put in the yellow bin.

3.

> Departure Information
>
> Please put belongings outside your door by 11:30 a.m. for the driver to load onto the bus.
> Lunch from 11:30
> Bus leaves at 13:00.
> Don't be late.

A. Passengers should put their belongings on the bus before lunch.

B. Belongings must be ready for loading onto the bus after lunch.

C. The driver will put passengers' belongings on the bus during lunch.

4.

Seeking for a better position?

At Future Career Service Centre, we specialize in career training and occupation introduction. Do you want to improve your vocational skills? Do you want to work in the world's top 500 enterprises? Contact us now on 369-9654-8820.

Future Career Service Centre _____

A. offers its employees good pay.

B. is an ideal place for who desires for a better career development.

C. wants to recruit several employees for itself.

5.

School Tennis Club Membership

If you'd like to join the new Tennis club, sign below by Tuesday (tomorrow). There are only 15 places left now. Practice evenings are Mondays and Wednesdays, Fridays sometimes.

A. There are three tennis sessions a week at the new club.

B. The new tennis club can only have 15 members.

C. Candidates need to apply for the club as soon as possible.

6.

From: David Museum

To: Sally

The museum tickets reserved through our online channel can now be cancelled free of charge. Notice period: minimum 7 days ahead of visit. And the ticket can't be changed within 48 hours of the original date.

A. Customers can receive full refunds, for cancelling one week or more before travelling.

B. On July 3rd, customers can change the tickets with the original date of July 4th.

C. Tickets reservation on the Internet must be completed at least 7 days before travel.

7.

> The deep water zone is dangerous. It is only available for adults and children over 10 years old with the company of the adult. For all the entrants, safeguards are required.

A. A 12 years old boy can enter the water area on his own.

B. Adults can enter the deep water zone without restriction.

C. This signal may be designed for a water park.

8.

> **From:** Susan Smith（Sales，Paris office）
> **To:** Billy Freeman
>
> Dear Billy,
> All is good here in the forest. We are on a very tight schedule, which is why I don't write to you as usual. We only have a few hours of daylight. My arm hurt and I had a cold, but I feel better now.
> I'll tell you my experience in detail tomorrow.
>
> Susan

A. Susan can't write to Billy very often because she lost her phone.

B. Susan's body is always well in the forest.

C. Another email from Susan may be sent to Billy tomorrow.

9.

Library Wi-Fi Policy

All the rooms in the building are equipped with routers, so that everyone can enjoy the best experience. We welcome all users to report any error to the main desk on the ground floor. We also warn you that improper use is not allowed. Our servers are constantly monitored and we retain our right to suspend any unusual online activity. Thank you for your cooperation.

A. Library readers can get access to the Wi-Fi from almost anywhere in the building.

B. Individual passwords for the library Wi-Fi are assigned to the readers at the main desk.

C. Readers can connect to the library Wi-Fi and use it for any purpose.

10.

Congratulations on enrolling on our Go Forward with Adversity Course! Graduating from this course, you will be calmer when facing the adversity and you will be more capable of making progress under pressure. Our course includes the treatment and prevention for the adversity from various aspects. We look forward to helping you achieve your own adversity overcoming goals.

A. The course focuses only on how to deal with adversity.

B. Adversity may be less formidable after you attend this course.

C. After graduating from this course, you will never encounter the adversity.

Part 2 句子填空

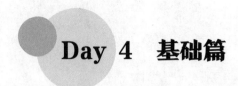

Day 4   基础篇

一、题型介绍

阅读第二类题型是句子填空。考生需要从四个选项中选择正确的单词给句子填空。

二、考试界面

✓   界面最上方是本部分的答题说明

✓   界面中间是需要填写的句子

✓   界面下方是四个选项，通过点击每个选项而进行选择

✓   点击右下角箭头可以切换到下一题（注意答完的题目不能再切换回来进行检查）

三、考查技能

本题型的题目只有一句话，也是阅读考试中相对简单的题型。这一题型的本质其实是对英语单词和语法的考查，具体包括词义辨析、固定搭配和习语以及语法基础知识，侧重考查考生平时的语言积累及知识运用的能力。

句子填空的出题类型主要包括以下三种：

1. 词义辨析

此类题型在考试中较为常见，在选项中会给出四个选项，考生则根据所给出的句子，选出置于句中最恰当的单词。根据选项设置方式的不同，词义辨析类题目可以分为以下三个类型。

一是对近义词的辨析，即从选项中四个含义相近的单词中，选择出最恰当的一项。这类题目侧重考查单词的具体应用情景，所以仅记住单词含义是不够的。这就要求考生在积累单词时，不仅要熟记单词自身的含义，还要着眼于应用角度，掌握单词的具体使用场景以及与近义词的区别。

二是对形近词的辨析，选项中的四个单词外观相似，可能是同根词，可能是前缀和后缀相同的单词，也可能是字母组合相近的单词。这一类题目侧重考查考生对单词记忆的熟练程度，考生是否能在形近词的干扰下，准确地选择正确选项，这就要求考生要加深对单词的记忆，同时在记忆单词时触类旁通，也记忆该单词的形近词。

还有一种类型的题目，选项既不是近义词，也不是形近词。这类题目中，选项中的单词往往比以上两种类型更加生僻，这类题目主要考查考生对难记单词的积累，要求考生不断积累单词。

通过以上内容，我们可以看到，在日常的单词积累中，仅记忆其含义是远远不够的，要全面系统地对单词进行学习和记忆。

2. 固定搭配

此类题型主要考查考生对于单词的固定用法及某些固定表达的运用。

固定搭配考查的是单词的固定用法及一些固定表达。这一题型要求考生注重日常积累，熟练掌握固定搭配，提升对固定搭配的敏感度，这样才能有效提高答题效率。

另外，一个单词可能会构成多种固定搭配，这一点在题目中也会涉及，这要求考生在掌握固定搭配的同时，还要掌握不同搭配的用法。

3. 语法基础

此类题型题目考查语法基础知识。

语法基础题考查语法基本功，要求考生根据句子中的信息，对其中出现的语法现象进行判断，这要求考生熟知语法规则，包括词法和句法。本题型在考试中占比相对较少，但考生不可掉以轻心，须系统地学习并熟练应用语法。

四、答题策略

针对本题型，建议采用以下答题思路：

1. 通读全句，判断题型

进行选择之前通读全句，结合句子内容和选项，预测考点，这样能够帮助我们调整思路，选择合适的解题方法。

比如：Please turn _____ the radio, because it's too noisy.

A. out   B. off   C. away   D. in

观察句子，可以看到空格前出现了动词，四个选项均可与空格前的动词构成固定搭配，可以推测出本题考查固定搭配。然后我们从句中寻找进行选择的依据，这就可以从句子的主干成分和非主干成分中同时寻找。

从形式上看，固定搭配题的选项往往属于同一词性，且选项间含义的关联性较小。词义辨析题的选项可能是含义相近的单词，可能是外观相似的单词，也可能是难度较大但不存在关联的单词。语法基础题的选项往往围绕动词展开，选项中往往出现be动词、情态动词、实意动词的各种形式。

2. 细致分析，进行选择

在初步判断试题的类型和考查点之后，我们就要着手选择正确答案。我们可以将这一步骤的任务分解为三个部分：

（1）明晰成分

这一步骤的主要任务在于将句子进行拆解，可以按照语法规则进行拆解，也可以按照意群进行拆解，只要将句子整体划分为若干个易于理解的个体即可。

（2）理清关系

这一步是在上一步的基础上继续进行分析，判断哪部分与空格处存在直接关系，如：主谓关系、动宾关系、修饰与被修饰关系等。此外，还要寻找对选项起到修饰限定作用的成分，这类成分往往起到提示作用，有助于进行选择。

（3）谨慎选择

在完成上两步的任务后，就可以着手进行选择了。这一步骤要坚持"一致"的思想。即与相关成分在时态、人称等方面保持一致，这一部分可以视作语法意义上的"一致"。二是结合语境，充分考虑待推理的部分与文章语境的关系，在语境上保持"一致"。

3. 代入答案，认真核对

完成选择后，要将选择出的答案代入原句中，再次检查语义是否通顺，语法是否正确，逻辑是否正确。在全句的语境下对答案再次验证。

五、典型例题及详解

1. 词义辨析例题

（1）My brother knows a number of _____ people in the major company who can address this issue.

A. negligible　　　B. influential　　　C. artificial　　　D. naughty

【答案】B

【解析】从本题的选项可以看出，本题考查词义辨析。四个选项均可做形容词使用，用来修饰句中的"people"。A选项意为"微不足道的；可忽略的"；B选项意为"有影响力的，有势力的"；C选项意为"人造的，人工的"；D选项意为"淘气的"。将四个选项代入句子后，B选项最为恰当，所以B选项正确。句意为"我的哥哥认识这家大公司里许多有势力的人，他们能解决这个问题"。

（2）We all need someone else's assistance at intervals, so you'd better correct that _____ attitude of yours while you still needn't.

A. pushy　　　B. roomy　　　C. sappy　　　D. haughty

【答案】D

【解析】本题的四个选项为外观相近的单词，可知本题考查词汇辨析。四个选项均为形容词词性，修饰句中的"attitude"。A选项意为"有进取心的；爱出风头的"；B选项意为"宽敞的，广阔的"；C选项意为"多汁液的；愚蠢的"；D选项意为"傲慢的，自大的"，将四个选项代入句子中，D选项最符合语境，所以D选项正确。本句意为"我们都会不时需要别人的帮助，所以就算你还不需要，最好还是改正一下你傲慢的态度"。

2. 固定搭配例题

（1）The volume that the charity has collected up to now to fund a kindergarten for children _____ at over ￡10,000.

A. counts　　　B. predicts　　　C. stands　　　D. aggregates

【答案】C

【解析】以上四个选项均有动词词性，且在原句空格处后面出现了"at"，可知空格处内容应该能与"at"构成搭配。A选项意为"计算"；B选项意为"预测，预计"；C选项意为"站立；忍受；高达"，该选项可以和at构成固定搭配，意为"达到"；D选项意为"聚集；共计"。从含义上看，D选项似乎也符合语境，但D选项无法与at构成搭配，所以C选项正确。句意为"截至目前，慈善机构为孩子们筹建幼儿园募集的资金已达到一万多英镑"。

（2）The rain was so heavy that the tennis game had to be _____ off.

A. called   B. taken   C. showed   D. brought

【答案】A

【解析】本题的四个选项均为动词，空格后为副词，所以本题考查动词与副词的搭配。A选项与off搭配意为"取消；放弃"；B选项与off搭配意为"起飞；脱下"；C选项与off搭配意为"炫耀，卖弄"；D选项与off搭配意为"完成；救出"，将这四个选项的含义代入句子中，A选项最符合语境，所以A选项正确。句意为"雨下得很大，网球比赛不得已而取消了"。

3. 语法基础例题

（1）Nick was ill last week and stayed in hospital. You _____ have seen him at the cafe.

A. shouldn't   B. can't   C. must   D. needn't

【答案】B

【解析】本题考查语法基础知识。四个选项均为情态动词，可知本题考查情态动词的用法。空格后出现了"have+过去分词"的结构，这是情态动词表示对过去推测的标志。逗号前的内容说到"尼克上周生病住院了"，逗号后的内容说到"在咖啡厅看见他"，所以空格处应该表示否定含义，首先排除C选项。A选项意为"不应该"，B选项意为"不可能"，D选项意为"不需要"，B选项最符合语境，所以B选项正确。句意为"尼克上周生病住院了，你不可能在咖啡厅看到他"。

（2）Numerous specialists _____ the seminar tomorrow.

A. have attended   B. are attending   C. were attended   D. attend

【答案】B

【解析】本题考查时态和语态的运用。由句末的"tomorrow"可知，事件发生在将来，所以本句应使用将来时。句中的主语"专家"，和谓语"参加"间应该是主动关系，所以排除C选项。A选项为现在完成时，D选项为一般现在时，均与语境不符。本题易将B选项视作现在进行时，其实这是一般将来时的表达方法之一，即be动词+现在分词表一般将来时，所以B选项正确。句意为"许多专家将在明天参加研讨会"。

Day 5 提分篇

一、词义辨析总结

1. 150组高频形近词辨析

(1) quite *adv.* 相当
quiet *adj.* 安静的

(2) affect *v.* 影响
effect *n.* 影响

(3) adapt *v.* 适应
adopt *v.* 采用
adept *adj.* 内行的

(4) angel *n.* 天使
angle *n.* 角度

(5) later *adv.* 后来
latter *adj.* 后来的
latest *adj.* 最新的

(6) context *n.* 上下文
contest *n.* 竞争

(7) principal *adj.* 主要的
principle *n.* 原则

(8) implicit *adj.* 含蓄的
explicit *adj.* 明白的

(9) desert *v.* 放弃
dissert *v.* 写论文

(10) pat *v.* 轻拍
tap *v.* 轻打

(11) decent *adj.* 正经的
descent *n.* 下降,降落
descend *v.* 下来,下降

(12) extensive *adj.* 广阔的
intensive *adj.* 深刻的

(13) sweet *adj.* 甜的
sweat *n.* 汗水

(14) costume *n.* 服装
custom *n.* 习俗

(15) dairy *n.*
牛奶场;乳制品
diary *n.* 日记

(16) altar *n.* 祭坛
alter *v.* 改变

(17) chore *n.* 家务活
chord *n.* 和弦
cord *n.* 细绳

(18) precede *v.* 领先
proceed *v.* 继续

(19) clash *n.* 撞击声
crash *v.* 坠落
crush *v.* 压坏

(20) aural *adj.* 听觉的
oral *adj.* 口头的

(21) abroad *adv.* 国外
aboard *v.*
上(船,飞机)

(22) beam *n.* 光束
bean *n.* 豆

(23) pray *v.* 祈祷
prey *n.* 猎物

(24) dose *n.* 一剂
dozen *n.* 一打

（25）confirm v. 确认
conform v. 使顺从

（26）assent n. 同意
ascent n. 上升
accent n. 口音

（27）champion n. 冠军
champagne n. 香槟
campaign n. 活动

（28）barn n. 谷仓
barren adj. 贫瘠的

（29）cite v. 引用
site n. 场所
sight n. 视觉

（30）compliment n. 赞美
complement n. 附加物

（31）contact n. 接触
contract n. 合同
contrast n. 对照

（32）council n. 委员会
counsel n. 忠告
consul n. 领事

（33）chicken n. 鸡
kitchen n. 厨房

（34）emigrant n.
移居外国的人
immigrant n.
（外来）移民

（35）vocation n. 职业
vacation n. 假期

（36）drought n. 旱灾
draught n. 通风气流

（37）scare v. 使惊恐
scarce adj. 缺乏的

（38）model n. 模型
meddle v. 干涉

（39）ensure v. 确保
assure v. 使确信
insure v. 为……投保

（40）latitude n. 纬度
altitude n. 海拔高度
gratitude n. 感激之情

（41）crow n. 乌鸦
crown n. 王冠
clown n. 小丑

（42）mortal adj. 终有一死的
metal n. 金属
mental adj. 精神的

（43）alone adj. 单独的
lonely adj. 寂寞的

（44）hotel n. 旅馆
hostel n. 青年旅舍

（45）excess n. 过量
exceed v. 超过
excel v. 擅长

（46）floor n. 地板
flour n. 面粉

（47）incident n. 事件
accident n. 意外

（48）inspiration n. 灵感
aspiration n. 抱负

（49）march v. 前进
match n. 比赛

（50）patent n. 专利（权）
potent adj. 有力的
potential adj. 潜在的

（51）revenge n. 报复
avenge v. 报复

（52）purpose n. 目的
suppose n. 猜想
propose n. 提议

（53）story n. 故事
storey n. 楼层
store n. 商店

（54）expand v. 扩大
expend v. 花费
extend v. 延伸

（55）commerce *n.* 商业
commence *v.* 开始

（56）protest *v.* 抗议
protect *v.* 保护

（57）strike *v.* 打；撞
stick *v.* 刺；戳；插入
strict *adj.* 严格的

（58）through *prep.* 穿过
thorough *adj.* 彻底的
(al)though *conj.* 虽然

（59）police *n.* 警察
policy *n.* 政策
politics *n.* 政治

（60）brown *adj.* 棕色的
brow *n.* 眉毛
blow *v.*（风）刮，吹

（61）carton *n.* 硬纸盒
cartoon *n.* 动画片

（62）acclaim *v.* 赞扬
declaim *v.* 慷慨陈词

（63）perfuse *v.* 使充满
profuse *adj.* 丰富的

（64）literacy *n.* 读写能力
literary *adj.* 文学的
literature *n.* 文学
literal *adj.* 字面上的

（65）expel *v.* 驱逐
repel *v.* 击退

（66）impel *v.* 推动
dispel *v.* 驱散

（67）confidant *n.* 知己
confident *adj.* 自信的

（68）dreg *n.* 渣滓
drag *v.* 拖，拽

（69）imprudence *n.* 轻率
impudence *n.* 厚颜无耻

（70）hanger *n.* 衣架
hunger *n.* 饥饿

（71）status *n.* 地位
stature *n.* 身高；名望

（72）exempt *adj.* 免除
excerpt *n.* 选录

（73）reject *v.* 拒绝
eject *v.* 赶出

（74）require *v.* 需要
inquire *v.* 调查；询问

（75）assert *v.* 断言
asset *n.* 资产

（76）expect *v.* 期望
aspect *n.* 方面
accept *v.* 接受

（77）respect *n.* 尊敬
inspect *v.* 检查
suspect *v.* 猜想；怀疑

（78）glide *v.* 滑行
slide *v.*（使）滑行
slip *v.* 滑倒

（79）strive *v.* 努力
stride *n.* 大步

（80）stationery *n.* 文具
stationary *adj.* 静止的

（81）prospect *n.* 可能性
perspective *n.* 视角

（82）steal *v.* 偷窃
steel *n.* 钢

（83）illusion *n.* 幻想
delusion *n.* 妄想
elusion *n.* 逃避

（84）loose *adj.* 松动的
lose *v.* 丢失
loss *n.* 损失

（85）amend v. 修订(法律)
　　emend v. 修订(文稿)

（86）amoral adj.
与道德无关的
unmoral adj.
与道德无关的
immoral adj.
不道德的
immortal adj.
不朽的

（87）capitol n. 美国国会大厦
capital n. 首都

（88）casual adj. 随便的
causal adj. 表原因的

（89）extend v. 延伸
extent n. 程度
extant adj. 现存的

（90）inability n. 无能
disability n. 残疾

（91）sock n. 袜子
stocking n. 长袜

（92）vision n. 幻想
version n. 版本

（93）phrase n. 短语
phase n. 阶段

（94）grim adj. 严酷的
grime n. 污垢

（95）mission n. 使命
emission n. 散发
mansion n. 大厦

（96）definite adj. 清晰的
infinite adj. 无限的

（97）recent adj. 最近的
resent v. 怨恨

（98）crayon n. 蜡笔
canyon n. 山谷

（99）widow n. 寡妇
window n. 窗

（100）ardour n. 热情
adore v. 非常喜欢
adorn v. 装饰

（101）statue n. 雕像
statute n. 法令

（102）tax n. 税款
taxi n. 出租车

（103）gasp n. 喘息
grasp v. 抓住

（104）delicate adj. 易碎的
dedicate v. 献身

（105）idle adj. 空闲的
idol n. 偶像

（106）baggage n. 行李
（尤用于北美英语中）
luggage n. 行李

（107）award n. 奖品
reward n. 回报

（108）attain v.获得
obtain v. (艰难地）得到
abstain v.戒除

（109）resemble v.
与……相似
assemble v. 集合；装配
assembly n.
立法机构；会议；议会

（110）area n. 区域
era n. 时代

（111）evocation n. 唤出
revocation n. 废除

（112）deduce v. 演绎
seduce v. 勾引

（113）lapse n. 过失
relapse v.
（旧病）复发
elapse v.
（时间）消逝
eclipse n. 日食

（114）personnel n. 全体人
员
personal adj. 私人的

（115）assume v. 假定
resume v.
恢复（职位）

（116）rude adj. 粗鲁的
crude adj. 粗略的

（117）sauce n. 调味汁
saucer n. 茶碟
source n. 来源

（118）resource n. 资源
recourse n. 求助

（119）stretch v. 伸展
sketch n. 素描

（120）propel v. 推进
proper adj. 真正的
compel v. 强迫

（121）stripe n. 条纹
strip v. 除去
trip n. 旅行

（122）badge n. 徽章
bandage n. 绷带

（123）blade n. 刀片
bald adj. 秃头的
bold adj. 大胆自信的

（124）bloom n. 花期
blossom n. 花
bosom n. 胸部

（125）contend v.
声称，主张
content n. 内容
contest n.
竞争，比赛
context n. 上下文

（126）intrude v. 闯入
extrude v. 挤出

（127）growl v. 低沉吼叫
howl v. 嚎叫

（128）depress v. 使抑郁
suppress v. 镇压
oppress v. 压迫

（129）dime n. 十分硬币
dim adj. 暗淡的

（130）bulletin n. 公告
bullet n. 子弹

（131）vanish v. 突然不见
evanish v. 使消失

（132）dizzy adj. 头晕目眩的
dazzle v. 使目眩

（133）decline v. 下降
recline v. 斜倚
incline v. 倾斜

（134）eminent adj.
卓越的
imminent adj.
即将发生的

（135）chivalry n. 骑士精神
cavalry n. 骑兵

(136) contort v. 扭曲　　(137) collar n. 衣领　　(138) edict n. 法令

distort v. 使失真　　　　cellar n. 地下室　　　indict n. 控告

retort v. 反驳　　　　　colour n. 颜色

(139) inject v. 注射　　(140) median adj.　　(141) rip v. 撕裂

deject v. 使沮丧　　　　中间值的　　　　　ripe adj. 成熟的

medium n. 媒介

(142) wench n. 姑娘　　(143) diner n. 进餐者　　(144) faint adj. 模糊的

wrench v. 猛扭　　　　dinner n. 晚餐　　　　feint n. 佯攻

(145) resign v. 辞（职）　　(146) suit n. 西装　　(147) enquire v. 询问

reject v. 拒绝，否决　　　suite n. 套房　　　　acquire v. 获得

(148) exclaim v. 呼喊　　(149) reduce v. 减少　　(150) bride n. 新娘

proclaim v.　　　　　induce v. 引起　　　　bribe n. 贿赂

（正式）宣告

acclaim v. 称赞

2. 80组高频近义词辨析

（1）接受，接纳：receive, accept, admit

receive 指收到了发送出去的信息、物品，强调收到这一事实。

accept 强调从主观意愿上接受，往往与抽象事物搭配。

admit 强调经过考核或批准后准许进入。

（2）精确的：exact, accurate, precise

exact 指数量或质量完全符合标准。

accurate 指符合事实，与事实没有出入，强调准确的程度高。

precise 指各项细节都丝毫不差，有时含有为追求准确而"吹毛求疵"的意思。

（3）获得：acquire, achieve, gain, obtain

acquire 指经过努力后，获得某物，强调获得的结果。

achieve 指实现目标或预期结果，强调过程的不易。

gain 指通过努力或发挥主观能动性，得到某种成就或获取利益。

obtain 指通过努力得到某件渴望的事物。

（4）使适合，适应：suit, fit, adapt, adjust, conform, accommodate

suit 侧重与某人的偏好相符，也指服装的颜色或款式与某人相配。

fit 强调大小、尺寸和形状上相配。

adapt 指为迎合客观条件的变化而进行调整或改变。

adjust 表示对人或物的某一方面进行小规模调整。

conform 指与某种固定模式或规范相符。

accommodate 侧重以使自己获得好处为目的，进行自我调整。

（5）附加物，增加物：attachment，addition，appendix，accessory，supplement

attachment 表示能使原有功能变得更强大的附属物。

addition 表示数量的增加。

appendix 特指书后的附录。

accessory 指物品的附件，同时也可表示增加美观度的配饰。

supplement 指为使物品功能更完善而进行的增补。

（6）另加的，额外的：extra，additional，supplementary

extra 指不包括本身而额外加上去的部分。

additional 指在原有部分上进行增加，增加的部分包含原有部分。

supplementary 指在原有基础上进行补充，使其更完整。

（7）演讲，讲话：speech，lecture，address，oration

speech 指个人演说或发言，可以是即兴的，也可以是经过准备的。

lecture 指学术性较强的演讲。

address 指在重要场合所做的正式演讲。

oration 指在一些特殊场合为引发听者共鸣而做的演讲。

（8）足够的，充足的：enough，sufficient，adequate

enough 表示数量和程度足够。

sufficient 指数量足够满足某种需要。

adequate 强调数量刚好满足，没有多余部分；质量符合要求。

（9）尊重；钦佩：respect，esteem，admire，honour

respect 指因某人的品德或成就而敬重某人，还指对前辈或长者的敬重。

esteem 指因某人的研究达到最高水准而敬重某人。

admire 指因某人或某物的超常之处而对其敬仰。

honour 指对某人十分尊敬，并引以为荣。

（10）承认：admit，acknowledge，confess，concede

admit 承认某种不容争辩的事实。

acknowledge 强调公开承认，多指承认过去发生的事实，对其进行澄清。

confess 承认罪行或不良行径。

concede强调不情愿的承认或在客观因素下被迫承认。

（11）意见，建议：advice, opinion, view, proposal, suggestion, recommendation

advice指经验更丰富，能力更强的人提出的建议。

opinion表示初步的，不深刻的看法。

view对重大事件或广受关注的事件的看法。

proposal 指可以探讨、验证或推行的成熟的建议。

suggestion指正确性有待考察，可以用来参考的建议。

recommendation指具有指导性或能让人信服的建议。

（12）劝告，忠告；警告：advise, warn, caution, admonish

advise泛指劝告。

warn对某种危险进行警告，如不听从可能会出现某种后果。

caution对危险进行提示，告诫他人注意。

admonish资历深厚者对资历尚浅者的忠告，含有语重心长之味。

（13）断言；声称：affirm, assert, allege, claim, testify

affirm侧重指在有确凿证据的情况下断言，态度极为坚决。

assert以自我认识为依据，向外宣称。

allege毫无根据地对外宣称。

claim说话者根据某种依据而提出的主张或要求。

testify在法庭上发表证言。

（14）同意，赞同：agree, approve, consent

agree指几人持有相同的看法或观点。

approve指赞成自身认为可行的观点或事件。

consent指个人从主观上愿意同意他人的主张或看法。

（15）协定；协议；契约，合同：agreement, contract, treaty, convention

agreement泛指国家、机构、个人之间订立的正式或非正式的合同或协议。

contract指明确规定了各方权利及义务的用于正式场合的合同。

treaty国家之间签订的合同或协议。

convention指国家之间就有关事项签订的条约，不及treaty正式。

（16）进攻；侵略：assault, attack, aggression, invasion

assault指猛烈的进攻。

attack使用暴力手段对某人或某地发起的攻击。

aggression指以侵略为目的的暴力袭击，强调故意发起袭击。

invasion 多指侵犯别国领土或领地。

（17）出现：show，appear，emerge，loom

show 指人或物完全显现。

appear 强调公开露面，被看见。

emerge 侧重缓缓出现的过程。

loom 指朦胧的出现，强调给人若隐若现的感觉。

（18）任命；委派：assign，appoint，designate，name，nominate

assign 指给一群人布置任务或分配某物。

appoint 指上级直接进行的任命。

designate 指定某人从事某项任务或担任某一职务。

name 普通用词，强调任命的结果，而不是过程。

nominate 通常指为某一公职选择候选人，并将其提交给有决定权的人做最后决定。

（19）要求；请求：ask，beg，demand，require，request，implore，claim，entreat

ask 适用范围广泛，指表明自己的想法，并想让其发生。

beg 指为了迫切的需要而降低身份去求某人。

demand 指以强硬的方式要求。

require 多指按照法律制度进行要求。

request 指以正式、恰当的方式提出要求。

implore 指运用情感打动对方而进行请求。

claim 表示要求享有某种权利。

entreat 表示以诚恳的方式请求。

（20）问，询问：ask，inquire，question

ask 为得到某一问题的答案，或存在疑惑而向他人发问。

inquire 较正式用词，指为得到真实情况而详细询问或调查、了解。

question 指在较严肃场合下的盘问和讯问，或对某事提出质疑。

（21）假设；猜想，推测：guess，assume，suppose，presume，guess，postulate

guess 指盲目的猜测。

assume 指脱离客观事实，主观臆想地去推测。

suppose 指对未知情况的假设，往往还会提及这种假设产生的影响。

presume 在不确定的情况下，给某件事下结论。

postulate 指为逻辑性较强的推理而作出的假设。

（22）试图；努力：try, attempt, strive, endeavour

try指希望做成某事，通过采取行动来实现此事。

attempt指动作正在进行中，希望得到预期结果但不一定会成功。

strive指实现目标的过程十分艰辛，为此会付出很多努力。

endeavour指尽最大努力来实现某事。

（23）吸引，引诱：attract, tempt, charm, enchant, fascinate

attract指能吸引某人注意的特质。

tempt常含贬义，采取手段诱导他人。

charm指个体具有某种有别于他人的特质，而让他人着迷。

enchant指能够把他人吸引过来，并使其高兴。

fascinate指某事引起了某人的兴趣，而对此关注。

（24）意识到的：aware, sensible, conscious

aware通过感知，能意识到某些信息。

sensible通过直觉或思考，能意识到某物的存在。

conscious侧重心理的认知，强调内心活动。

（25）禁止：ban, forbid, prohibit

ban语气强烈，表示明令禁止，往往由官方发布。

forbid官方或非官方发布的、适用范围较小的禁令，常含劝导之意。

prohibit通过法律或规章制度进行禁止。

（26）基本的，基础的：basic, essential, fundamental

basic指一方的存在是以另一方为基础。

essential指事物的某一部分具有奠基性的作用，不可缺少、不可替代。

fundamental指事物的某一部分能反映出事物的特征。

（27）相信，信任：belief, faith, trust, confidence, conviction

belief由主观想法决定的信念，可能会与事实存在出入。

faith强调无条件、完全的相信。

trust由于双方互相接触而产生的信任。

confidence指因某人或某物具有某种特征或能力而给予其信任。

conviction强调坚定不移地相信，不会被外界所动摇。

（28）改变：change, alter, vary, shift, convert, modify, transform

change可以指任何变化，强调与原有状态存在不同。

alter指浅层次或表面上的变化，基本上维持原有状态。

convert强调为了达到某一目的，对原有事物进行一定程度的改造，使之呈现出新的状态。

modify强调在事物原有的状态上进行微调。

shift指事物的位置或人的态度发生转变，侧重变化的过程。

transform指全方位、彻底的变化。

vary指无规则、不连续的变化。

（29）价格；费用：price, cost, expense, charge, fee, fare

price指通过货币所表现出的商品价值，即商品的价格。

cost指进行某项活动所需的各项费用。

expense指在某一事项的开销。

charge指某些额外服务所收取的数额较小的费用。

fee指为专业性服务而支付的费用。

fare指乘坐交通工具而产生的费用。

（30）宣称；断言：claim, affirm, assert

claim往往表示说话者反对或不同意某一观点。

affirm指根据事实坚定不移地宣称，有无可争辩之意。

assert指不管事实如何，主观自信地宣称。

（31）明显的：clear, obvious, evident, apparent, visible

clear指事物清晰或明显，能够被人洞察或理解。

apparent指事物十分明显，不费力就能感知到。

evident指抽象事物或推理出的结果较为明显。

obvious指不言自明、不用费力去感知的事物。

visible侧重某事物是能够让人看见的。

（32）社团，会社，协会：club, union, association, institute, league

club指将拥有共同兴趣的人聚集在一起，方便进行交流和活动的团体。

union指工人为维护共同利益而建立的工会。

association指有特定的、同一目的的人们聚集在一起而形成的官方组织。

institute指为从事某种专业性工作而建立的合作组织。

league指共同利益一致的个人、团体或国家之间建立的同盟。

（33）组成，构成：consist, compose, constitute, comprise

consist含被动含义，表示"由……组成"。

compose表示多个个体一起构成的一个整体。

constitute表示"构成"时，暗指构成整体的个体在性质上与整体相同。

comprise在表示"组成"时，侧重"包含""涵盖"之意。

（34）明确的：definite，specific，explicit

definite强调事物范围明确、界限清晰，不会与其他事物混为一谈。

specific强调内容确切具体，与抽象相对。

explicit指内容十分清晰，不让人存在疑惑。

（35）放弃：abandon，desert，forsake

abandon指不承担自己的责任，彻底放弃，且不会回头。

desert指为逃避责任，离开依靠自己的人或物，且这种行为会受到谴责。

forsake强调在情感上的断离。

（36）分配，分发：distribute，allocate，divide，assign

distribute指将物品分发给很多人。

allocate指为某种特定目的而进行的分配。

divide侧重将物品分成多份的分配。

assign常指分配任务、作业。

（37）怀疑的，不确定的：uncertain，doubtful，questionable，ambiguous

uncertain指了解不透彻或对某事没有把握而无法做出定论。

doubtful指对某事持疑问态度。

questionable指某物的合理性有待考证，往往是有依据的。

ambiguous认为多种理解方式都有道理，无法做出明确判断。

（38）努力：effort，endeavour，struggle

effort指做某事需要付出体力或脑力上的努力。

endeavour指为困难的任务付出长久的努力或面对新任务时付出开创性的努力。

struggle指面对困境和问题时，付出具有抗争意义的努力。

（39）初级的：primary，elementary，elemental

primary指在重要性上占据首位。

elementary指事物的初步或起始阶段。

elemental强调事物具有基础或本质的特征。

（40）鼓励，激励：encourage，inspire，excite，stimulate

encourage指给予某人信心和希望，使其继续从事某种活动。

inspire常指通过言语使某人受到启发，使其继续前行。

excite强调激发某人做某事的情绪。

stimulate强调某人或某物受到外界刺激后产生的行动。

（41）增加，增大，扩大，提高：increase，expand，enhance，enlarge，amplify，magnify

increase指数量的增加或水平的提升。

expand指范围、数量、尺码的增加。

enhance指质量、价格、地位的提高。

enlarge指范围的扩大或将图像的放大。

amplify指放大声音或增强信号。

magnify指让显示出来的物体变得更大。

（42）保证：ensure，assure，guarantee，promise

ensure确认某事一定会发生。

assure向他人保证事件一定会发生，消除他人的疑虑。

guarantee指对产品质量或个人品质，需承担的责任所做的保证。

promise主观上认为自己一定会做某事并向他人承诺。

（43）完整的，全部的，整个的：all，entire，whole，complete，full，total

all表示群体中的所有的个体。

entire表示整体中的个体不可或缺，强调事物的完整性。

whole强调每个组成部分都包括在内，无一漏掉或舍去。

complete强调事物在内容、程度或数量方面完整，已达标准。

full侧重内容的完整。

total指把所有数目累计在一起得到的总数。

（44）器具：equipment，facility，instrument，appliance，device，tool

equipment多指成套的大型装备。

facility指为某种特定用途所用的设施。

instrument指完成某项任务所需的仪器，尤指科学研究所用的仪器。

appliance指家庭使用的，需要能源驱动的设备。

device指用于测量、记录的小型装备。

tool指进行手工作业时所需的工具。

（45）估计：estimate，assess，evaluate

estimate指对金额、数量进行的大致测算。

assess指对财产、收入、损失做出评估（make an assessment）。

evaluate指对事物的价值给予评定。

（46）检查：examine，inspect，scan

examine指检查事物是否存在问题或对其正确性进行检查。

inspect将某一事物与标准进行比较，观察其与标准的异同。

scan原指仔细地检查分析，现指细看或浏览。

（47）感情，情感：feeling，emotion，passion，affection，sentiment

feeling指接触外界后所产生的内心情感。

emotion泛指较为强烈的情感。

passion指十分强烈，甚至无法控制的情感。

affection指较深厚的喜爱之情。

sentiment指基于思想所产生的情绪。

（48）力：force，energy，power，might，strength，vigour

force指使某人或某物的外观或性质发生变化的力量，也可指武力。

energy指维持某人或某物正常活动的能量或精力。

power泛指各种动力、力量和能力。

might多指超乎寻常的巨大力量。

strength指身体内部的力量。

vigour指支撑生命体活动的精力、体力。

（49）目标：aim，goal，target，object，objective

aim对未来结果的理想预期，并指导未来的行动。

goal指某人需要付出巨大努力才能实现的目标。

target常指被攻击或批判的目标。

object指通过具体行动而实现的目标。

objective指尽力争取获得的事物。

（50）思想；观点，观念：idea，concept，conception，thought，notion

idea通过思维活动产生的想法、见解、假设。

concept指从大量具体事物中总结出的抽象的、具有普适性的概念。

conception指通过思维加工进行的设想或构思。

thought指经过长时间的认真思考得出的表明立场或态度的观点。

notion指经过初步了解或思考后产生的不清晰的想法。

（51）影响：effect，impact，influence

effect强调某人或某物带来的直接作用。

impact指带来强烈冲击的巨大影响。

influence指经过长时间、潜移默化的影响。

（52）通知，告知：inform，advise，notify

inform常指在正式场合下将信息传递给他人。

notify指用正式的书面材料告知他人某事。

advise指通知、告知与该事件直接相关的人员。

（53）坚持：insist，persist，persevere，cling

insist坚持某一主张，且难以劝说。

persist指事物持续存在，或坚持做某事。

persevere指在困难面前不放弃，继续坚持。

cling表示坚持信念、原则、理念等，含墨守成规之意。

（54）参加，加入：join，attend，participate，take part in

join指加入组织或团体，成为其中一员。

attend指出席活动。

participate指以某种身份积极参加团体活动。

take part in参加某一活动或实践并从中发挥作用。

（55）保持，保存：keep，retain，reserve，conserve，preserve

keep使用范围较广，可指某人或某物保持在某种状态。

retain强调留住，即不让现状发生变化。

reserve强调留存或保留某物以便未来使用。

conserve强调节约和保护自然资源。

preserve指为防止受到破坏而进行保留。

（56）限制，限定：limit，confine，restrict

limit指不可逾越，已经确定的极限。

confine强调以束缚、阻挠的方式进行限制。

restrict指在一定范围内进行活动。

（57）连接，结合，联合：link，unite，connect，combine，associate

link指将不同事物用连接物连接起来，强调连接得较为牢固。

unite指某人或某物为某一目的而联合在一起，组成联合体。

connect指不同事物在某一点相互连接，但依然保持各自特性。

combine将多个人或事物联结在一起，使之处于一种并存的状态。

associate将本来就存在联系的事物和人联系起来。

（58）看起来；好像是：look，appear，seem

look 指从视觉获得的直观印象。

appear 指初步的、较浅显的印象，可能与真实情况有所出入。

seem 指有一定依据，在内心中形成的判断。

（59）主要地；大量地：mainly, chiefly, largely, mostly, primarily, principally, generally

mainly 指整体中相对重要，影响重大的部分。

chiefly 指某一个体在整体中处于首要地位，最应该受到关注。

largely 强调在多数情况下所处的状态，但不完全如此。

mostly 强调在数量或比重上占有绝对的优势。

primarily 侧重基本地、首要地。

principally 侧重处于最重要地位。

generally 通常强调普遍性。

（60）方法，方式：way, method, means, approach, manner

way 适用范围较广，指做某事的方式或方法。

method 指较为具体的、具有针对性的做某事的方法。

means 指做某事的方法、工具和手段。

approach 指为解决问题或达到某一效果而精心设计的方法。

manner 指开展行动时较为特殊的方法。

（61）事情：thing, matter, business, concern, affair

thing 泛指所有的事件、物品，多指不具体的事物。

matter 指应该引起关注并进行处理的事情。

business 指较为重要，需要耗费较大精力去处理的事情。

concern 与某一方的切身利益直接相关的事情。

affair 常指与公众利益相关，较为严肃的事情。

（62）反对：oppose, object, resist, protest

oppose 通过采取行动进行反对，反对的对象一般有着较大影响。

object 指反对某个人的观念，并且往往通过言语进行表现。

resist 通过采取行动，尽力阻止事物朝着自己反对的方向发展。

protest 通过文字或行动，在较大范围内宣布自己对某事的反对。

（63）正常的，常规的；平常的：normal, usual, ordinary, average, regular

normal 指符合标准或规范，没有异常。

usual 强调事情经常发生而习以为常。

ordinary强调事情普通平常，不存在特别之处。

average强调数值处于居中位置，不高也不低。

regular指事情遵循已有模式，有规律或定期的。

（64）整体的一部分：part，piece，section，division，portion，fraction，fragment，segment

part适用范围较为广泛，泛指能从整体中剥离的部分或从整体中划分成的部分。

piece指从整体上分割下来的部分，也可指构成复杂整体的部件。

section按照较为明确的标准划分出的部分。

division将整体分割后形成的部分。

portion指分得整体中的一部分。

fraction指虽包含在整体中，但较为微小的部分。

fragment指在外力作用下，整体破碎成碎片。

segment指自然力量分割后形成的一部分。

（65）执行，实施：perform，conduct，execute，fulfil

perform指执行较为复杂或难度较大的任务。

conduct指组织某一活动并实施。

execute指按照已有计划，执行某项任务或进行活动。

fulfil指为满足需要、愿望、要求而实施某事。

（66）个人的，私人的：personal，private，individual

personal指与特定的人或物有关，与他人无关。

private指事物为私人所有，也指活动只在几人间展开，不对外公开。

individual指单独的、个别的，不是群体的。

（67）之前的，先前的：former，prior，previous

former形容某人过去的身份、职位或多者之中的前者。

prior侧重对比事件发生的先后顺序。

previous指之前存在的事物或状态。

（68）前进，行进；进展：progress，advance，proceed

progress指逐步改进并接近预期目标的过程。

advance指队伍的前进，尤指武装部队的前进。

proceed指继续做某事或下一步要做某事。

（69）明智的；合情合理的：reasonable，sensible，rational

reasonable 表示事实清楚，证据充分且合情合理。

sensible 指理性而非感性地做出了正确的判断或选择。

rational 指人清醒理智，不受蒙蔽。

（70）拒绝：refuse, decline, reject, repel

refuse 指直截了当、毫不避讳的拒绝。

decline 指以委婉的方式谢绝他人的帮助、邀请。

reject 指因不接受或不赞同而拒绝。

repel 指十分强烈的拒绝，还会采取相应行动。

（71）除掉，去掉：remove, eliminate, dismiss, expel, eradicate

remove 指把某物从某处移开。

eliminate 让某种事物或现象消失。

dismiss 指摒弃某物或某种思想、观点。

expel 指开除某人，或将某人或某物驱逐出某一区域。

eradicate 意为"根除"，强调彻底地去除。

（72）工资，收入：pay, income, wage, salary, earnings, allowance

pay 适用范围较为广泛，泛指付出劳动后得到的报酬。

income 指从劳动、投资中获得的收入。

wage 指按小时、天、周计算的报酬。

salary 多指专业技术人员或脑力劳动者获得的劳动报酬。

earnings 可指劳动者获得的报酬，也可指组织机构所获得的利润。

allowance 指收入中的补贴部分。

（73）显示，显露，展现：show, exhibit, display, indicate, reveal, manifest, demonstrate

show 适用范围较为广泛，可指表明某种结果或将某物给某人看。

exhibit 侧重指较为正式的展出，将某物公开展示，以供欣赏或了解。

display 侧重指列举某物的优势或特点，不如 exhibit 正式。

indicate 指显示的内容是经过一定调查研究而获得的，不是显而易见的。

reveal 指把之前只有少部分人了解或保密的事情公布出来，让更多人了解。

manifest 指清楚地显示出某种结果或论断。

demonstrate 指为某人的行为、态度或外在特征提供证据，表明其合理性。

（74）策略，战术：strategy, tactic

strategy 表示为完成某事而制定的系统性、全局性的计划。

tactic 指在特殊场景下为完成某事而采取的方法。

（75）趋势，倾向：trend，tendency，inclination

　　trend 指事物发展变化的大体方向。

　　tendency 指人或事物在行动、习惯上表现出的特定模式。

　　inclination 多指思想态度存在偏好。

（76）经历，经受，遭受：experience，undergo，suffer

　　experience 指经历了某一特定事件或情况。

　　undergo 多指经历变化或让人不愉快的事。

　　suffer 指经历灾难、疾病、困境，并受到折磨。

（77）理解，明白：understand，apprehend，comprehend

　　understand 指明白某人的话语或事物的本质及意义。

　　apprehend 指能明白事物的核心要义。

　　comprehend 指对事物有透彻的理解。

（78）使用，应用：use，apply，employ，utilize，exploit

　　use 为达到某一目的而使用某种方法或工具。

　　apply 多指在特殊场景下运用政策、制度、技术，使其发挥作用。

　　employ 多指雇佣人员，也指为某种原因而使用某物。

　　utilize 侧重指为实际性的目的而使用。

　　exploit 多指为了谋取利益而使用。

（79）视力，视觉：sight，vision，eyesight

　　sight 表示能看见事物的能力。

　　vision 指人的视力或视野，也可指远见或幻象。

　　eyesight 指视力。

（80）财产，财富：property，wealth，asset

　　property 指个人、机构或国家所拥有的财富。

　　wealth 可指物质财富或抽象的精神财富。

　　asset 指能够用来支撑组织发展的资本或资产。

二、固定搭配积累

1. 常考固定搭配汇总

➢ 常考动词固定搭配（一）

（1）break away from 逃脱，脱离；背叛

（2）break down 出故障，坏掉；失败；垮掉

（3）break even 收支平衡

（4）break into 强行闯入；突然开始；顺利打入

（5）break off 断开；停顿，中断

（6）break out 突然开始；爆发

（7）break through 取得突破

（8）break up 破碎；结束；解散

（9）break with 与……断绝关系；脱离

（10）bring up 养育；提出

（11）bring in 引入；推行；赚得

（12）bring out 生产；出版；推出；使显现

（13）bring to 使恢复知觉

（14）bring on 引起；导致

（15）call away 叫走

（16）call back 回电话

（17）call for 需要；（公开）要求

（18）call in 打电话来；顺路拜访

（19）call off 取消

（20）call on 呼吁；（短暂）拜访，探访

（21）call out 号召；喊叫

（22）call up 打电话；征召入伍

（23）carry back 使回想起，使回忆

（24）carry on 继续；举行，开展

（25）carry out 实施，执行

（26）carry forward 发扬；推进

（27）catch on 受欢迎，流行起来

（28）catch up 赶上，追上

（29）catch up with 产生（曾设法避免的）问题；捕获

（30）（be）caught up in 牵扯进

（31）come about 发生

（32）come across 被理解；给人以……印象

（33）come after 追赶，追逐

（34）come along 到达，抵达；跟随，跟着来

（35）come around 改变心态，改变观点

（36）come back 回来；再度流行

（37）come by（为看望某人）作短暂拜访

（38）come down 崩塌；（雨、雪等）落下；着陆；下降

（39）come from 来自

（40）come in（赛跑等比赛中）取得（名次）；在……中起作用；到达

（41）come to 恢复知觉；苏醒

（42）come up 发生；被提及；即将发生

（43）come up with 想出，提出；设法拿出（所需钱款）

（44）drive away 驱车离开

（45）drive back 驾车返回

（46）drive off 驱车离去

（47）drive down 降低，减少

（48）drive in 驶进

（49）get on/along with（与某人）和睦相处

（50）get away 离开，脱身；度假，休假

（51）get away from 摆脱（旧思维）

（52）get back 回去

（53）get back to 恢复（原来的状态）；回到（原来的话题）

（54）get down 使沮丧；写下，记下；俯身；跪下

（55）get in 当选；（火车、公共汽车或飞机）到达，抵达

（56）get in one's way 妨碍某人

（57）get off 下车；出发；走开；把手拿开；免受惩

（58）get on 上车；取得成功

（59）go away 走开；离家外出（尤指度假）；消失

（60）go back 追溯到；回到（过去），回顾

（61）go in for 爱好（某活动）；参加（考试）；从事（某种活动）

（62）go into 描述，叙述；调查；从事（某工作或职业）；（时间、精力或钱）被用在

（63）go on（灯）亮，通（电）；继续；（时间）流逝；

（64）go out 外出交际；送出；发出，（广播或电视节目）播放；（新闻或消息）发布；（火或灯光）熄灭

（65）go over 仔细检查；认真讨论；用心思考

（66）give away 赠送；丧失，失去；泄露（秘密）

（67）give back 归还

（68）give in 投降，屈从

（69）give out 用完；分发；公开，宣布（消息等）；停止运转

（70）give over 停止

（71）give up 放弃；辞去（工作）

（72）hold back（使）犹豫，踌躇

（73）hold down 按住某人；保住（工作或位置）

（74）hold out 伸出（手），递出；维持，坚持；抵抗，幸存

（75）hold up 举起，抬起；支持住，承受住；耽搁

（76）keep at 继续做某事

（77）keep back 留存，保留（……的一部分）；隐瞒

（78）keep in touch with（与……）保持联系；了解（某课题或领域的情况）

（79）keep on 继续；继续雇用

（80）keep up（天气）持续不变

（81）keep up with（与……）齐步前进；跟上（变化等）；了解

（82）lay back 向后靠；躺下

（83）lay off 辞退，解雇

（84）lay out（整齐地）铺开，展开；阐述，讲解；规划，布置

（85）lay up 贮备

（86）look about 四下观望

（87）look after 照顾；（尤指为工作）料理，打理

（88）look ahead 展望未来

（89）look back 回顾

（90）look down 俯视

（91）look down on 蔑视，轻视

（92）look for 寻找

（93）look into 调查

（94）look through 逐一查看……；浏览；（因生气、沉思等）对……视而不见

（95）look out 小心，当心

（96）look over 检查；（快速）翻阅，浏览

（97）make out（勉强地）辨认出；把……弄清楚；举例证明（……是最好的）

（98）make up 组成；编造；（给……）化妆；凑足

（99）make up for 弥补，补偿

（100）start from 从……开始

（101）start off 动身；进行（或开展）起来；首先进行

（102）start up（使）启动，发动

（103）pass along 沿……向前走

（104）pass around（一群人）传，传递

（105）pass away 去世，逝世

（106）pass by 经过（……旁边）

（107）pass down 使世代相传，流传

（108）pass out 昏迷

（109）pass through 经过，路过

（110）pay back 偿还；报复，惩罚

（111）pay for 为……付钱

（112）pay off 还清（债务）；成功

（113）pick off 选择（目标）射击

（114）pick on（跟某人）闹别扭，故意刁难挑剔；挑选，选中

（115）pick out 精心挑选；认出来

（116）pick up 拿起，捡起；（通常指开车）接载，取走；（不费力地）获得，学会；（贸易或经济）好转，改善

（117）put away 把……收起

（118）put down 写下，记录；付（定金）；镇压（暴乱或叛乱）

（119）put forward 提出（计划、建议）；推荐

（120）put off 推迟；敷衍；使对……失去兴趣；使分心

（121）put on 穿，戴；上演，举办；开动（设备、装置等）

（122）put out 离港，起航

（123）put up 建造，搭建；张贴

（124）put up with 忍受，容忍

（125）run about 跑来跑去

（126）run across 偶然碰见

（127）run after 追逐，追赶

（128）run away 逃离；逃避，躲避

（129）run down 耗尽能量，停止工作；压缩，削减；降低；（车辆）把……撞伤

（130）run out 用完，耗尽；过期，失效

（131）run over（车辆）撞倒，碾过

（132）send away 邮购，函购

（133）send back 寄回，送回

（134）send for 请……来，派人去叫；写信索要

（135）send out 分发；发出（信号、声音、光、热）；生出，长出（根茎、枝芽）

（136）set about 着手做，攻击

（137）set down 制定，规定（规则）；把（思想、经历）写下来，记下

（138）set off 动身，出发；引发，触发

（139）set out 动身，出发；开始，着手；安排，摆放；陈述，阐述

（140）set up 创建，建立；安排

（141）sign in 签到，登记

（142）sign off（在信的结尾）写结束语；（挂电话、广播节目结束时）就说到这

（143）sign out 签退

（144）sign up（和……）签约，雇用；报名（参加课程）

（145）take along 随身携带

（146）take away 拿走；从……中减去；带走，抓走

（147）take back 退还，归还；收回，撤回；使回想起

（148）take in 收留；理解，领会；观看；摄入，吸收；容纳；收入，进账

（149）take off（飞机）起飞；腾飞，突然成功；（突然）离开；脱掉；请假

（150）take on 承担，接受；呈现，显出；雇用

（151）take out 去除；取得，获得（贷款、执照、保单等）；邀请……外出

（152）take up 开始从事；喜欢上；开始处理；占用，花费

（153）think about 考虑到，关心；考虑，打算

（154）think of 想象到；想出；记得

（155）think out 仔细思考

（156）think over（尤指在做出决定前）仔细考虑

（157）turn away 把某人拒之门外

（158）turn back 往回走；回头

（159）turn down 拒绝（某人或其请求、提议等）；调低；（比率）减少，（水平）

降低

（160）turn off 关掉；拐弯；使失去兴趣

（161）turn on 打开（设备）；突然表现得

（162）turn over 翻转；发动，继续运转

（163）turn over a new leaf 重新开始

（164）turn over to 交，移交

（165）turn to 翻到；向……求助

（166）use up 用尽，吃光

（167）used to 过去常常

（168）（be）used to do 被用作

（169）（be）used to doing 习惯于做某事

（170）work as 任……职，做……工作

（171）work at 在……工作；致力于

（172）work out 想出，得到（解决方法）；计算出；（如期）发生；锻炼

（173）write back (给某人）写回信，复信

（174）write down 写下，记下

（175）write to 给……写信

（176）write out 写出（篇幅较长的报告或清单）

➤ 常考动词固定搭配（二）

（1）（be）about to 刚要，即将

（2）account for 说明（原因）

（3）accuse sb. of sth. 因某事控告某人，谴责某人

（4）acquaint with 熟悉，熟知

（5）adapt to (使）适应，适合；改编，改写

（6）add up to 合计达，总计

（7）adhere to 附着，黏附

（8）adjust to (使）适应于

（9）agree to sth. 同意，赞成某事

（10）agree with sb. 同意，赞成某人

（11）aim at 瞄准，对准；旨在

（12）aim to 目的是

（13）amount to 合计，共计，等于

（14）appeal to 诉诸，求助

（15）apply for 申请，请求

（16）approve of 赞成，同意；批准，核准

（17）arise from 由……引起，由……产生

（18）arrive at 到达（小地方）；达成，得出

（19）arrive in 到达（大地方）

（20）ask for 询问，要求

（21）assign to 指派，选派

（22）associate with 使联系，使联合；交往

（23）attach to 系上，贴上；使附属，使依恋

（24）attempt at 企图；努力

（25）attend to 照顾，护理；专心于

（26）attribute to 把……归因于，归咎于

（27）bear/keep in mind 记住

（28）begin with 从……开始

（29）believe in 相信，信任

（30）belong to (在所有权关系等方面）属于

（31）benefit from 受益，获益

（32）blame for/on 责备；因……而受到责备

（33）check in 办理登记手续

（34）check out 记账后离开；检验，核查

（35）combine with 结合，联合

（36）comment on 评论

（37）communicate with 与……通讯；交流

（38）compare to 比较，对比；把……比作

（39）compensate for 补偿，赔偿

（40）complain about/of 抱怨，申诉

（41）comply with 照做，遵照；应允

（42）concentrate on 集中，专心

（43）(be) concerned with 关心，挂念；从事于

（44）confine to/with 限制

（45）conflict with 冲突，抵触

（46）congratulate on祝贺，向……致祝词

（47）consent to同意，赞成

（48）consist of由……组成

（49）consist in在于；存在于

（50）consult with商量，商议

（51）contrast with对比，和……形成对照

（52）contribute to捐献，捐助，贡献；投稿

（53）control over控制，支配

（54）convert to变化，变换，转换

（55）convince of使确信，使信服

（56）cope with对付，应付

（57）correspond to相当，相类似

（58）correspond with相符合，相一致

（59）count on倚靠，指望

（60）count up算出……的总数，共计

（61）cover up掩饰，掩盖

（62）deal in经营

（63）deal with处理；论述；涉及

（64）dedicate to奉献，把……用在

（65）depend on/upon依靠，信赖，取决于

（66）devote to致力于，把……奉献给

（67）differ from不同

（68）differ with与……意见不同

（69）disagree with不同意，不一致

（70）disappoint at/with对……失望

（71）dispose of 处理，销毁，去掉

（72）distinguish from区别，辨别，辨认

（73）do away with废除，取消；结束

（74）do without没有也行

（75）engage in使从事于，使忙于

（76）equip with装备，配备

（77）exchange for交换，调换；兑换

（78）expose to 使暴露，受到，使曝光；

（79）figure out 计算出；领会到

（80）fill in/out 填充，填写

（81）find out 查明，发现

（82）free of/from 不受……之苦，免去

（83）focus on（使）聚焦，（使）集中

（84）hurry up 匆匆完成，（使）赶快

（85）identify with 认为等同于

（86）impose on 把……强加给；利用；欺骗

（87）impress on 印，留下印象

（88）improve on/upon 改进，超过

（89）inform of/about 通知，告诉

（90）inquire of/about 询问，打听，调查

（91）insist on/upon 坚决要求，坚持

（92）interfere in/with 干涉，介入；妨碍，干扰

（93）involve in 卷入，陷入；牵涉，包含

（94）lead to 导致，通往

（95）leave behind 留下；忘记带

（96）leave for 动身去

（97）lie in 在于

（98）limit to 限制，限定

（99）line up 排成一行

（100）long for 渴望，极想

（101）major in 主修，专攻

（102）meet with 遇见，碰到

（103）name after 用……取名，命名

（104）object to 反对，不赞成

（105）occur to 被想到，被想起

（106）owe to 应把……归功于

（107）participate in 参与，参加

（108）persist in 坚持不懈，执意；持续

（109）persuade of（使）相信

（110）prefer to更喜欢，宁愿

（111）prevent from预防，防止

（112）profit by/from利，获益

（113）provide sb. with sth.向某人提供某物

（114）provide sth. for sb.把某物提供给某人

（115）refer to参考，查阅；涉及，提到

（116）refer to...as把……称作，把……当作

（117）regard...as把……看作，认为

（118）register with注册，登记

（119）relate to有关联

（120）rely on/upon依靠，依赖

（121）remark about/on评论，议论

（122）remind sb. of sth.使某人想起某事

（123）remind sb. to do sth.提醒某人做某事

（124）reply to回答，答复

（125）report to报到；报告

（126）resign to辞职；辞去，放弃；托付给

（127）resort to求助，诉诸；采取；凭借

（128）respond to响应，回答

（129）rest on依靠，依赖；被搁在，停留在

（130）restrain from阻碍，控制，抑制

（131）result from起因于，由……产生

（132）result in导致，结果是

（133）search for寻找，探查；搜查，搜索

（134）seek after/for寻找，追求；探索；试图，企图

（135）select from挑选，选择

（136）separate from（使）分离；（使）分开

（137）settle down定居；平静下来，专心于；解决，调停

（138）share in分享，分担

（139）share with分派；分配；分享，共用

（140）specialize in擅长于；专门研究，专攻

（141）speed up加速

（142）stick to粘在……上，粘住，坚持，信守

（143）subject to使服从；使遭受

（144）submit to使受到；服从，屈服，忍受，顺从；呈送，递交

（145）succeed in在……方面成功

➢ 常考动词和名词固定搭配

（1）have access to可以接近；可以利用

（2）make the acquaintance of sb.结识某人

（3）take advantage of利用，趁……之机

（4）make an agreement with与……达成协议

（5）make an appeal to sb.向某人发出呼吁

（6）application for申请

（7）at pains尽力

（8）make an appointment with sb.与某人约会

（9）approach to通往……的方法；接近

（10）pay attention to注意

（11）pay a visit to参观，访问

（12）do/try one's best努力，尽力

（13）make the best of充分利用

（14）give a challenge挑战

（15）take a chance冒险；投机

（16）take charge of管理，接管

（17）combination with与……结合

（18）get command of控制

（19）communication with与……通讯，与……交流

（20）keep company with和……结交；和……亲热

（21）keep sb. company陪伴某人，陪某人同走

（22）competition with/against sb.与某人竞争

（23）complaint about/of对……抱怨

（24）come to a conclusion得出结论

（25）take...into consideration考虑到……

（26）be in contact with与……接触

（27）have contact with和……接触

（28）lose contact with 与……失去联系

（29）have control over/of 对……控制

（30）lose control of 失去对……控制

（31）have/hold a conversation with 与……谈话

（32）commit a crime 犯罪

（33）do damage to 损害

（34）come to a decision 决定下来

（35）arrive at a decision 决定下来

（36）make a decision 做决定

（37）make a difference 有影响，有关系

（38）have difficulty in doing sth. 做某事有困难

（39）come into effect 生效；实施

（40）put into effect 实行；使生效，使起作用

（41）take effect 生效，起作用

（42）make a mistake 犯错误

（43）set a good example to sb. 为某人树立榜样

（44）catch sb.'s eye 引人注目

（45）keep an eye on 留意，照看

（46）have faith in 对……信任

（47）lose faith in 失去对……的信任

（48）come into fashion 开始流行

（49）follow the fashion 赶时髦

（50）set the fashion 创立新式样

（51）make a fortune 发财

（52）try one's fortune 碰运气

（53）get hold of 抓住，得到

（54）hunger for/after 渴望

（55）have an influence on/upon 对……有影响

（56）make inquiries of sb. about sth. 向某人询问某事

（57）throw light on/upon sth. 阐明某事，使人了解某事

（58）make up one's mind 下决心，决意

（59）make the most of 充分利用

（60）come to sb.'s notice 引起某人的注意

（61）take notice of 注意到

（62）make/take an objection to 对……表示反对

（63）bring/put...into operation 做手术；操作，运转；运算

（64）come/go into operation 实行，生效

（65）keep pace with 与……并驾齐驱，共同前进

（66）take pains 努力，尽力，下苦功

（67）play a part（in）(在……中）扮演角色，参与

（68）take part in 参加

（69）take place 发生，进行，举行

（70）take the place of 取代，代替

（71）keep to the point 扣住主题

（72）make a point 立论，证明论点

（73）make a living 谋生

（74）hold the position of（as）担任……职务

（75）put...in/into practice 实施，实行

（76）make preparations for 为……做准备

（77）make a promise 许下诺言

（78）make a reduction 减小，缩小

（79）make reference to 提到

（80）have no reference to 与……无关

（81）have resort/recourse to sb. 求助于某人

（82）make a response 对……做出响应

（83）take the responsibility for 对……负起责任

（84）give rise to 引起，使发生

（85）run/take a risk 冒险

（86）play a role in 在……中扮演角色（起作用）

（87）make sense 讲得通，言之有理

（88）take stock 清查存货，盘存

（89）lay/place/put stress on/upon 把重点放在……上

（90）substitute for sth. 替代某物

（91）have a talk with sb. 与某人交谈

（92）thanks to 由于，多亏

（93）take one's time 不着急，不慌忙

（94）keep in touch with sb. 与某人保持联系

（95）keep track of 记录；与……保持联系

（96）get into trouble 陷入困境，招致不幸

（97）have trouble with 同……闹纠纷

（98）make use of 使用，利用

（99）night shift 夜班

➤ 常考形容词固定搭配

（1）absent from 缺席，不在

（2）accustomed to 习惯于

（3）applicable to 可应用于，适应于

（4）aware of 意识到，知道

（5）beneficial to 对……有益，对……有利

（6）blind to 对……视而不见；盲目的

（7）capable of 有能力/技能的；能……的，可……的

（8）common to 共同的，共有的

（9）confident of 确信，相信

（10）conscious of 意识到，知道

（11）consistent with 与……相符，与……一致

（12）content with 对……感到满意

（13）contrary to 和……相反

（14）convenient to/for 对……方便

（15）crazy about/on 对……着迷，热衷

（16）critical of 对……感到不满，对……表示谴责

（17）dependent on/upon 依靠，依赖

（18）distinct from 与……不同

（19）diverse from 和……不一样

（20）doubtful about/of 对……怀疑

（21）due to 因为，由于；应归于

（22）eager for/after 渴求

（23）equivalent to 等于，相当于

（24）essential to/for必要的，基本的，不可少的

（25）familiar to/with熟悉

（26）fit for适合，能胜任……

（27）fond of喜欢

（28）good at擅长

（29）grateful to sb. for对某人表示感谢

（30）helpful to对……有益，对……有帮助

（31）independent of不依赖，不依靠

（32）inferior to不如，劣于

（33）in the public eye受公众瞩目的

（34）keen on对……着迷，喜爱

（35）liable to易患……的；应受法律制裁的

（36）loyal to对……忠诚的

（37）opposite to相反的；对立的，对面的

（38）preferable to更可取的，更好的

（39）prior to在……之前，居先

（40）proportional to与……相称，与……成比例

（41）qualified in胜任，合适

（42）relative to相对于；和……相应，和……有关

（43）relevant to与……有关

（44）representative of代表

（45）resistant to对……有抵抗力的，耐……的

（46）responsible to sb. for sth.向某人对某事负责

（47）ripe for时机成熟；准备好

（48）sensitive to对……敏感，对……灵敏

（49）similar to和……相似

（50）skillful at/in精于，善于

（51）strict with对……要求严格

（52）subject to易受……的，受……支配的；将会……的

（53）sufficient for足够，满足

（54）suitable for/to适合的

（55）superior to比……好，优于

（56）suspicious of 对……起疑心，猜疑

（57）tired of 厌倦，厌烦

（58）typical of 典型的，有代表性的

（59）uncertain of/about 对……不确定

（60）worthy of 值得

➤　常考介词固定搭配

（1）above all 最重要的是，尤其是

（2）after all 毕竟，终究

（3）ahead of 在……之前

（4）all at once 突然；同时，一起

（5）all but 除了……都；几乎，差不多

（6）all of a sudden 忽然，突然

（7）all over 到处，遍及

（8）all over again 再一次，重新

（9）all the same 仍然，照样地

（10）all the time 一直，始终

（11）and so on/forth 诸如此类，等等

（12）anything but 根本不；除……以外任何事情

（13）apart from 除……以外（别无，尚有）

（14）around the clock 夜以继日

（15）as a matter of fact 事实上，其实

（16）as a result 因此，作为结果

（17）as a result of 作为……的结果，由于

（18）as a rule 通常，多半；照例

（19）as for/to 至于，关于

（20）as usual 像往常一样，照例

（21）aside from 除了……以外

（22）at a loss 不知所措，困惑；亏本地

（23）at all costs 不惜任何代价，无论如何

（24）at best 充其量，至多

（25）at first 起先，最初

（26）at last 终于

（27）at least 至少；无论如何

（28）at most 至多，不超过

（29）at no time 从不，决不

（30）at once 立刻，马上；同时，一起

（31）at one time 曾经；一度

（32）at present 现在，目前

（33）at the cost of 以……为代价

（34）at the same time 同时；然而，不过

（35）at times 有时，不时，间或

（36）back and forth 来回地，反复地

（37）because of 因为，由于

（38）before long 不久（以后）

（39）by accident 偶然

（40）by all means 尽一切办法；一定，务必

（41）by chance 偶然；意外地，碰巧

（42）by means of 用，依靠

（43）by mistake 错误地；无意中（做了某件错事）

（44）by no means 决不，并没有

（45）by reason of 由于，因为

（46）by the way 顺便地；附带说说

（47）for instance 例如，比如

（48）for the better 好转，向好的方向发展

（49）for the moment/present 暂时；目前

（50）for the sake of 为了，为了……的利益

（51）from time to time 有时；偶尔

（52）from now on 今后，从今以后

（53）in a hurry 匆忙；很快地；急于

（54）in a moment 立即，马上

（55）in a sense 从某种意义上说

（56）in a/one word 简言之，总之，一句话

（57）in accordance with 与……一致；按照，依据

（58）in addition 另外，加之

（59）in addition to 除……之外（还）

（60）in advance 预先，事先

（61）in all 总共，合计

（62）in any case 无论如何；不管怎样

（63）in brief 简言之，以简洁的形式

（64）in case of 假使……，如果发生

（65）in charge of 主管，负责

（66）in common 共用的，共有的

（67）in consequence of 结果，因此

（68）in debt 欠债

（69）in detail 详细地

（70）in difficulty 处境困难

（71）in effect 实际上；事实上

（72）in favour of 赞同，支持

（73）in future 今后，从今以后

（74）in general 一般来说，大体上

（75）in hand（工作等）正在进行中；待办理

（76）in honour of 向……表示敬意；为纪念

（77）in itself 本质上，就其本身而言

（78）in line with 跟……一致，符合

（79）in memory of 以纪念，为了纪念

（80）in no case 决不，无论如何不

（81）in no way 一点也不；决不

（82）in order to 为了……，以……为目的

（83）in other words 也就是说，换句话说

（84）in part 在某种程度上；部分地

（85）in particular 特别地；尤其

（86）in place 在合适的位置；适当的

（87）in place of 代替，取代

（88）in practice 在实践中；在不断练习中

（89）in proportion to 与……成比例；与……相称

（90）in quantity（=in large quantities）大量

（91）in relation to 与……相关，沙及，有关

（92）in return for 作为……的交换；作为……的报答

（93）in short 总之，简言之

（94）in sight of 被见到，看得见；在望，在即

（95）in spite of 不管，不顾

（96）in step with 与……合步调，与……步调一致

（97）in the course of 在……期间，在过程中

（98）in the end 最后，终于

（99）in the first place 首先，第一点

（100）in the future 未来

（101）in the light of 鉴于，由于；按照，根据

（102）in the way 挡道，妨碍人

（103）in time 及时，最后，终于

（104）in touch with 与有联系；有……的消息

（105）in turn 依次，轮流；反过来

（106）in vain 徒劳

（107）instead of 代替，而不是

（108）more or less 或多或少；左右

（109）no doubt 无疑地

（110）no longer 不再

（111）no more 不再；不再存在；也不

（112）now and then 时而，不时

（113）of course 当然，自然

（114）off duty 下班

（115）on a large scale 大规模地

（116）on account of 因为；由于

（117）on the average 平均而言，通常

（118）on behalf of 代表；为了

（119）on board 在船（或车、飞机）上

（120）on business 因事，因公

（121）on condition that 如果，在……条件下

（122）on duty 值班，当班

（123）on earth 究竟；到底；在世界上

（124）on occasion 间或，有时

（125）on one's own 独自地，独立地

（126）on purpose 有意，故意地

（127）on sale 出售；上市；廉价出售

（128）on schedule 按时间表；准时

（129）on second thoughts 进一步考虑后，继而一想

（130）on the contrary 正相反

（131）on the grounds of 以……为理由，根据

（132）on the one hand...on the other hand...一方面……另一方面……

（133）on/upon the point of 即将……之时，正要……的时候

（134）on the whole 总的看来，大体上

（135）once in a while 偶尔，间或

（136）once more/again 再一次

（137）once upon a time(常用于故事开头) 从前，很久以前

（138）out of control 失去控制

（139）out of date 过时的；废弃的

（140）out of order 不整齐；（工作）不正常，出故障

（141）out of place 不在合适的位置；不恰当的

（142）out of practice 生疏；久不练习

（143）out of question 没问题

（144）out of touch（with）与……失去联系；没有……的消息

（145）over and over（again）反复，再三

（146）so as to 为的是，以便

（147）so...as to 如此……以至于

（148）so far 迄今为止；就此说来

（149）so/as far as...be concerned 就……而言

（150）sooner or later 迟早，早晚

（151）to the point 切题，中肯；切中要害

（152）under control 被控制住

（153）under/in the circumstances 在这种情况下；（情况）既然如此

（154）under way 在进行中；（船）在行进

（155）up to 忙于，从事于；胜任，适于；直到

（156）up to date 最新的；现代的

（157）with/in regard to 关于，至于

（158）with relation to 关于，涉及；与……相比

（159）with respect to 关于，至于

（160）word for word 逐字地，一字不变地

2. 常考动词接宾语/宾补的不同形式

  ➤ 接不定式做宾语/宾补的常考动词

首字母	接不定式做宾语的常考动词	接不定式做宾补的常考动词
A	afford to do sth. 负担得起做某事 agree to do sth. 同意做某事 aim to do sth. 目的是做某事 appear to do sth. 似乎要做某事 arrange to do sth. 安排做某事 ask to do sth. 要求做某事 attempt to do sth. 尝试做某事	advise sb. to do sth. 建议某人做某事 allow sb. to do sth. 允许某人做某事 ask sb. to do sth. 要求某人做某事
C	can't afford to do sth. 负担不起做某事 can't wait to do sth. 等不及做某事 choose to do sth. 选择去做某事 consent to do sth. 同意做某事 continue to do sth. 继续做某事	cause sb. to do sth. 导致某人做某事 challenge sb. to do sth. 挑战某人做某事 choose sb. to do sth. 选择某人做某事 convince sb. to do sth. 说服某人做某事
D	decide to do sth. 决定做某事 deserve to do sth. 值得做某事	/
E	expect to do sth. 期望做某事	enable sb. to do sth. 使某人做某事 encourage sb. to do sth. 鼓励某人做某事
F	fail to do sth. 未能做某事	forbid sb. to do sth. 禁止某人做某事 force sb. to do sth. 迫使某人做某事
G	/	get sb. to do sth. 使（要）某人做某事
H	help（to）do sth. 帮忙做某事 hesitate to do sth. 犹豫做某事 hope to do sth. 希望做某事 hurry to do sth. 匆忙去做某事	help sb.（to）do sth. 帮助某人做某事 hire sb. to do sth. 雇用某人做某事
I	intend to do sth. 打算做某事	invite sb. to do sth. 邀请某人做某事

首字母	接不定式做宾语的常考动词	接不定式做宾补的常考动词
L	learn to do sth. 学做某事	/
M	manage to do sth. 设法做某事	/
N	need to do sth. 需要做某事 neglect to do sth. 忽略做某事	need sb. to do sth. 需要某人做某事
O	offer to do sth. 主动提出做某事	order sb. to do sth. 命令某人做某事
P	plan to do sth. 计划做某事 prepare to do sth. 准备做某事 pretend to do sth. 假装做某事 promise to do sth. 承诺做某事	pay sb. to do sth. 付钱给某人做某事 permit sb. to do sth. 允许某人做某事 persuade sb. to do sth. 劝说某人做某事 promise sb. to do sth. 承诺某人做某事
R	refuse to do sth. 拒绝做某事 request to do sth. 要求做某事	remind sb. to do sth. 提醒某人做某事 request sb. to do sth. 要求某人做某事 require sb. to do sth. 需要某人做某事
S	seem to do sth. 似乎要做某事 struggle to do sth. 努力做某事 swear to do sth. 发誓做某事	/
T	/	teach sb. to do sth. 教某人做某事 tell sb. to do sth. 告诉某人做某事
U	/	urge sb. to do sth. 催促某人做某事
V	volunteer to do sth. 自愿做某事	/
W	wait to do sth. 等待做某事 want to do sth. 想要做某事 wish to do sth. 希望做某事 would like to do sth. 愿意做某事	warn sb. to do sth. 警告某人做某事 wish sb. to do sth. 希望某人做某事 would like sb. to do sth. 想要某人做某事 want sb. to do sth. 想要某人做某事
Y	yearn to do sth. 渴望做某事	/

➤ 接动名词做宾语/宾补的常考动词

首字母	接动名词做宾语的常考动词	接动名词做宾补的常考动词
A	acknowledge doing sth. 承认做（了）某事 admit doing sth. 承认做（了）某事 advise doing sth. 建议做某事 appreciate doing sth. 感激做某事 avoid doing sth. 避免做某事	/

首字母	接动名词做宾语的常考动词	接动名词做宾补的常考动词
C	celebrate doing sth. 庆祝做某事 consider doing sth. 考虑做某事	catch sb. doing sth. 碰上某人做某事
D	delay doing sth. 推迟做某事 deny doing sth. 否认做了某事 detest doing sth. 讨厌做某事 discontinue doing sth. 停止做某事 discuss doing sth. 讨论做某事 dislike doing sth. 不喜欢做某事	discover sb. doing sth. 发现某人做某事
E	endure doing sth. 忍受做某事 enjoy doing sth. 享受做某事 escape doing sth. 逃避做某事 explain doing sth. 解释做某事	/
F	feel like doing sth. 喜欢做某事 finish doing sth. 完成做某事 forgive doing sth. 原谅做某事	feel sb. doing sth. 感觉某人正在做某事 find sb. doing sth. 发现某人正在做某事
G	give up doing sth. 放弃做某事	get sb. doing sth. 使某人做某事
H	/	have sb. doing sth. 使某人做某事 hear sb. doing sth. 听见某人做某事
I	imagine doing sth. 想象做某事	/
J	justify doing sth. 证明做某事是正确的	/
K	keep doing sth. 继续做某事	keep sb. doing sth. 使某人不停地做某事
M	mention doing sth. 提及做某事 mind doing sth. 介意做某事 miss doing sth. 错过做某事	/
N	/	notice sb. doing sth. 注意到某人做某事
O	object doing sth. 反对做某事	observe sb. doing sth. 观察某人做某事
P	postpone doing sth. 推迟做某事 practice doing sth. 练习做某事 prevent doing sth. 阻止做某事 prohibit doing sth. 禁止做某事 propose doing sth. 提议做某事 permit doing sth. 允许做某事	prevent sb. from doing sth. 阻止某人做某事
Q	quit doing sth. 停止做某事	/

首字母	接动名词做宾语的常考动词	接动名词做宾补的常考动词
R	recall doing sth. 记得做某事 recommend doing sth. 建议做某事 report doing sth. 报告做某事 resent doing sth. 讨厌做某事 resist doing sth. 抵制做某事 risk doing sth. 冒险做某事	/
S	suggest doing sth. 建议做某事 support doing sth. 支持做某事	see sb. doing sth. 看见某人正在做某事 send sb. doing sth. 使某人（突然）做某事 set sb. doing sth. 使（引起）某人做某事 start sb. doing sth. 使某人开始做某事 stop sb. doing sth. 阻止某人做某事
T	tolerate doing sth. 忍受做某事	/
U	understand doing sth. 理解做某事	/
W	/	watch sb. doing sth. 观看某人做某事

➤ 接动词原形做宾补的常考动词

（1）feel sb. do sth. 感觉某人做某事

（2）have sb. do sth. 使某人做某事

（3）hear sb. do sth. 听见某人做某事

（4）let sb. do sth. 让某人做某事

（5）listen to sb. do sth. 听着某人做某事

（6）look at sb. do sth. 看着某人做某事

（7）make sb. do sth. 使某人做某事

（8）notice sb. do sth. 注意某人做某事

（9）observe sb. do sth. 观察到某人做某事

（10）see sb. do sth. 看见某人做某事

（11）watch sb. do sth. 看着某人做某事

➤ 接不定式或动名词做宾语意思有区别的常考动词

（1）remember to do sth. 记住要去做某事

   remember doing sth. 记住曾做过某事

（2）forget to do sth. 忘记要去做某事

forget doing sth. 忘记曾做过某事

（3）regret to do sth. 遗憾要去做某事

regret doing sth. 后悔曾做过某事

（4）try to do sth. 设法要做某事

try doing sth. 试图做某事

（5）mean to do sth. 打算做某事

mean doing sth. 意味着做某事

（6）can't help to do sth. 不能帮助做某事

can't help doing sth. 禁不住做某事

（7）go on to do sth. 做完某事后接着做另一件事

go on doing sth. 继续做一直在做的事

（8）stop to do sth. 停下来去做某事

stop doing sth. 停止正在做的事

三、重点语法讲解

1. 介词

在领思阅读考试中，介词的考点十分常见，考查的是对介词的理解和运用，这里给大家列举一些最基础的介词用法，请大家熟记。

（1）时间介词

① in 表示时间段

in the morning/evening/afternoon 在早上/晚上/下午

in the daytime 在白天

in a day/week/month/year 在一天/一周/一个月/一年

in May 在五月

in spring/summer/autumn/winter 在春天/夏天/秋天/冬天

in 2019 在2019年

in the Christmas Holiday 在圣诞假期

in one's life 在某人的一生

② at 表示时刻、钟点

at half past five 在五点半

at seven o'clock 在七点钟

at noon 在中午

at the moment　现在

at that time　在那时

at the end of the holiday　在假期结束时

③ on表示特定的日子、具体日期、星期几

on Wednesday　在周三

on my birthday　在我生日那天

on that day　在那天

on September 1st　在9月1日

on a rainy morning　在一个下雨的早上

on a cold day in December　在12月的一个寒冷的日子

④ during和in都表示一段时间，但during更强调时间的延续，可以表示某段时间内自始至终的状态。

例：I want to relax in the summer vacation.

我想在暑假时放松一下。

She hadn't been attending during the lesson.

上课时她一直不专心。

⑤ for和since引导的时间状语都有延续之意，但侧重点不同。for+时间段，其侧重点是现在，表示延续到现在的一段时间（与现在完成时连用），或表示一段已经终结的时间（与过去时连用），或表示将要延续的一段时间（与将来时连用）。

例：They've been best mates since school.

他们从上学时期以来就是最要好的朋友。（现在完成时）

The room will be available for 3 days.

接下来的三天房间都可用。（一般将来时）

⑥ since+时间段，其侧重点是过去某时，意为"自从（过去某时）以来"，表示自过去某时延续至今的一段时间，常与现在完成时连用。

例：I have received 5 messages since I refused him.

自从我拒绝了他，我已经收到了5条信息了。（现在完成时）

It was the worst flood since records began.

这是有记录以来最严重的水灾（一般过去时）

⑦ 时间介词by表示不迟于某时，某时包括在内。before表示在某时之前，不包括某时。

例：The paper should be handed in by May 5th.

论文应该在5月5日或之前上交。（5月5日为最后期限）

The paper should be handed in before May 5th.

论文应该在5月5日前上交。（5月4日为最后期限）

（2）地点介词

① on指与物体表面接触，在某物的表面上。

例：There is a bird on the tree.

　　树上有一只鸟。

② in表示在……之上时，暗示占去了某物的一部分。

例：There are some impurities in the rice.

　　大米里有些杂质。

③ above指离开物体表面，在其上方，但不是正上方。

例：He lifted his hands above his head.

　　他双手举过头顶。

④ over指在物体正上方，还有"覆盖，越过"之意。

例：Water washed over the deck.

　　水从甲板上流过。

⑤ through表示从内部穿过；across表示从表面穿过；past表示从旁边经过；over表示从上方跨过。

例：I zoomed through the hall because I am late.

　　我快速穿过大厅，因为我迟到了。

　　We walked across the springy grass.

　　我们走过松软的草地。

　　He just walked straight past us!

　　他刚刚与我们擦肩而过！

　　She climbed over the wall.

　　她翻过墙去。

（3）表示工具、手段、材料的介词

with、by、in都可以表示"用"工具、手段和材料。with多指用具体的工具；by指使用的某种手段、交通工具等；in指使用语言或工具的具体类型。

例：The students cut the paper with scissors.

　　学生们用剪刀剪纸。

　　If you're travelling by car, ask whether there are parking spaces nearby.

如果你开汽车旅行，问问附近是否有停车位。

Please answer me in English.

请用英文回答我。

2. 可数名词、不可数名词的修饰词总结

可数名词、不可数名词的修饰词是语法中一大极易混淆的知识点，也是常出现的考点。因此，考生需仔细辨析，熟记在心。

（1）只能修饰可数名词的表达有：

few、a few、many、many a（n）、a good / great many、a（great/ large）number of、scores of、dozens of 等。

例：They've gone away for a few days.

他们已外出几天了。

The project was carried out in a great number of cities.

这个项目已经在多个城市实施。

Dozens of homes had been completely destroyed.

数十家房屋已被完全毁坏了。

注意：

① a good/great many后直接跟名词，没有介词of。

例：A good many books were bought from that bookstore.

许多书都是从那家书店里买的。

但是，若其后所接名词有the、these、my等限定词修饰，则要用介词of表示"……中的很多"。

例：a great many of my friends 我朋友中的许多人

② Many a修饰主语时，主语虽为复数含义，但要用单数形式，同时谓语动词也要用单数。

例：Many a student has（=many students have）passed the rigorous test.

许多同学都通过了严格的测试。

（2）只能修饰不可数名词的表达有：

little、a little、a bit of、much、a great deal of、a great/large amount of 等。

例：A great deal of information was neglected.

许多信息都被忽视了。

He has little money to buy food.

他几乎没有钱买食物。

I don't have much free time.

我没有多少空闲时间。

She's done quite a bit of work this past year.

她在过去的这一年里做了很多工作。

（3）既能修饰可数名词又能修饰不可数名词的词语有：

a lot of、lots of、plenty of（以上三个词语后谓语动词的单复数需依据of后名词的单复数而定）；

a great/large quantity of（谓语动词用单数）；

quantities of（谓语动词用复数）；

all、some、enough（谓语动词的单复数视所修饰的名词而定）

例：All five men are hard workers.

五个人都是辛勤的工人。

3. 被动语态

被动语态是本题型中的常考考点，考生不仅需要知道其基本结构，还需要学会随具体题目进行变化，灵活运用。

（1）被动语态的基本时态变化

被动语态由be+动词过去分词构成，通常依托于各时态而变化。

以do为例，各种时态的被动语态形式为：

① 一般现在时

基本形式：am/is/are+done（过去分词）

例：Audiences are requested to keep quiet.

听众被要求保持肃静。

② 现在完成时

基本形式：has/have been+done

例：Many experiments have been done to test the link.

人们做了许多实验来检测这一联系。

③ 现在进行时

基本形式：am/is/are+being done

例：The bus is being repaired.

公交车正在维修。

④ 一般过去时

基本形式：was/were+done

例：He was asked to send the message at once.

　　他被命令立刻发送信息。

⑤ 过去完成时

基本形式：had been+done

例：He got home to find that his flat had been done over.

　　他到家后发现公寓已经装修过了。

⑥ 过去进行时

基本形式：was/were+being done

例：They were assured that everything possible was being done.

　　已经向他们保证，凡是可能做的都做到了。

⑦ 一般将来时

基本形式：shall/will be+done

例：In 20 minutes, the dishes will be done.

　　20分钟后菜就熟了。

⑧ 过去将来时

基本形式：should/would be+done

例：The car would be cleaned because today is fine.

　　今天天气很好，所以应该洗车。

⑨ 将来完成时

基本形式：shall/will have been+done（少用）

例：The class will have been finished before next month.

　　课程将在下个月之前结束。

（2）被动语态的特殊结构形式

① 带情态动词的被动结构

其形式为：情态动词+be+动词过去分词

例：The ID card should be reserved in a safe place.

　　身份证应该妥善保管。

② 有些动词可以有两个宾语，在用于被动结构时，可以把主动结构中的一个宾语变为主语，另一个宾语仍然保留在谓语后面。通常变为主语的是间接宾语。

例：He gave me a doll for my birthday present.

　　他给了我一个洋娃娃作为我的生日礼物。

可改为 I was given a doll for my birthday present.

③ 当"动词+宾语+宾语补足语"结构变为被动后忘叶，将宾语变为被动结构中的主语，其余不动。

例：The teacher caught the student playing the cell phone in the class.

　　老师抓住学生在课上玩手机。

可改为The student was caught playing the cell phone in the class.

④ 在使役动词have、make、get 以及感官动词see、watch、notice、hear、feel、observe等后面的不定式做宾语补语时，在主动结构中不定式to要省略，但变为被动结构时，要加to。

例：Lucy saw Tom enter the apartment.

　　露西看见汤姆进入了公寓。

可改为：Tom was seen to enter the apartment by Lucy.

⑤ 有些相当于及物动词的动词词组，如"动词+介词""动词+副词"等，也可以用于被动结构，但要把它们看作一个整体，不能分开。其中的介词或副词也不能省略。

例：The concert is called off due to the equipment trouble.

　　由于设备故障，音乐会被取消了。

4. 定语从句

英语的三大从句分别是定语从句、状语从句和名词性从句，其中定语从句是领思阅读考试中考查最多的从句。

定语从句的概念：

要弄清楚什么是定语从句，首先要清楚什么是定语。用来修饰或限定名词或代词的成分叫作定语，当定语是一个句子时就是定语从句。

例：I was told that the book I bought yesterday was piratic.

　　我被告知我昨天买的书是盗版的。（I bought yesterday做定语修饰book）

（1）先行词的概念

定语从句所修饰的那个名词或代词叫作先行词。我们可以这样理解，之所以它叫先行词，是因为修饰它的定语从句总是放在它的后面，而不同于普通形容词放在被修饰词的前面。

（2）常见的关系代词和关系副词

关系代词应具有代词的特点，在句子中主要做主语、宾语、表语，常见的关系代词有who、whom、whose、that、which、as。关系副词应具有副词的特点，在句子中做状语，常见的关系副词有where、when、why。

（3）由关系代词引导的定语从句

① who/whom

两者都用于指人，who在定语从句中可做主语、宾语、表语，而whom只能做宾语。

例：The club welcomes the one who is interested in dancing.

　　俱乐部欢迎对舞蹈感兴趣的人。（who在从句中做主语，修饰the one）

　　The man with whom you have lived was my father's friend.

　　和你住在一起的那个男人是我父亲的朋友。（whom在从句中做宾语，修饰the man）

② whose

whose可以指人，也可以指物，在定语从句中做定语。

例：He has a friend whose father is a doctor.

　　他有一位父亲是医生的朋友。（whose指人）

　　The classroom whose door is broken will be repaired.

　　门坏了的那间教室会被修好。（whose指物）

③ which

which用于指物，在定语从句中做主语、宾语、表语、定语。

例：The major which is related to the computer is popular now.

　　现在，和计算机相关的专业很受欢迎。（which在从句中做主语）

　　I can't see the picture（which）you showed to me.

　　我没看见你向我展示的那张照片。（which在从句中做宾语，可省略）

④ that

that既可指人又可指物，在定语从句中做主语、宾语、表语。

例：The professor that delivered a speech is my tutor.

　　发表演讲的那位教授是我的导师。（that指人，在从句中做主语）

　　The man that I mentioned is there.

　　我刚刚提到的那个人在那里。（that指人，在从句中做宾语）

　　The printer that broke yesterday is under repair now.

　　昨天坏了的那台打印机现在正在维修。（that指物，在从句中做主语）

　　I can't get the point that you said just now.

　　我没明白你刚才所讲的要点。（that指物，在从句中做宾语）

⑤ as

as引导定语从句常出现在the same…as…、such…as、as…as…、so…as…等句型

中，as在定语从句中既可指人和物，也可以指整个句子了。

例：Let's meet at the same coffee shop as we did last week.

我们还是在上周那个咖啡厅见面吧。（as指物）

Such people as have made great contributions to the world should be remembered forever.

那些对世界做出巨大贡献的人应该被永远铭记。（as指人）

As we all know, true gold does not fear fire.

众所周知，真金不怕火炼。（as指整个句子）

⑥ "介词+关系代词"的结构

定语从句中的介词可以提前，这时不能用that/who，指物用which，指人用whom。

例：Ben is the example that/who/whom all of us learned a lesson from.

本是我们所有人学习的典型。

介词提前：Ben is the example from whom all of us learned a lesson.

This is the school which/that I learned in.

这就是我学习过的学校。

介词提前：This is the school in which I learned.

⑦ 介词+关系代词which =when（表时间）/where（表地点）/why（表原因）

例：I can still remember the day when/on which I met my wife.

我仍然可以记得我见到我妻子的那天。

This is the room where/in which I grow flowers.

这就是我养花的房间。

⑧ 关系代词的省略

关系代词做宾语、表语时可省略，做主语时不能省略。

例：They are the suspects（whom/who/that）policemen are finding.

他们就是警察正在找的嫌疑人。（关系代词在从句中做宾语）

He is not the person（whom/who/that）he was.

他已不是过去的他了。（关系代词在定语从句中做表语）

（4）由关系副词引导的定语从句

① where

在定语从句中做地点状语，指代地点。

例：The housing estate where I lived was redecorated.

我之前居住的小区重新装修了。

You reach a point where medicine can't help.

你已到了药物无法治疗的地步。

② when

在定语从句中做时间状语，指代时间。

例：The night when we took a stroll in the park was so cold.

我们在公园散步的那个晚上好冷。

The day when I got the admission was unforgettable.

我被录取的那天是令我难忘的。

③ why

在定语从句中做原因状语，why指原因或理由，它的先行词只有reason。

例：It's not the reason why you fail a math test.

这不是你数学考试不及格的理由。

He didn't tell me the reason why he was so upset.

他没有告诉我他为什么那样心烦意乱。

（5）限制性定语从句和非限制性定语从句

① 限制性定语从句用来修饰或限定先行词，与先行词的关系非常紧密，用于说明先行词的性质、身份、特征等，如果去掉会使句子意思含糊不清。

例：He is the man who wins a lottery.

他就是中彩票的那个人。（说明身份）

This is the tree which can survive below minus twenty degrees.

这就是那种在零下二十度以下还能存活的树。（说明性质）

② 非限制性定语从句对先行词没有特别的限定作用，常按并列句进行翻译，即使去掉，主句的意思依然清楚。非限制性定语从句与主句之间用逗号隔开，不能用that引导。

例：The note was left by Jim, who was here a moment ago.

这个便条是吉姆留的，他刚才来过。

Have you seen the film, whose leading actor is world famous?

你看过这部电影吗？它的主演可是世界闻名。

（6）宜用that而不宜用which的情况

① 先行词是不定代词 all、little、few、much、anything、something、everything、nothing、none等。

例：He did everything that he could do to help us.

他做了一切他所能做的来帮助我们。

All that can be done has been done.

一切能做的都已经做完了。

② 先行词被 all、every、no、some、any、little、much、few、just、the only、the very、the right、the last 等修饰。

例：All the things that I can do is to bless you.

我所能做的就是祝福你。

③ 先行词被序数词或形容词最高级修饰，或先行词本身就是序数词或形容词最高级。

例：This is the most wonderful film that I have ever seen.

这是我看过最精彩的电影。

④ 先行词中既有人又有物时

例：He talked about things and persons that he remembered in the hometown.

他谈到了他记得的家乡的人和事。

The writer and his novel that you have just talked about are really well known.

你刚才谈起的那位作家以及他的小说确实很著名。

（7）宜用 which 而不宜用 that 的情况

① 关系代词前有介词且指事物

例：This is the building in which he lives.

这就是他住的房子。

② 在非限制性定语从句中

例：She missed the train, which depressed her greatly.

她没赶上火车，这让她很沮丧。

③ 先行词本身就是 that

例：What is that which they introduce to me?

他们向我介绍的是什么？

④ 先行词后有插入语

例：Here is the flavour which, as I've told you, will make the dish more delicious.

这是我告诉过你的那个调料，它能让菜肴更美味。

（8）宜用 who 而不宜用 that 的情况

① 先行词是指人的不定代词 one、ones、anyone

例：The ones who can always keep fit are perseverant.

能一直保持身材的人是有毅力的。

② 先行词为 those

例：Those who want to get the gift should queue up.

那些想领取礼品的人应该排队。

5. 名词性从句

名词性从句的概念：

在句子中起名词作用的句子叫名词性从句。名词性从句分为主语从句、宾语从句、表语从句和同位语从句。

（1）名词性从句的连接词

引导名词性从句的连接词有三类：从属连接词、连接代词、连接副词。

① 从属连接词

that、whether、if 既不是连接代词也不是连接副词，在从句中不充当任何成分。作为从属连接词，that 没有实际意义，whether 和 if 表示"是否"。

例：The writer thinks that all readers will be moved by the story.

作者认为所有读者都会被这个故事打动。

I want to ask whether the ticket was sold out.

我想问一下票是否售空了。

② 连接代词

连接代词指既具有代词特点，又能引导从句的词，主要有 what、whatever、who、whoever、whom、whose、which、whichever，在句子中既有具体含义，又做特定成分，不能省略。

例：Whoever violates the rule will be punished.

任何违反规则的人都会受到惩罚。

My question is which is the best one.

我的问题是哪一个是最好的。

③ 连接副词

连接副词指既具有副词特点，又能引导从句的词，主要有 when、where、how、why、whenever、wherever，在句子中既有具体含义，又做特定成分，不能省略。

例：Where we should go for the vacation is undetermined.

我们应该去哪度假还没决定。

The puzzle why he is out of touch with me makes me annoyed.

他为什么和我失去联系这个谜题让我恼火。

（2）主语从句

在句子中起主语作用的从句叫主语从句。

例：That you are coming to Paris is the best news I have heard this long time.

你将来巴黎是我好久以来听到的最好消息。

How this happened is not clear to anyone.

这件事怎样发生的，谁也不清楚。

What struck me was that they have all suffered a lot.

给我留下很深印象的是他们都受过很多苦。

（3）表语从句

在句子中起表语作用的从句叫表语从句。

例：The reality is that the party must be cancelled because of the storm.

现实就是因为暴风雨，这个聚会必须得取消了。

It sounds as if someone is knocking at the door.

听起来好像有人在敲门。

It appears that he wants to teach us all he has.

他似乎想要把他所会的都教给我们。

（4）同位语从句

在句子中起同位语作用的从句叫同位语从句。

例：The news got about that he had won a car in the lottery.

消息传开说他中彩得了一辆汽车。

We have no idea at all where he has gone.

我们根本不知道他去哪里了。

Her mother was worried about the possibility that her daughter disliked to go to school.

她的母亲担心她女儿有可能不喜欢上学。

（5）宾语从句

在句子中起宾语作用的从句叫宾语从句。

例：Can you tell me whom you are waiting for?

你能告诉我你在等谁吗？

I think it necessary that we take enough exercise every day.（it 做形式宾语）

我认为我们每天进行足够的锻炼是有必要的。

We discussed whether we had a sports meeting next week.

我们讨论了下周是否要召开运动会。

6. 状语从句

状语从句的概念：状语从句指句子用作状语时，起副词作用的句子。状语从句可以修饰谓语、非谓语动词、定语、状语或整个句子。

状语从句可以分为：时间状语从句、地点状语从句、原因状语从句、条件状语从句、目的状语从句、让步状语从句、比较状语从句、方式状语从句、结果状语从句。

（1）时间状语从句

用表示时间的连词连接一个句子做状语，这样的主从复合句就是时间状语从句，连接时间状语从句的连接词有when、before、after、while、as soon as、until、since等。

We were going to leave when he reached. 我们就要离开时，他到了。

I had gone out before he visited me. 我在他来拜访之前出门了。

It was not until the film was over that he replied me. 直到电影结束后，他才回复我。

（2）地点状语从句

地点状语从句表示地点、方位。这类从句通常由where、wherever引导。地点状语从句可置于句首、句中或句尾。

Go back where you came from. 你从何处来就到何处去。

You should have put the book where you found it. 你本来应该把书放回你发现它的地方。

You should be diligent wherever you are. 不论你在哪，你都应该勤奋。

（3）原因状语从句

原因状语从句指在句中用来说明主句原因的从句。引导原因状语从句的从属连词有because、as、since、when、seeing（that）、considering（that）、given（that）等。

I can't get to sleep because he is singing. 由于他在唱歌，我睡不着。

Since it's raining, we'd better stay indoors. 既然外边在下雨，我们最好待在室内。

I can't do housework, as I was exhausted. 我不能做家务了，因为我已筋疲力尽了。

（4）条件状语从句

条件状语从句中的内容是主句内容成立的条件，通常由if、unless、on condition（that）、provided（that）引导。条件状语从句要注意"主将从现"这一原则，即从句用一般现在时，主句用一般将来时。有时从句也可以用祈使句或情态动词。

If you can't find the way, please contact me. 如果你找不到路，请联系我。

You will fail to arrive there in time unless you start earlier. 如果你不早点动身，你就不能及时赶到那儿。

I can set off immediately on condition that there are tickets left. 如果有剩余的票，我可以马上出发。

Provided that he is forced to do so, will you blame him? 倘若他是被迫这样做的，你会怪他吗?

（5）目的状语从句

目的状语从句是用来补充说明主句中谓语动词发生的目的的状语从句，通常用that、so that、in order that等连接。

I get up early in order that I can catch the early bus. 为了赶早班车，我起得很早。

I'll give you a key so that you can let yourself in. 我把钥匙给你，你可以自己开门进去。

（6）让步状语从句

让步状语从句往往意为"尽管……"或"即使……"等，有"退一步说……"的含义，通常由though、although、while、even if、even though引导。其中特别注意although、though 不可与but连用，但可以与still和yet连用。

Although/Though he is 80 years old, he is quite strong. 他虽然80岁了，他还很健壮。

Even if I can't take care of him, I will find others to help me. 即使我不能照顾他，我会找别人帮我。

（7）比较状语从句

比较状语从句用来表达人或物的属性的不同程度，经常用as...as...、not as / so...、than等进行引导。

She thinks more about her appearance than her personality. 比起个性，她更注重外表。

This book is twice as thin as that one. 这本书的厚度是那本书的二分之一。

（8）方式状语从句

方式状语从句表示做某事的方式，通常用as、as if、as though引导。

As they treated us, we should give them a warm welcome. 就像他们对待我们那样，我们要热烈欢迎他们。

It looked as if there would be an exciting race. 看起来会有一场激动人心的比赛。

（9）结果状语从句

结果状语从句表示从句的内容是主句的结果，通常由 so、so...that、such...that 引导。

This room has a seating capacity of 30 people, so I choose this for my birthday party. 这个房间能坐下 30 个人，所以我选择在此举办我的生日聚会。

The dog is so cute that many people can't help touching it. 这只狗太可爱了，以至于很多人都忍不住摸它。

Day 6　实战篇

1. The specialist's new research result will _____ his conjecture, which is wonderful news.

   A. overturn　　　B. consider　　　　C. vindicate　　　　D. suspect

2. He was so _____ that Tom reminded him three times to check his belongings.

   A. regretful　　　B. faithful　　　　C. fruitful　　　　　D. forgetful

3. ——I'm so hungry. Shall we have a hotdog?

   ———— _____.

   A. Yes, we have.　　　　　　　　B. No, I haven't.

   C. Yes, let's.　　　　　　　　　D. No, you mustn't.

4. One of the worries of the celebrity is being consistently in the public _____.

   A. sight　　　　B. eye　　　　　　C. focus　　　　　D. attention

5. Lucy's parents _____ with her not to work in another city, but no one can persuade her.

   A. begged　　　B. pleaded　　　　C. urged　　　　　D. implored

6. The France's education minister had friendly discussions with his _____ in the Italy government.

   A. replacement　　B. complement　　C. counterpart　　D. duplicate

7. In spite of trivial faults, Sally's solo at the school concert went very well, _____ all accounts.

   A. on　　　　　B. by　　　　　　C. at　　　　　　D. with

8. The student's obscure answer to the oral test _____ doubt on his way of understanding the question.

   A. laid　　　　B. launched　　　C. cast　　　　　D. delivered

9. My credit card is entitled to open _____ function so I can spend more money than I actually have.

   A. profit　　　　B. exchange　　　C. overdraft　　　D. budget

10. She had to _____ some money so she could afford the car, but all of her friends were poor.

　　A. lend　　　　　B. save　　　　　C. rent　　　　　D. borrow

11. She ought _____ more time to review before the test, but she can't help watching films.

　　A. have had　　B. to do　　　　C. to have had　　D. have

12. Daniel didn't understand what I was talking about and he completely _____ the point.

　　A. saw　　　　　B. missed　　　　C. blunted　　　　D. acquired

13. If a citizen does not follow certain laws, there can be serious legal _____ in the future.

　　A. upshots　　B. effects　　　C. consequences　　D. results

14. My parents named me _____ my grandfather, and he's called Bill too.

　　A. by　　　　　B. to　　　　　C. after　　　　　D. from

15. I'm really sorry to let you down at such short notice, but something comes _____ so I won't be able to keep an appointment.

　　A. up　　　　　B. on　　　　　C. across　　　　D. over

16. The White Food Group launched as a small bakeshop and _____ has become one of the most well-known brands of food around the world.

　　A. therefore　　B. subsequently　　C. besides　　D. although

17. This housing estate is very safe, so everyone needs to _____ a password to get in.

　　A. enter　　　B. come　　　　C. move　　　　D. record

18. The number of fossils discovered by experts is probably the _____ fraction of the total number that exists under the ground.

　　A. utmost　　B. closest　　　C. merest　　　D. purest

19. The professor _____ pride in his student's research achievement on the world-class problems.

　　A. verified　　B. took　　　　C. appeared　　D. indicated

20. It took a team of engineers three years to invent a camera that was lightweight, and could _____ the natural handicap of space.

　　A. battle　　　B. struggle　　　C. persist　　　D. withstand

Part 3　完形填空

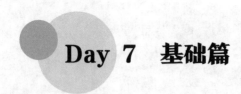

Day 7　基础篇

一、题型介绍

  阅读第三类题型是完形填空。题目中会给出一段短文，内容一般涉及生活纪实、知识科普、观点探讨、日常通信等。短文中通常有五道题目，要求考生分别从四个选项中选择正确的单词或短语，给短文中的句子填空。这类题型也是考生相对熟悉的题型，短文的篇幅较短，平均在70~200词之间，总体难度中等。

二、考试界面

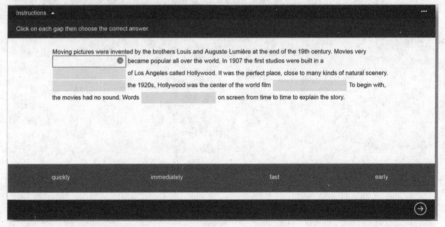

 ✓ 界面最上方是本部分的答题说明

 ✓ 点击每个空格，界面下方会出现该题对应的四个选项，点击选项内容进行选择

 ✓ 点击右下角箭头可以切换到下一题（注意答完的题目不能再切换回来进行检查）

三、考查技能

完形填空主要考查考生的以下技能：

 ✓ 对于日常生活英语文章的理解，包括对内容以及逻辑关系的理解

 ✓ 语法基础知识运用

✓　词义辨析、固定搭配和习语

本题型的出题类型主要包括以下四种：

1. 词义辨析

词义辨析考查的是考生对近义词、形近词或难度较高单词的掌握程度。该命题方式对考生的单词掌握程度有较高的要求，要求考生在日常积累单词时不仅要牢记单词含义，还要明确其适用的场景，区分其近义词，能够辨别与其拼写相似的单词，并不断提高单词的涉猎广度和难度。在句子填空中也会出现这种类型的题目，但与之相比，文章中涉及的语境信息更为复杂多样，这对考生的能力也提出了更高的要求。

2. 固定搭配

固定搭配考查某些单词的固定用法或者某些固定表达。这类题目的特点是要么很快就能得出答案，要么毫无思路。这类题目的关键在于考生日常对于固定搭配的积累。由于固定搭配的含义不是通过自行推理分析而得出的，所以注重积累是帮助解答这一题目的有效方法。

3. 内容理解

这类题目要求考生能在空格处填入使句子逻辑正确、内容完整的成分。这类题目的选项一般为代词、介词和连词。这类题目的特点是有时不能通过空格所在句进行判断，需结合上下文，这就要求考生充分理解文章内容。

4. 语法基础

这类题目要求考生熟练掌握并运用语法规则。这类题目的选项往往就能反映出试题所考查的语法知识，所以在解答这类题目时，考生要将选项与文章的已有信息联系起来，选择既符合语法规则，又符合文章内容的选项。

四、答题策略

针对本题型，建议采用以下答题思路：

1. 通读全文，了解大意

选择之前要先将文章快速通读一遍，了解文章的题材和大意。通常在阅读完第一句话之后，考生基本就能了解文章的主题。阅读的同时要对空格处填的内容进行初步的判断，对空格处的含义进行适当的猜测。同时还可以对文章的内容进行划分，明确文章中各部分的写作目的。

注意这一步骤要采取"略读"的方式，把握大意即可，如遇到难以理解的内容，不要过分纠结，应继续阅读。

2. 寻找线索，恰当选择

这一步骤的任务要求与句子填空类似，但相比之下，这一步骤更加复杂，具体可按以下方法进行：

（1）仔细阅读空格所在句子，明确句子成分，并判断空格处在句中充当什么成分。根据空格处所充当的成分和选项，判断题目从哪方面进行考查。

（2）之后在文中寻找线索，即能够帮助考生选择正确答案的依据。一般而言，线索存在于句中或前后句中。句中的多种成分都可以充当线索，主语、谓语、宾语等句子的主干成分可以帮助我们缩小选项的范围，而句中的非主干成分，如：定语、状语、补语等可以帮助我们最终确定选项。

（3）对于语法基础和固定搭配类题目，寻找到线索后，可直接选择出正确答案。因为这两类题目的命题依据都是固定的规则和表达，在考虑到文章的语境后，可以直接依据语法规则或固定表达进行选择。而词义辨析和内容理解类题目并没有约定俗成的规则可以遵循，往往采取"代入——对比"的方法，即将选项代入原文，对比它们间的差别，选择出最适合的一项。

3. 重读短文，复核答案

完成所有选择后需要通读全文，通读全文验证答案的正确性，确保意思通顺、逻辑合理，句子之间和段落之间的衔接自然连贯。同时注意上下文的一致性，即语态和时态的一致、主语和谓语的一致、代词与被指代成分的一致等。

这一步骤还要关注那些难以判断的题目，这类题目的判断依据通常距离所在句子较远，或需要整合全文内容进行选择，所以要学会"瞻前顾后"。

五、典型例题及详解

Esperanto—a modern language

The first 'planned language' was born in 1878 by a Polish man called Lazarus Ludwig Zamenhof. He firmly believed that there would be fewer conflicts if all people spoke a (1) _____ language. In constructing his language, he excluded the most influential European languages of the time (English, French, German and Russian), in (2) _____ not to give their speakers an advantage. For this purpose, he based it on other languages employing a twenty-eight letter alphabet and a lucid set of grammar rules. In 1887 his first book (3) _____ people in the language was published. (4) _____ using his own name as the author, Zamenhof (5) _____ himself the name 'Esperanto', which represents 'person is hoping' in Lingvo Internacia. The language which was then called 'Dr. Esperanto's International Language' soon became abbreviated to 'Esperanto'.

(1) A. simple   B. normal   C. general   D. common

(2) A. addition   B. fact   C. order   D. turn

(3) A. informing   B. instructing   C. noticing   D. demonstrating

(4) A. Regardless of   B. In contrast to   C. Instead of   D. So that

(5) A. offered   B. called   C. identified   D. gave

➤ 试题详解

(1)【答案】D

【出题类型】词义辨析

【解析】本题考查词义辨析，四个选项均为形容词。A选项意为"简单的，朴素的"，B选项意为"正常的；标准的"，C选项意为"总体的；普遍的"，D选项意为"共同的"。结合文章内容可知，本处表达的是"都讲同一种语言"的含义。D选项符合题意，所以D选项正确。本句意为"如果所有人都说同一种语言，冲突就会减少"。

(2)【答案】C

【出题类型】固定搭配

【解析】本题考查固定搭配，A选项意为"增加；增加物"，B选项意为"事实，真相"，C选项意为"命令；顺序"，D选项意为"转动"。结合句意可知，空格后内容为空格前内容的目的，所以C选项正确。in order to表示目的，本句意为"他把当时最具影响力的欧洲语言（英语、法语、德语和俄语）排除在外，这是为了不给以这些语言为母语的人优势"。

(3)【答案】B

【出题类型】词义辨析

【解析】本题考查词义辨析，四个选项均为动词的变形，A选项意为"通知，告知"，B选项意为"指示；指导"，C选项意为"注意；通知"，D选项意为"证明，证实"。其中B选项能够与句中的"in"构成搭配，表示"指导……"，所以B选项正确。本句意为"1887年他的第一本指导人们掌握这门语言的书出版了"。

(4)【答案】C

【出题类型】内容理解

【解析】本题考查对文章内容的理解。A选项意为"不顾，不管"，B选项意为"相比之下"，C选项意为"而不是"，D选项意为"以便"。四个选项含义各不相同，所以结合文章内容是解题的关键。逗号前内容说到，用自己的名字作为作者名，逗号后的内容中提到了另一个名字，所以C选项正确。本句意为"扎门霍夫没有使用自己的名字作为作者名"。

（5）【答案】D

【出题类型】词义辨析

【解析】本题考查词义辨析。A选项意为"提供，给予"，B选项意为"叫；召唤"，C选项意为"认出；识别"，D选项意为"给，给予"，结合句意可知，本句应表示为自己起笔名的含义，give与name搭配，可表示"命名"，所以D选项正确。本句意为"而是给自己起了'世界语'这个名字"。

➢ 全文翻译

世界语——一种现代语言

第一种"计划语言"诞生于1878年，由一个名叫拉扎勒斯·路德维希·扎门霍夫的波兰人发明。他坚信，如果所有人都说同一种语言，冲突就会减少。在构建语言时，他把当时最具影响力的欧洲语言（英语、法语、德语和俄语）排除在外，这是为了不给以这些语言为母语的人优势。为此，他以其他语言为基础，使用28个字母的字母表和一套简单明了的语法规则。1887年他的第一本指导人们掌握这门语言的书出版了。扎门霍夫没有使用自己的名字作为作者名，而是给自己起了"世界语"这个名字，它的意思在国际语中是"充满希望的人"。这种语言当时被称为"扎门霍夫博士的国际语言"，很快就被缩写为"世界语"。

➢ 词汇笔记

conflict /ˈkɒnflɪkt/ *n.* 争执；分歧

v. 冲突；抵触

例：Their versions of how the accident happened conflict.

他们对事故是如何发生的说法相互矛盾。

近：clash

exclude /ɪkˈskluːd/ *v.* 不包括，把……排除在外

例：This was intended to exclude the direct rays of the sun.

这是用来阻挡太阳直射光线的。

派：exclusive *adj.* 独享的，独家的；高档的

exclusion *n.* 排斥；被排除的人或物

lucid /ˈluːsɪd/ *adj.* 明晰的；易懂的

例：He wasn't very lucid, and he didn't quite know where he was.

他神志不太清醒，不太清楚自己在哪儿。

近：clear

abbreviate /əˈbriːvieɪt/ v. 缩写；使简短

例：The teacher asked me to abbreviate my report to one page.

老师让我把我的报告缩短为一页。

派：abbreviation n. 缩写；缩略词；缩写形式

Day 8 提分篇

1. 文章特点

纪实类文本从客观角度对某一对象进行介绍，所涉猎的话题较为广泛，包括：人物或物品介绍、事件介绍、地点介绍等。

2. 例题及详解

Smith College, Annual Report

This has been a prosperous year for the college. The number of part-time students went up to a history high, (1) _____ there was a small decrease in the number of full-time students, which was a pity. Higher fees for full-time courses were almost certainly the primary (2) _____ for this decline, but we are confident it will be temporary. We are delighted, nevertheless, that the results our students (3) _____ in public examinations continued to be better.

Plans for the next year (4) _____ launching new part-time courses in medicine and in French. Besides, the college will collaborate with local firms on (5) _____ more curriculums that will prepare students for development in the future.

（1）A. despite   B. although   C. therefore   D. if

（2）A. outcome   B. objective   C. opinion   D. reason

（3）A. achieved   B. finished   C. arrived   D. defeated

（4）A. hold   B. contain   C. include   D. consist

（5）A. targeting   B. prohibiting   C. formulating   D. becoming

➤ 试题详解

（1）【答案】B

【出题类型】内容理解

【解析】A选项、B选项均意为"尽管"；C选项意为"因此"；D选项意为"如果"。根据文章内容可知，空格前后的句子存在转折关系，A选项和B选项均可表达转折含义，但空格前后均为完整的句子。A选项是介词，无法连接两个句子；B选项为连词，所以B选项正确。本句意为"非全日制学生的数量达到历史最高，尽管全日制学生人数略有下降，这是令人遗憾的"。

（2）【答案】D

【出题类型】内容理解

【解析】A选项意为"结果；效果"；B选项意为"目的，目标"；C选项意为"观点"；D选项意为"原因"。分析可知，二者为因果关系，首先排除B选项和C选项。同时，本句中的"Higher fees for full-time courses"是"decline"的原因，所以D选项正确。本句意为"全日制课程学费的增加是该类学生数量下降的主要原因"。

（3）【答案】A

【出题类型】词义辨析

【解析】A选项意为"取得"；B选项意为"完成"；C选项意为"到达"；D选项意为"击败，战胜"。正确选项应该能与句中的"results"搭配，A选项与之搭配最为合理，意为"取得成果"，所以A选项正确。本句意为"然而，学生在公开考试中取得的成绩持续提升，这让我们振奋"。

（4）【答案】C

【出题类型】词义辨析

【解析】四个选项的词义相近，都有"包含"的含义。A选项多指容纳之意；B选项多指含有或某物里面有……；C选项多指整体所包括的部分；D选项表达此含义须与介词of连用。结合文章内容可知，句子表达的是"plan"这一整体中包括的个体，C选项最符合文章语境，所以C选项正确。本句意为"明年的计划包括开设新的非全日制医学和法语课程"。

（5）【答案】C

【出题类型】词义辨析

【解析】A选项意为"瞄准；旨在"；B选项意为"阻止；禁止"；C选项意为"规划；制订"；D选项意为"成为，变成"。观察本句可知，空格处内容要能与句中的"curriculums"搭配，C选项与之搭配最为合理，意为"规划课程"，所以C选项正确。本句意为"此外，学院将与当地公司合作，规划更多为学生未来发展做准备的课程"。

➢　全文翻译

史密斯学院，年度报告

今年是学院成功的一年。非全日制学生的数量达到历史最高，尽管全日制学生人数略有下降，这是令人遗憾的。可以肯定的是，全日制课程学费的增加是该类学生数量下降的主要原因，但我们相信这将是暂时的。然而，学生在公开考试中取得的成绩持续提升，这让我们振奋。

明年的计划包括开设新的非全日制医学和法语课程。此外，学院将与当地公司合作，规划更多为学生未来发展做准备的课程。

➢ 词汇笔记

prosperous /ˈprɒspərəs/ *adj.* 繁荣的；成功的

例：Suzhou has become one of the most dynamic and prosperous cities.

　　苏州已经成为最具活力、最为繁荣的城市之一。

派：prosperity *n.* 繁荣

temporary /ˈtemprəri/ *adj.* 临时的，暂时的，短期的

例：They had to move into temporary accommodation.

　　他们不得不搬进临时住所。

近：occasional

collaborate /kəˈlæbəreɪt/ *v.* 合作；勾结

搭：collaborate with 合作；勾结

例：We have collaborated on many projects over the years.

　　这些年来我们合作了许多项目。

派：collaboration *n.* 合作，协作

近：cooperate

curriculum /kəˈrɪkjələm/ *n.* 课程

例：The school curriculum is not always geared to the needs of all students.

　　学校课程并不总能适应所有学生的需要。

近：course

二、阐释说明类

1. 文章特点

阐释说明类文本起到解释说明的作用，让读者明白事物背后的原理。这类文本的客观性较强，逻辑较为严谨，文章的内容可以是对某种现象或问题的解释，或是对某种概念的介绍。

2. 例题及详解

Reading Habits

One of the important things that have changed as a direct result of technological advance is our way of (1) _____ new information. Technology has even changed the way we use libraries. Now, instead of searching the shelves one by one, you can simply reserve the book you want online, before (2) _____ it up in person. This saves a lot of time. (3) _____, libraries which are reluctant to introduce the advanced technology face the risk of shutting down. Over the last few years, many people seem to have cultivated a (4) _____ to avoid book shops that don't have their own website. These individuals are, in fact, also less (5) _____ to buy printed books when they can easily download a digital copy of the novel they want to read.

(1) A. conquering   B. obtaining   C. winning   D. earning

(2) A. grabbing   B. showing   C. picking   D. holding

(3) A. Although   B. Nevertheless   C. Despite   D. Besides

(4) A. attraction   B. tendency   C. custom   D. bending

(5) A. gladly   B. possibly   C. nicely   D. likely

➤ 试题详解

(1)【答案】B

【出题类型】词义辨析

【解析】A选项意为"攻克；征服"；B选项意为"得到，获得"；C选项意为"获胜；赢得"；D选项意为"赚得"。空格处在句中与"new information"进行搭配，B选项最为恰当，意为"获取新信息"，所以B选项正确。句意为"技术进步带来的直接重要变化之一是我们获取新信息的方式"。

(2)【答案】C

【出题类型】词义辨析

【解析】本题的四个选项均为动词的分词形式，空格后出现了"up"，可知正确选项与up构成搭配。A选项与up搭配意为"把……抓起"；B选项与up搭配意为"露面"；C选项与up搭配意为"捡起；习得"；D选项意为"举起；阻碍"。原句中这一动词短语的宾语为"book"，C选项最符合语境，所以C选项正确。句意为"你可以仅在网上预订你想要的书，而不是在书架上一个一个地寻找，然后亲自去取书"。

(3)【答案】D

【出题类型】内容理解

【解析】本题中的四个选项可体现前后内容间存在的关系，进行选择时需全面把握相关内容。A选项意为"尽管"，表示让步关系；B选项意为"然而"，表示转折关系；C选项意为"尽管"，表示让步关系；D选项意为"此外"，表示并列关系。空格前说的是如今的阅读方式，空格后说到不愿意采用新技术的图书馆有倒闭的风险。D选项置于此处最符合语境，所以D选项正确。句意为"此外，不愿意引进先进技术的图书馆会面临倒闭的风险"。

（4）【答案】B

【出题类型】词义辨析

【解析】A选项意为"吸引；有吸引力的事物"；B选项意为"趋势；偏好"；C选项意为"风俗；习惯"；D选项意为"弯曲"。结合句中的已知信息，B选项最符合语境，所以B选项正确。句意为"在过去的几年里，许多人似乎已经形成了一种偏好——不去没有自己网站的书店"。

（5）【答案】D

【出题类型】固定搭配

【解析】A选项意为"乐意地，高兴地"；B选项意为"可能，也许"；C选项意为"漂亮地；恰好地"；D选项意为"大概，可能"。结合语境，可以将A和C两项排除。本句中，空格后出现了"to"，在句首部分出现了be动词are，D选项可以与句中的上述单词构成固定搭配，意为"很可能；倾向于"，所以D选项正确。句意为"事实上，当这些人可以很容易地下载他们想读的小说的电子版时，他们也不太可能购买纸质书"。

➢ 全文翻译

阅读习惯

技术进步带来的直接重要变化之一是我们获取新信息的方式。科技甚至改变了我们使用图书馆的方式。现在，你可以仅在网上预订你想要的书，而不是在书架上一个一个地寻找，然后亲自去取书。这节省了很多时间。此外，不愿意引进先进技术的图书馆会面临倒闭的风险。在过去的几年里，许多人似乎已经形成了一种偏好——不去没有自己网站的书店。事实上，当这些人可以很容易地下载他们想读的小说的电子版时，他们也不太可能购买纸质书。

➢ 词汇笔记

reserve /rɪˈzɜːv/ *v.* 预订；保留；储藏

     n. 储藏；保护区；替补队员

搭：in reserve 备用

例：You can reserve seats over the telephone.

  你可以打电话预订座位。

派：reservation *n.* 保留，保护

in person 亲自

例：It was the first time she had seen him in person.

　　这是她第一次见到他本人。

reluctant /rɪˈlʌktənt/ *adj.* 勉强的，不情愿的

例：She is reluctant to admit her fault.

　　她不愿意承认自己的错误。

派：reluctance *n.* 不愿意，不情愿

近：unwilling

shut /ʃʌt/ *v.* 关闭，合上

搭：shut up 住口

例：Please shut the door when you go out.

　　你出去的时候请把门关上。

cultivate /ˈkʌltɪveɪt/ *v.* 培养；耕作；养成

搭：cultivate talents 培养人才

例：This area mainly cultivates rice.

　　这片区域主要种植水稻。

派：cultivation *n.* 耕作；种植

近：breed

三、观点建议类

1. 文章特点

　　观点建议类文本从日常生活的某一问题出发，表明自己的观点或提出建议，可能会加以论证从而让读者接受其观点或建议。这类文本往往具有主客观相结合的特点，即从客观事实出发，再加以自己的观点。

2. 例题及详解

Is There a Future in Agriculture?

　　No matter how scornful people are of the notion of a career in farming, there can be no (1) _____ the obvious fact that we can't live without food. Therefore, although no one is saying the agricultural industry will remain the same as it is today, what is apparent is that the industry is extremely crucial and will continue to be so. So of course there is a future for the agricultural industry. But farmers must understand that the world is technology (2) _____ and new farming technologies must be introduced in order to advance. The owners of small farms must be pragmatic and admit that they cannot possibly compete with larger (3) _____ unless they pool their re-sources. Farmers should also realize that they must specialize in one type of farming. Mixed farms where crops are cultivated, cattle are raised for meat and cows are milked are largely a thing of the past. Farmers must (4) _____ what activity gives them a competitive advantage and pay attention to this. The farms of tomorrow will be highly sophisticated and specialized; the cosy (5) _____ of the family farm is almost extinct.

(1) A. denying   B. realizing   C. asserting   D. refusing

(2) A. invested   B. driven   C. loaded   D. crucial

(3) A. products   B. farmers   C. enterprises   D. entrepreneurs

(4) A. organize   B. decide   C. inspect   D. understand

(5) A. notion   B. angle   C. predicament   D. mentality

➤ 试题详解

(1)【答案】A

【出题类型】词义辨析

【解析】本题的四个选项均为动词的分词形式。A选项意为"否定，否认"；B选项意为"认识到，明白"；C选项意为"断言"；D选项意为"拒绝"。由逗号前的句子中的"No matter how"可知，本句中包含让步关系，那么逗号后的句子应该表示肯定含义，即双重否定表示肯定。A选项和D选项均含有否定含义，A选项更符合语境，所以A选项正确。句意为"不管人们对农业这个职业的概念有多不屑一顾，也不会有人否认我们的生存离不开食物这个显而易见的事实"。

(2)【答案】B

【出题类型】内容理解

【解析】A选项为动词的分词形式，意为"投资；投入"；B选项意为"受……影响的"；C选项意为"载有……的"；D选项意为"重要的"。driven用在名词后，可表示"由……驱动的"，符合语境，所以B选项正确。句意为"但是农民必须意识到世界是由技术驱动的"。

(3)【答案】B

【出题类型】内容理解

【解析】A选项意为"产品"；B选项意为"农夫，农民"；C选项意为"企业"；D选项意为"企业家"。由空格前出现的"owners of small farms"可知，空格处内容应与其形成对照，所以B选项正确。句意为"小农场的所有者必须要务实，并认识到除非汇集资源，否则他们不可能与大农场主竞争"。

（4）【答案】D

【出题类型】词义辨析

【解析】A选项意为"组织"；B选项意为"决定"；C选项意为"检查；审视"；D选项意为"理解；清楚"。根据空格后的内容可知，D选项最为恰当，所以D选项正确。句意为"农民必须要清楚什么活动能给他们带来竞争优势，并深耕于此"。

（5）【答案】A

【出题类型】词义辨析

【解析】四个选项均为名词。A选项意为"概念；想法"；B选项意为"角度；立场"；C选项意为"困境"；D选项意为"心智；心态"，将四个选项带入到空格处，A选项最符合语境，所以A选项正确。句意为"温馨的家庭农场的概念几乎不复存在"。

➤　全文翻译

农业有未来吗?

不管人们对农业这个职业的概念有多不屑一顾，也不会有人否认我们的生存离不开食物这个显而易见的事实。所以，尽管没有人断言农业会维持今天的状态，但可以肯定的是，农业绝对是至关重要的，并且以后也是如此。因此，农业当然是有未来的。但是农民必须意识到世界是由技术驱动的，为了发展，他们必须引进新的农业技术。小农场的所有者必须要务实，并认识到除非汇集资源，否则他们不可能与大农场主竞争。农民也应该意识到，他们必须专门从事一种作物的耕作。既种植农作物，又饲养牛和奶牛的混合农场基本已经成为过去。农民必须要清楚什么活动能给他们带来竞争优势，并深耕于此。未来的农场会是高度复杂且专业化的。温馨的家庭农场的概念几乎不复存在。

➤　词汇笔记

scornful /ˈskɔːnfl/ *adj.* 轻蔑的，蔑视的

搭：scornful laugh 轻蔑的笑

例：He is deeply scornful of the rival's progress.

　　他对对手所取得的进步很不屑。

近：contemptuous

agricultural /ˌæɡrɪˈkʌltʃərəl/ *adj.* 农业的；与农业有关的；务农的

搭：agricultural products 农产品

例：This could be useful to the agricultural industry.

　　这可能对农业有帮助。

crucial /ˈkruːʃl/ *adj.* 至关重要的

搭：crucial factor 关键因素

例：The next few weeks are going to be crucial.

接下来的几个星期将是关键。

近：vital

pragmatic /prægˈmætɪk/ *adj.* 务实的；实用的

搭：pragmatic approach 实用的方法

例：We should take a pragmatic look at this problem.

我们应该以实用主义的眼光看待这个问题。

近：practical

sophisticated /səˈfɪstɪkeɪtɪd/ *adj.* 复杂的；精密的；精于世故的

搭：sophisticated technology 尖端技术

例：Mark is a sophisticated guy.

马克是一个精于世故的家伙。

近：ingenious

cosy /ˈkəʊzi/ *adj.* 温暖的；舒适的

搭：cosy room 温馨的房间

例：Lying in the beach, I feel very cosy.

躺在沙滩上，我感到十分惬意。

近：comfortable

extinct /ɪkˈstɪŋkt/ *adj.* 灭绝的；消亡的

搭：extinct species 灭绝的物种

例：The flunkey is extinct in the modern society.

仆人在现代社会中已经不复存在。

Day 9 实战篇

1.

Teenager and Music

In recent years, more attention is being caught to the (1) _____ music plays in life. There is also a research into how it affects children's (2) _____. The market was deluged with educational toys, videos, and a wide (3) _____ of recreation equipment that plays popular songs or classical music. Why? Music is enjoyable and interesting, and latest research has proved that (4) _____ children to music is conducive to their overall intelligence and brain development. Encouraging children to listen to disparate styles of music also (5) _____ their self-confidence and nurtures the ability to creat and explore.

(1) A. role   B. function   C. position   D. status

(2) A. improvement   B. development   C. result   D. change

(3) A. series   B. area   C. extent   D. range

(4) A. sending   B. showing   C. exposing   D. displaying

(5) A. increases   B. rises   C. enlarges   D. adds

2.

Skateboards

The one who made the first skateboard can't be confirmed; it seems that a few people came up with similar (1) _____ in the meanwhile. These first skateboards started (2) _____ wooden boxes or boards with roller skate wheels fixed to the bottom. The earliest manufactured skateboards were used by surfers during their break, when an ambitious surf shop owner made a (3) _____ with a roller skate company to construct equipment from sets of roller skate wheels and square wooden boards. By the 1960s surfing manufacturers in Southern California were building skateboards on a large (4) _____ and hiring batches of skateboarders to (5) _____ their products in sports grounds and parks.

（1）A. purposes   B. reasons   C. ideas   D. meanings

（2）A. with   B. for   C. over   D. out

（3）A. sale   B. business   C. deal   D. work

（4）A. degree   B. scale   C. size   D. amount

（5）A. demonstrate   B. propose   C. inform   D. instruct

3.

The Power of Sunlight

Hippocrates argued that the （1）_____ season is associated with health and that the key was how much available daylight there was during different times of the year. Some people have inferred that our modern lifestyle, which keeps people indoors under （2）_____ light for so many hours, may be inducing feelings of sorrow and hopelessness. Messing up the normal light and dark cycles by sleeping during the day and being awake at night can （3）_____ the body's metabolism. That can influence nearly everything: how we break down energy from food, and how （4）_____ our immune systems are and several substances that contribute to mood and weight. For （5）_____, people who often work night shifts tend to be heavier than people who don't.

（1）A. varying   B. changing   C. altering   D. growing

（2）A. fabricated   B. crafted   C. artificial   D. false

（3）A. puzzle   B. disrupt   C. ruin   D. prevent

（4）A. strong   B. hard   C. solid   D. firm

（5）A. proof   B. instance   C. evidence   D. sample

4.

Exploring Bilingual Minds

A study launched by psychologist and cognitive neuroscientist Megan Zirnstein indicates that bilinguals who are highly （1）_____ in their second language, such as international students who have come to the United States to （2）_____ higher education, can not only overcome the difficulty that is immersed in their non-native language environment, but also engage in reading strategies in their second language just like their monolingual peers. "When we （3）_____ for the challenges that skillful bilinguals must face on account of knowing more than one language and being exposed to variable language input, we see evidence in brain activity that some second-language readers can actively forecast the meaning of following words. In order to research how bilingualism might impact cognitive and brain health later in life, we first need to understand what cognitive and environmental pressures bilinguals confront when using language every day." The study underlines the need to acknowledge the variability and diversity (4) _____ in bilingual communities—an approach that has the potential to significantly (5) _____ conceptions of what it means to use language.

(1) A. practical　　　B. prolific　　　C. profitable　　　D. proficient

(2) A. oversee　　　B. pursue　　　C. badger　　　D. haunt

(3) A. deem　　　B. judge　　　C. account　　　D. yearn

(4) A. inherent　　　B. enveloped　　　C. wedged　　　D. shattered

(5) A. invoke　　　B. alter　　　C. subtract　　　D. deflate

Part 4 开放式完形填空

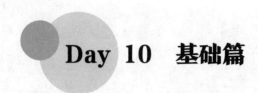

Day 10　基础篇

一、题型介绍

　　阅读第四类题型是开放式完形填空。本题型和第三类题型类似，都是给考生一篇短文，篇幅也和第三类题型的长度相当。文中一般有5处空格，需要考生将合适的单词填入空格中，本题型和第三类题型的不同之处在于，第三类题型是提供了选项让考生去选择，而本题则是要考生自己思考需填入的单词。每处空格只填一个单词，答案不唯一，合理即可。

二、考试界面

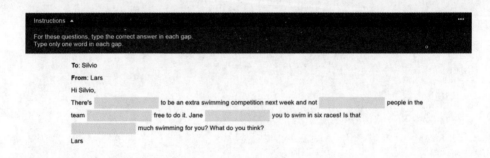

✓　界面最上方是本部分的答题说明

✓　点击每个空格，输入单词，每个空只填一个单词

✓　点击右下角箭头可以切换到下一题（注意答完的题目不能再切换回来进行检查或修改）

三、考查技能

开放式完形填空主要考查考生的以下技能：

✓　对于英语文章的理解，包括内容理解、句子间的逻辑衔接

✓　语法基础知识的掌握

✓　固定搭配的运用

✓　单词的掌握，包括单词正确拼写、大小写等

本题型和第三类题型类似，考查要点的相同之处在于，都会考查对文章内容的理解、语法基础知识的掌握和固定搭配的运用。不同之处在于，由于本题型不设选项，所以本题型不考查词义辨析。从解题思路来看，第三类题型往往采用"代入—对比"的模式，即将选项代入文中，经过对比选出最恰当的一项。而本题型需要从文章中抽取信息，通过自己的理解，填写合适的答案。换言之，没有了选项的提示，该题型在文章的理解能力，知识掌握的广度和熟练度的方面，给考生都提出了更高的要求。同时因为需要自己填写单词，所以也涉及对单词正确拼写和大小写的考查。

本题型的命题类型主要包括以下三种：

1. 内容理解

本题型需要考生在空格处填入单词，使句子的意义完整、逻辑正确。本题要求考生根据上下文语境写出最合适的词语，这类题目侧重考查考生对情景的理解能力及总结归纳能力。考生需充分理解文章内容，并且具备一定的推断、预判能力。

这类题目通常从以下两方面进行考查：

（1）填入使内容完整的单词

这类题目的句子可能缺少必要成分，导致语义不完整或不正确。如：The percentage of suburbanites identifying themselves in his research as feeling lonely is no higher than _____ of city centre residents. 这个句子明显缺少必要成分。

也有可能空格处所在句的含义与其他句子存在矛盾，含义不同。如：With the decrease of the salary, the employees can _____ earn their life.

（2）填入使逻辑正确的单词

这类题目往往在句首或两个句子之间设置空格，要求考生根据相关内容，填写正确的连词，使逻辑通顺。如：Their initial friendliness may not sustain for long, _____ the warm welcome they give you at first meetings.

2. 固定搭配

固定搭配考查的是单词的固定用法和一些固定表达，缺少了选项的提示，要求考生对固定搭配有着更高的敏感度，所以考生要加强对固定搭配的记忆，这样能有效提高解题效率。此类题目往往考查动词与介词的搭配，动词与不定式或分词结构的搭配以及一些固定的表达。

3. 语法基础

语法基础考查语法基本功，要求考生熟知语法规则（包括词法和句法），并熟练应用。这类题目往往都会在文中找到提示信息，所以考生要明确各语法现象的适用范围和判断依据，提高对语法规则运用的熟练度。经常考查的内容包括：时态、语态、主谓一致、定语从句、名词性从句、情态动词、冠词等。

四、答题策略

针对本题型，建议采用以下答题思路：

1. 通读全文，了解短文大意

开始做题之前先快速阅读整篇短文，把握文章大意。本类型题由于不设置选项，所以考生只需将注意力集中于文章即可。同时我们可以从内容和结构两个角度观察原文内容的特点，如：原文涉及了哪些人或事？原文采用了什么时态和语态？原文哪部分是总体叙述？哪部分是具体说明等。这可以帮助我们了解原文的表达特点和行文方式，能够为解题提供帮助。同时在这一过程中也可以完成一些较简单的固定搭配题和语法基础题，尽可能恢复短文的完整性。

2. 细读空格前后，填入合适的单词

仔细阅读空格所在的句子，理解句子要表达的含义，根据空格前后内容的特点判断题目要考查的要点，与上一种题型相比，由于缺乏选项的提示，所以文章内容是预测考点的唯一依据。

一般而言，内容理解类题目所在句会出现含义不完整、含义与前后句子存在矛盾或句子间缺乏连词的状况；固定搭配类题目在空格处附近往往会出现动词、介词（结构）；语法基础类题目往往在句子的谓语部分设空。

（1）内容理解类题目首先判断是含义的不完整还是逻辑的不完整。如为含义的不完整，可以通过参照前后句的含义，判断空格处所在句缺乏哪一层面的信息，并根据空格处所在句的结构，填入恰当的单词使句意完整。

如果缺少连词，我们需要概括出前后相关句子的含义，比较二者内容间的关系，如并列关系、因果关系等，然后再填写最适合文中句子的连词。

（2）语法基础类题目首先需判断题目考查的语法现象，句中出现的一些内容可以作为判断的依据。如考查时态的题目，句中往往会出现一些关于时间的表达；考查被动语态的题目会在句中出现过去分词；考查从句的题目，空格后的句子可以在主句中充当成分。在明确考查的语法现象后，需将语法规则与句子内容结合进行判断。

（3）固定搭配类题目要重视空格前后出现的单词，根据句中的已知信息，并结合句

中的提示，填写最恰当的搭配。

3. 重读短文，进行检查

　　完成所有填空后需要再通读一遍短文，确保文章意思通顺、逻辑合理。重点关注所填入的内容在全文的语境下是否成立。同时检查单词拼写和首字母大写。

五、典型例题及详解

The Sami Reindeer Herders

　　I was recently fortunate to follow a Sami reindeer herdsman to the 150-kilometre annual migration, a torturous and perilous journey into Norway's frozen north.

　　"How many reindeer do you have?" I asked Ulrich, the herdsman. He answered that he didn't know, but in fact he did really. I (1) ＿＿＿＿＿ have known better. You don't ask a Sami reindeer herder how many animals he possesses; I might as (2) ＿＿＿＿＿ have demanded to see his bankbook.

　　(3) ＿＿＿＿＿ had been Ulrich who had granted admission to me and a batch of tourists to accompany him. He firmly believed that it's crucial to propagate the reindeer herders' barely known way of life to the public. Ulrich explained, "We cannot keep our culture to (4) ＿＿＿＿＿ any more. I want to share it with outsiders because letting the outside world know is the best way (5) ＿＿＿＿＿ us to conserve our identity."

　　➢　参考答案

　　(1)【参考答案】should

　　【出题类型】内容理解

　　【解析】根据前文内容可知，作者询问当地人问题，对方回答不知道，而其实对方并非不知道。根据后一句，可知作者认为自己的提问方式存在问题。本句作者表达一种懊悔的情绪，所以本题应填"should"，表示"本该"。本句意为"我要是早知道就好了"。

　　(2)【参考答案】well

　　【出题类型】固定搭配

　　【解析】根据前文可知，作者发现不能问当地人拥有多少动物，根据本句可知作者认为看当地人的存折都比他之前的提问好。句中出现了"might as"，"might as well"为固定搭配，意为"还不如"，符合语境，所以本题应填"well"。本句意为"我还不如看他的存折呢"。

　　(3)【参考答案】It

　　【出题类型】语法基础

【解析】本题考查强调句式，强调句式的基本结构为"It is/was + 被强调部分（通常是主语、宾语或状语）+ that/who（当强调主语且主语指人）+ 其他部分"，且空格位于句首，首字母应大写，所以本题应填"It"。本句意为"是乌尔里希允许我和一批游客陪在他身边的"。

（4）【参考答案】ourselves

【出题类型】内容理解

【解析】作者在前一句说到"他坚信，向公众宣传驯鹿牧民鲜为人知的生活方式至关重要"，可知当地人认为让外界了解自己的文化至关重要，所以本题应填"ourselves"。本句意为"我们不能再封锁我们的文化了"。

（5）【参考答案】for

【出题类型】固定搭配

【解析】本题考查固定搭配。"the way for sb. to do"意为"某人做某事的方法"，所以本题应填"for"。本句意为"我想与外界分享，因为让外界了解我们是我们保存自己身份的最好方式"。

➤ 全文翻译

萨米驯鹿牧人

最近，我幸运地跟随一位萨米驯鹿牧人进行了150公里的年度迁徙，这是一段痛苦而危险的旅程，进入了挪威冰冷的北部。

"你有多少只驯鹿？"我问牧民乌尔里希。他回答说他不知道，虽然实际上他知道。我要是早知道就好了。你不能问萨米驯鹿牧人他有多少动物，我还不如看他的存折呢。

是乌尔里希允许我和一批游客陪在他身边的。他坚信，向公众宣传驯鹿牧民鲜为人知的生活方式至关重要。乌尔里希解释说："我们不能再封锁我们的文化了。我想与外界分享，因为让外界了解我们是我们保存自己身份的最好方式。"

➤ 词汇笔记

migration /maɪˈɡreɪʃn/ *n.* 迁徙

例：Considerations of this sort lead to the development of migration flow.

这类考虑导致了迁徙潮的发展。

torturous /ˈtɔːtʃərəs/ *adj.* 折磨人的，痛苦的

例：Yes, it is beautiful, but the roads are torturous.

是的，这是美丽的，但道路是曲折的。

perilous /ˈperələs/ *adj.* 危险的

例：The road grew even steeper and more perilous.

这条路变得更陡、更险了。

近：dangerous

propagate /ˈprɒpəgeɪt/ *v.* 散播，宣传

例：They propagated political doctrines that promised to tear apart the fabric of society.

他们宣传有可能摧毁社会结构的政治学说。

近：disseminate

Day 11 提分篇

一、日常通信类

1. 文章特点

此类型的内容通常为邮件或书信，话题通常与日常生活相关，表示问候、咨询、回答、歉意等。这类题材的表达较为固定，考生注重日常积累有助于提高解题效率。

2. 例题及详解

Dear Mr. Brown,

Thank you for your suggestion on our sign language course. We are always dedicated to poring over what portions of our courses we should focus more (1) _____ , and what parts our students pay most attention (2) _____ . We are also relieved to learn that you were, generally, satisfied with the course, (3) _____ some minor issues. We would like to offer you a special promotion. If you register for the next level, you (4) _____ get a 30% discount on the course fees. Our courses will be reserved fast, and we do not want you to miss (5) _____ on any chances, so let us know as soon as possible if you would like to join.

Yours sincerely,

Lily Smith

Smith Language School

➢ 参考答案

（1）【参考答案】on

【出题类型】固定搭配

【解析】"focus on" 为固定搭配，意为"集中于"，符合语境，所以本题应填"on"。句意为"我们一直致力于研究我们应该关注课程中的哪些部分"。

（2）【参考答案】to

【出题类型】固定搭配

【解析】本句与逗号前的内容为并列关系，空格处也应该表示"关注"的含义。"pay attention to"意为"关注，重视"，符合语境，所以本题应填"to"。句意为"我们一直致力于研究我们应该关注课程中的哪些部分以及我们的学生最关注哪些部分"。

（3）【参考答案】despite

【出题类型】内容理解

【解析】空格前提到对课程满意，空格所在句提到存在小问题。可知前后内容存在转折。由于逗号后并不是完整的句子，所以空格处不能填入连词。despite意为"尽管"，同时为介词词性，符合语境及语法规则，所以本题应填"despite"。句意为"我们也很欣慰地得知，尽管有些小问题，您对这门课程总体上是满意的"。

（4）【参考答案】will

【出题类型】语法基础

【解析】本题考查if引导的条件状语从句。if引导的条件状语从句采用"主将从现"的时态，空格处为从句，应采用一般将来时，所以本题应填"will"。句意为"如果您注册进入下一阶段，您将得到课程费用的7折优惠"。

（5）【参考答案】out

【出题类型】固定搭配

【解析】逗号前的内容说到，课程预订得很快。空格处前为动词"miss"，后为介词"on"，可推断出本题考查固定搭配。"miss out on"表示"错失……"，能够与空格后的"chances"搭配，所以本题应填"out"。句意为"我们不想让您错过任何机会"。

➢ 全文翻译

亲爱的布朗先生：

谢谢您对我们手语课程的建议。我们一直致力于研究我们应该关注课程中的哪些部分以及我们的学生最关注些哪部分。我们也很欣慰地得知，尽管有些小问题，您对这门课程总体上是满意的。我们想为您提供一个特别优惠。如果您注册进入下一阶段，您将得到课程费用的7折优惠。我们的课程预订得很快，我们不想让您错过任何机会，所以如果您想参加，请尽快告诉我们。

真诚的，

莉莉·史密斯

史密斯语言学校

➢ 词汇笔记

dedicated /ˈdedɪkeɪtɪd/ *adj.* 专心的；献身的

搭：be dedicated to 专心做……；投身于……

例：Mary is dedicated to her job.

玛丽对工作专心致志。

派：dedication *n.* 奉献，献身

近：devoted

pore over 集中精力阅读；沉思

例：He would rather pore over a book than play.

他宁可专心致志地读书，也不愿意去玩。

relieved /rɪˈliːvd/ *adj.* 放心的，宽慰的

例：I'm relieved that nobody was hurt.

谁都没有受伤，我深感宽慰。

近：comforting

promotion /prəˈməʊʃn/ *n.* 提拔，晋升；促销

例：The promotion of that supermarket attracts many customers.

那家超市的促销活动吸引了很多顾客。

派：promotional *adj.* 促销的；推广的

二、纪实类

1. 文章特点

纪实类文本语言较为平实，以真实地记录某一事件或人物为主要目的。这类文本往往按时间或方位的顺序进行叙述。

2. 例题及详解

Jason Hotel

The Jason Hotel has had a fame for wonderful food ever (1) _____ the day it opened in 1962. It was launched by a businessman called Jason Buth, who received an leaflet for a house overlooking a garden. He had been planning to convert a residence (2) _____ a hotel, and this house appeared to be optimal.

Buth (3) _____ soon managing the hotel on his own, but employed a superb chef, Danny White. Within three months, the restaurant was (4) _____ heavily booked that Buth had to hired new staff. The hotel gained several prizes for the its specialty. The current owner, Sam Brown, has personally trained (5) _____ number of chefs who have gone on to become famous.

➢ **参考答案**

（1）【参考答案】since

【出题类型】语法基础

【解析】 本句使用了现在完成时，且在空格后出现了关于时间的表达。since通常与现在完成时连用，表示"自从……"的含义，所以本题应填"since"。句意为"杰森酒店自1962年开业以来就以美味的食物而闻名"。

（2）【参考答案】to

【出题类型】固定搭配

【解析】句中出现了"convert"，意为"转换"，该单词与介词"to"连用，可表示"转换至……"的含义，所以本题应填"to"。句意为"他一直在计划把民宅改成酒店，这所房子似乎是最佳选择"。

（3）【参考答案】wasn't

【出题类型】内容理解

【解析】空格处是谓语，通过阅读逗号后的句子，可知布斯没有自己经营，所以逗号前的句子应该表示否定含义，逗号后的句子使用了一般过去时，所以本题应填"wasn't"。句意为"布斯并没有马上自己经营这家酒店，而是聘请了一位顶级厨师丹尼·怀特”。

（4）【参考答案】so

【出题类型】固定搭配

【解析】空格后出现了副词和"that"，可推断出此处应该是"so…that…"结构，表示"如此……以至于……"，所以本题应填"so"。句意为"不到三个月，餐厅就被订满了，布斯不得不雇佣新员工"。

（5）【参考答案】a

【出题类型】固定搭配

【解析】结合空格后的内容可以联想到此处应该是固定搭配"a number of"，意为"许多"，所以本题应填"a"。句意为"现在的老板，山姆·布朗亲自培训许多厨师，他们中的很多人已经成为著名厨师"。

➤ 全文翻译

杰森酒店

杰森酒店自1962年开业以来就以美味的食物而闻名。它是由一个名叫杰森·布斯的商人创办的，他收到了一张能俯瞰花园的房子的宣传单。他一直在计划把民宅改成酒店，这所房子似乎是最佳选择。

布斯并没有马上自己经营这家酒店，而是聘请了一位顶级厨师丹尼·怀特。不到三个月，餐厅就被订满了，布斯不得不雇佣新员工。这家酒店因其特色菜肴而获得好几项大奖。现在的老板，山姆·布朗亲自培训许多厨师，他们中的很多人已经成为著名厨师。

➤ 词汇笔记

fame /feɪm/ *n.* 名誉，名气

搭：wealth and fame 名利

例：Wealth and fame hold no attraction for Green.

　　名利对格林没有吸引力。

近：reputation

leaflet /ˈliːflət/ *n.* 宣传单，小册子

例：You can request a free copy of the leaflet.

　　你可以索要一份免费的宣传单。

residence /ˈrezɪdəns/ *n.* 住宅，住所

例：Meet outside of your residence and wait for further instructions.

　　请在住所外集合，等待进一步指示。

convert /kənˈvɜːt/ *v.* 转变，转换

搭：convert into/to sth. 转变为某物

例：By converting the attic, they were able to have two extra bedrooms.

　　通过改建阁楼，他们能有两间额外的卧室。

派：conversion *n.* 转变

近：change/transform

optimal /ˈɒptɪməl/ *adj.* 最佳的，最适合的

搭：optimal solution 最优解，最佳方案

例：This restaurant is optimal for tomorrow's party.

　　这家饭店最适合举办明天的聚会。

派：optimize *v.* 优化

三、阐释说明类

1. 文章特点

　　阐释说明类文章的写作目的在于向读者解释某一事件或物品的原理。该类文章的客观性较强，具有层次分明的特点。

2. 例题及详解

The Touchscreen Technology

It is no wonder to say that, currently, people are literally surrounded by touchscreens. This technology has become an indispensable part of society and it is now difficult to imagine life (1) _____ it. Due to common assumptions, the first touchscreen was invented in 1965 in the UK, so this technology is (2) _____ than half a century old. The first prototypes were only able to process one touch at a (3) _____, so, what will later be called "multitouch" technology was still a long way away. Touchscreen technology really started to take (4) _____ at the beginning of the new millennium as developers explored ways (5) _____combining this technology with daily life.

➤　参考答案

（1）【参考答案】without

【出题类型】内容理解

【解析】根据本句中的已知信息，触屏技术已经成为生活中不可或缺的部分，可知这项技术对我们很重要，所以本题应填"without"，表示"没有"的含义。句意为"这

项技术已经成为社会不可缺少的一部分，现在很难想象没有它的生活"。

（2）【参考答案】more

【出题类型】内容理解

【解析】结合句中的时间"1965"和空格后的内容可知，句中的时间状语应表示"半个多世纪"，所以本题应填"more"。句意为"人们普遍认为触摸屏是1965年在英国发明的，所以这项技术已经有半个多世纪的历史了"。

（3）【参考答案】time

【出题类型】内容理解

【解析】本句意在说明触控屏开始的形态。根据句中出现的"multitouch"可知，起初触控屏每次只能对一个触点进行反应。所以本题应填"time"，表示"每次"的含义。句意为"第一个原型机每次只能对一个触控点进行反应"。

（4）【参考答案】off

【出题类型】固定搭配

【解析】空格处前出现了take，可以推测空格处与take能够进行搭配。本句"as"后的内容是对之前内容的解释，这部分内容对触控屏的发展有推动作用。所以空格处内容应该表示"发展"的含义。"take off"意为"起飞；脱下；突然成功"，符合语境，所以本题应填"off"。句意为"触屏技术真正开始腾飞是在新千年之初"。

（5）【参考答案】of

【出题类型】固定搭配

【解析】空格处所在句应该表示"……的方式"，"way of"为固定搭配，表示这一含义，所以本题应填"of"。句意为"开发人员探索了将这项技术与日常生活相结合的方法"。

➢ 全文翻译

触屏技术

毫无疑问，现在人们确实被触屏包围着。这项技术已经成为社会不可缺少的一部分，现在很难想象没有它的生活。人们普遍认为触摸屏是1965年在英国发明的，所以这项技术已经有半个多世纪的历史了。第一个原型机每次只能对一个触控点进行反应，所以，后来被称为"多点触控"的技术还有很长的路要走。触屏技术真正开始腾飞是在新千年之初，开发人员探索了将这项技术与日常生活相结合的方法。

➢ 词汇笔记

literally /ˈlɪtərəli/ *adv.* 逐字地，字面含义地；确实地

例：I literally jumped out of my skin.

我简直被吓了一大跳

派：literate *adj.* 有读写能力的；受过良好教育的

indispensable /ˌɪndɪˈspensəbl/ *adj.* 不可或缺的，必需的

例：A good dictionary is indispensable for learning a foreign language.

　　一本好词典是学习外语必备的。

派：indispensability *n.* 不可缺少，必要

近：necessary

assumption /əˈsʌmpʃn/ *n.* 假定，设想

例：The truth may lie in the reasonable assumption.

　　真相可能就存在于合理的假设之中。

近：hypothesis

prototype /ˈprəʊtətaɪp/ *n.* 原型；雏形

搭：prototype system 原型系统

例：The prototype of the machine is being displayed.

　　这个机器的原型正在展出。

派：prototypical *adj.* 原型的；典型的

millennium /mɪˈleniəm/ *n.* 一千年；千禧年

例：People celebrating the millennium filled the plaza.

　　广场上挤满了庆祝千禧年的人。

四、观点建议类

1. 文章特点

　　观点建议类文本从日常生活的某一问题出发，表明自己的观点或提出建议，可能会加以论证从而让读者接受其观点或建议。这类文本往往具有主客观相结合的特点，即从客观事实出发，再加以自己的观点。

2. 例题及详解

Advice for Cloze Exercises

Read the heading and entire text first（1）_____ acquire a general understanding of the topic and content. Next, read seriously around the first space. It is important to analyze the words directly on（2）_____ side of the space as well as at sentence and paragraph level, because the missing word may be part of a broader structure.

（3）_____ you are hesitant about the answer, make a reasonable conjecture on the basis of the likely part of speech of the missing word. Do not leave the space blank. You will （4）_____ be penalized for giving an incorrect answer，and if you guess，you may be right! Repeat the procedure with the rest （5）_____ the spaces，before reading through the text one final time to check.

➢ 参考答案

（1）【参考答案】to

【出题类型】内容理解

【解析】通过阅读，可以发现空格后的内容是空格前内容的目的，且空格后的动词为原形，所以本题应填"to"，表示"为了……"，句意为"首先阅读标题和全文以对主题和内容有一个大致的了解"，符合语境。

（2）【参考答案】either

【出题类型】内容理解

【解析】在空格后出现了"sentence and paragraph level"，即句子和文章的层面，空格处的内容应该对这两个层面进行指代。"either"可表示两者之中的任意一个，符合语境，所以本题应填"either"。句意为"重要的是分析在空格的左右两侧，并在句子和段落层面上直接分析单词"。

（3）【参考答案】If

【出题类型】内容理解

【解析】本句逗号前的部分说到对答案犹豫，选项后的内容说到进行猜测，可知前者为条件，后者为结果。所以空格应填表示"如果"的连词，且空格位于句首，所以本题应填"If"。句意为"如果你不能确定答案，根据所缺单词可能的词性做出合理的猜测"。

（4）【参考答案】not

【出题类型】内容理解

【解析】本题需要结合前后文的内容进行判断，前文的内容主要鼓励人们对不确定的题目进行推测，后文说到"如果你进行猜测，那还有对的可能"，可以推断出本句想表达的是"如果你的答案不正确，你也不会受到惩罚"的含义，所以本题应填"not"。

（5）【参考答案】of

【出题类型】固定搭配

【解析】空格前出现了"the rest"，可联想到固定搭配"the rest of"，表示"剩下的"，符合语境，所以本题应填"of"。本句意为"在最后一次检查文本之前，对剩下的空格重复上述步骤"。

➢ 全文翻译

完形填空练习的建议

首先阅读标题和全文以对主题和内容有一个大致的了解。接下来，认真阅读第一个空格。重要的是分析空格的左右两侧，并在句子和段落层面上直接分析单词，因为缺失的单词可能是更广泛结构的一部分。

如果你不能确定答案，根据所缺单词可能的词性做出合理的猜测。不要留有空格。如果你的答案不正确，你也不会受到惩罚，如果你进行猜测，那还有对的可能！在最后一次检查文本之前，对剩下的空格重复上述步骤。

➢ 词汇笔记

structure /ˈstrʌktʃə(r)/ *n.* 结构，构造

搭：industrial structure 产业结构

例：Your essay needs a better structure.

你这篇文章的结构有待提升。

派：structural *adj.* 结构的

近：framework

hesitant /ˈhezɪtənt/ *adj.* 犹豫的

搭：be hesitant about 不情愿的

例：She was hesitant about coming forward with her story.

她迟迟不愿说出自己的经历。

派：hesitancy *n.* 犹豫不决

近：tentative

conjecture /kənˈdʒektʃə(r)/ *n.* 猜测；猜测的结果

例：We should learn to distinguish the conjecture and fact.

我们应该学会区分猜测和事实。

派：conjectural *adj.* 猜测的

近：speculation

penalize /ˈpiːnəlaɪz/ *v.* 惩罚，处罚；使处于不利地位

例：Some councils issued smaller bins to penalize those who produced lots of rubbish.

一些委员会分发更小的垃圾箱，来惩罚那些制造许多垃圾的人。

近：punish

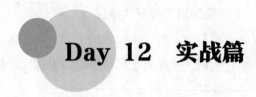

Day 12 实战篇

1.

Unprecedented Filming—From Non-human Photographers!

How tough would it be for a wild animal to make a film? In fact, a sea mew in Northern Canada recently made it. The juvenile sea mew picked (1) _____ a video camera that had originally (2) _____ planned to record whales. (3) _____ accidentally turning it on, the mew then made a brief wildlife documentary of the zone as it flew overhead. The mew managed to cover an amazing distance of 150 km while grabbing the camera. It then approached its nest, (4) _____ which point it felt tired. The bird simply discarded the camera and dropped it. Finally, it was found by (5) _____ local birdwatcher.

2.

From: Tom Black
To: Michael Beasley
Subject: Decoration designer

Hi Beasley,
I have some exciting news. I managed to get the phone number of the decoration designer (1) _____ worked for my house. Her name is Nancy. I stayed (2) _____ all night to look up my contacts and old receipts. At the beginning, I couldn't find the name of her company, but then I remembered that she named it (3) _____ her mother, so I basically spent two hours looking for the wrong surname! When you call her, tell her that you are a friend of (4) _____ and I'm sure she'll treat you well.
(5) _____ me know how it goes.

Take care,
Black

3.

It has long been accepted that swimming is beneficial to the body. It has many advantages (1) _____ a form of exercise: it keeps your heart healthy and strengthens your lungs. But whether or (2) _____ it's the best workout for different individuals is determined by your needs and preferences. A common consensus about swimming (3) _____ that it exercises your whole body, but the truth of this really leans on exactly how you swim. It's possible to get into a pool and swim on your back without using much energy (4) _____ all, meaning you miss out on the health benefits that swimming faster brings. Swimming fails to strengthen bones or build large muscles, so (5) _____ that's your aspiration, you're better off heading to the gym instead.

4.

Visitors to the USA may benefit (1) _____ grasping these cultural tips to help interaction. At first, Americans may seem very amicable, and smile and use first names when meeting you. However, they have a strong sense of personal space, and if you stand too close, you (2) _____ risk making them feel upset or restless. Their initial friendliness may not sustain for long (3) _____ the warm welcome they give you at first meetings. Americans don't feel the necessity to build a close personal relationship soon. They see connections as being between old friends rather than new acquaintances. Their frankness and aspiration to get straight to the (4) _____ indicate their attitude of "time is money" and they typically do not waste a lot of time (5) _____ small talk.

Part 5 拓展阅读

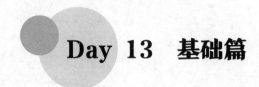

Day 13　基础篇

一、题型介绍

　　阅读第五类题型是拓展阅读。考生读一篇较长的文章，完成4~6道选择题。题目顺序与文章顺序一致，通常一个段落对应一道题。这类题型是多数考生比较熟悉的传统阅读理解题，文章主题与日常生活相关，比如回忆录、游记、书评影评、知识科普、历史故事等。文章篇幅较长，一般400~700词，总体难度较高。

二、考试界面

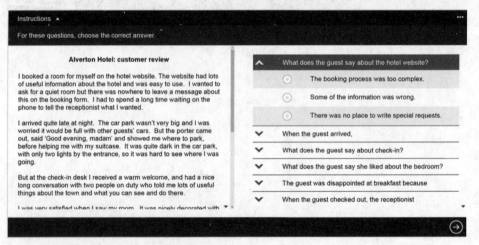

✓　界面最上方是本部分的答题说明

✓　界面左侧是文章，通过滚动条来阅读

✓　界面右侧是题目和选项，通过点击每道题前面的箭头来展开和折叠选项

✓　点击每个选项前的○进行选择

✓　点击右下角箭头可以切换到下一题（注意答完的题目不能再切换回来进行检查）

三、考查技能

拓展阅读主要考查考生的以下技能：

✓　理解主旨大意，包括整篇文章的主旨和各个段落的主旨

✓　理解段落内的逻辑结构

✓　抓取和理解文中的细节信息

✓　掌握作者观点以及文章中人物的态度及观点

✓　掌握同义改写

本题型的出题类型主要包括以下三种：

1. 主旨大意

主旨大意类题目的问题形式通常为"在第几段中，作者表达了什么"。由于题干中没有关键词，因此考生需要通读全段，将文中内容与选项进行对比，从而得出答案。

这类题目还有一种设问方式，即"最适合这篇文章的标题是什么"，这种题目要求考生要充分把握整篇文章的内容，对文章的核心要义进行概括，选择出最能概括文章内容的标题。

2. 细节理解

细节理解类题目是考试中出现频率最高的，会针对文中的某一细节进行提问，设问形式一般为"关于……的说法正确/错误的是"或"哪项说法未在文中提及"。在做此类题目时，要通过题目中的关键词进行定位，找到答案所在句子，有时根据一句话就能得出答案，有时也需要将两三句话结合起来进行理解分析。

3. 观点态度

观点态度类题目出现的位置通常靠后，提问形式一般为"在第几段中，作者/文中人物表达了什么观点/态度"或"哪项与……的态度相符/不符"。这类题目要注意问题问的是谁的态度，明确对象。

四、答题策略

针对拓展阅读，建议采用以下答题思路：

1. 快速浏览全文，了解文章大意

开始做题之前先快速浏览整篇文章，把握文章大意，可以重点读每段第一句话。

2. 仔细阅读题干，把握关键词

仔细阅读题目的题干和选项，理解题干的意思，把握题干和选项的关键词。大部分题目的题干中会直接问到"在某段中……"或"根据某段……"，考生可以直接去细读

对应的段落，而且本题型基本遵循一段一题的规律，所以建议考生按顺序做题。如果题干中没有明确的段落提示，考生则要把握住关键词，关键词通常是名词。除了题干之外，也要仔细阅读每个选项，把握选项中的关键词，充分理解选项的意思。

3. 细读每段，定位答案句，进行选择

根据上一步确定的段落和关键词进行细读，定位到答案所在句，将选项和答案句进行对比，确认答案。正确的选项往往是对文章内容的同义改写，错误的选项意思往往与文章表述不符，或者文章中没有提及。有些考查主旨大意的题目，无法直接定位到某一句，这种题目需要考生理解整段的主旨并进行选择。

4. 再次细读答案句，进行复核

题目都完成之后，建议考生再回到原文进行复核。注意选择的答案一定要在文中有据可依，千万不要加入自己的主观想法。

在日常学习中，考生要注意积累单词，本题型的文章中经常会出现难度较大的单词，平常练习时一定要将不认识的单词记录下来并掌握。同时，考生也要提高长难句的理解能力。遇到长难句时，可以从结构入手，牢记先主干后分支，即先分析主谓宾，再研究定状补。

五、典型例题及详解

I recently had an unforgettable trip with my friends—going to watch gray foxes in Columbia! We stayed in a small house in a deserted location in southern Columbia. We were in an area where there were no settlements and very few people, but numerous gray foxes, wolves, squirrels, hares and other wildlife. We were told that due to the gray foxes having rare contact with people there, we'd be able to watch them in natural surroundings. And it was astonishing, walking across the trees, muddy ground or along the path towards gray foxes!

Very fortunately, the gray foxes we saw were a family. We were told that it was time for the gray fox cubs to grow up, and during this period, the father provided food for the entire family. Little foxes can only hunt on their own when they are four months old. The mother fox was cleaning her paws and squinting towards our camera as she was surrounded by her cubs chasing and playing! We didn't get too close, for fear of disturbing this comfortable moment.

Our two guides, Mary and Billy, were highly trained in how to survive in damp conditions of the forest. They also made us feel be at ease as we got closer to the gray foxes. They taught us a very moderate and respectful approach so that the gray foxes didn't notice too much that we were there. Although our guides weren't originally from southern Columbia, they apparently loved the forest environment and shared so much with us. They are cautious not only about our safety, but about the well-being of the gray foxes.

We were really lucky on the tour as we had a professional photographer with us, and we were all given techniques on how to get the best photos. For my part, I finally acquired how to use some of the complicated equipment I'd brought along. However, while we were there, we had to deal with everything from bright sunshine to thick fog, so regrettably we weren't always able to benefit from her advice on taking great photos, as the conditions sometimes weren't very suitable for photography.

As for our accommodation, it was a bit basic. But although it was short of luxury, the staff offered considerate service and tasty local food. They were continually improving it, and they'd just built a new reception area that was really beautiful, and a perfect place to spend time when we weren't out looking for gray foxes! It was a trip I'll remember for years to come.

(1) In the first paragraph, the writer describes that the place she stayed in

A. prepared exclusive constructions for tourists to watch gray foxes safely.

B. had more gray foxes than other areas in the country.

C. was distant from the regions that indigenes inhabit.

D. was hard to get around because of the poor transportation.

(2) What does the writer tell us about the gray foxes she saw?

A. They were often surrounded by their babies.

B. Fox cubs are usually taken care of by their fathers.

C. They were closer to humans than other creatures were.

D. The writer witnessed that they were going hunting in the forest.

(3) What does the writer say about the guides?

A. They made the route shifty on the basis of actual situation.

B. They were the native who were adaptive to the humid climate.

C. They made the visitors thoroughly understand the matters that need attention.

D. They adhered to the concept that avoids interfering with the gray fox.

（4）How did the writer feel about having a photographer with them on the trip?

A. Dispirited when the adverse condition stops her from using the trick.

B. Delighted because the photographer took so many wonderful photos for her.

C. Despondent when she found the photographer was not very professional.

D. Appreciative very much because the sophisticated equipment was repaired.

（5）What did the writer think of the accommodation she had?

A. It made her wakeful because of the noisy from the construction.

B. It provided local food which failed to meet the writer's tastes.

C. It was managed by some very accommodating people.

D. It was less cost-effective compared with another one.

➢ 试题详解

题号	出题类型	答案	解析
（1）	细节理解	C	题目：第一段，作者说到她所处的地方_____ A 为游客安全地观赏灰狐准备了专门的建筑。 B 比这个国家别的地区的灰狐多。 **C 远离当地人居住的区域。** D 由于交通不便难以出行。 从题干可知，该题目考查对细节信息的理解，并且可将答案定位到第一段。在第一段第三句，作者提到"We were in an area where there were no settlements and very few people, but numerous gray foxes, wolves, squirrels, hares and other wildlife.（我们所在的地方没有村落，人口很少，但有很多灰狐、狼、松鼠、野兔和其他野生动物。）"，由此可知作者所处的地方远离居住区，所以C选项正确。 本段第四句说到"We were told that due to the gray foxes having rare contact with people there, we'd be able to watch them in natural surroundings.（我们得知，由于灰狐很少与那里的人接触，我们可以在自然环境中观察它们。）"，可知作者在自然环境中观赏灰狐，所以A选项错误。本段并未比较本地区灰狐和这个国家其他地区灰狐的数量，所以B选项错误。文中并未提到交通不便的问题，所以D选项错误。
（2）	细节理解	A	题目：关于作者看到的灰狐，她告诉我们什么？ **A 它们的孩子经常环绕身边。** B 狐狸幼崽们通常由爸爸照看。 C 和其他动物相比，它们和人类更亲近。 D 作者看到它们正在森林里狩猎。 根据关键词"the gray foxes she saw"可将答案定位到第二段。由本段第二句"We were told that it was time for the gray fox cubs to grow up（我们得知当时正是灰狐幼崽成长的时候）"以及第四句"she was surrounded

题号	出题类型	答案	解析
（2）	细节理解	A	by her cubs chasing and playing!（幼崽们正在她的身边追逐打闹！）"可知，作者看到的灰狐幼崽经常在父母的身边，所以A选项正确。 根据本段第二句可知，狐狸爸爸负责提供食物，并非照顾幼崽，所以B选项错误。C选项相关内容未在文中提及，可排除。文章并未提到灰狐正在打猎，所以D选项错误。
（3）	细节理解	D	**题目：关于她的导游，作者说了什么？** A 他们会根据实际情况改变路线。 B 他们是适应潮湿气候的本地人。 C 他们让游客充分理解需要注意的事项。 **D 他们坚持避免干扰灰狐这一理念。** 根据关键词"guides"可定位到第三段。由第三段第三句"They taught us a very moderate and respectful approach so that the gray foxes didn't notice too much that we were there.（他们教我们一种非常温和且尊重的方式，这样灰狐就不太会注意到我们在那里。）"可知，导游以不让灰狐受到影响的方式接近它们，所以D选项正确。 A选项相关内容未在文中提及，可排除。根据本段第四句"Although our guides weren't originally from southern Columbia（尽管我们的导游并非来自哥伦比亚南部）"，可知导游并非来自本地，所以B选项错误。C选项的相关内容未在文中提及，可排除。
（4）	细节理解	A	**题目：与摄影师一起旅行，作者感觉如何？** **A 不利的条件阻碍作者使用摄影师的建议，她感到沮丧。** B 摄影师为她拍了很多不错的照片，她感到高兴。 C 当她发现摄影师不专业时，感到沮丧。 D 高级的设备修好了，她很感激。 根据关键词"photographer"可将答案定位到第四段。由第四段最后一句"However, while we were there, we had to deal with everything from bright sunshine to thick fog, so regrettably we weren't always able to benefit from her advice on taking great photos（然而，当我们在那里的时候，我们不仅要应对刺眼的阳光，还要应对浓雾，所以遗憾的是，我们无法一直从她关于拍好照片的建议中获益）"可知，这与A选项说法相符，所以A选项为正确答案。 B选项和C选项相关内容均未在文中提及，可排除。本段中第二句提到了"高端设备"，但并未提及对其进行修理，所以D选项错误。

题号	出题类型	答案	解析
(5)	细节理解	C	题目：作者认为住宿怎样？ A 施工带来的噪声让她失眠。 B 这里提供的当地食物不能满足作者的口味。 C 经营者非常乐于助人。 **D 和另一家相比，性价比较低。** 由关键词"accommodation"，可定位至最后一段。本段第二句说到"But although it was short of luxury, the staff offered considerate service and tasty local food.（虽然不够豪华，但工作人员提供了周到的服务和美味的当地食物。）"，可知这里的服务很周到，所以C选项正确。 本段中第三句提到"they'd just built a new reception area that was really beautiful（他们刚建了一个新的接待区，十分漂亮）"，可知这里的确在进行施工，但并未提及是否带来噪声，所以A选项错误。其余两项均未在文中提及，可排除。

➢ **全文翻译**

最近我和朋友们的旅行经历让我难忘——我们去哥伦比亚看灰狐！我们住在哥伦比亚南部一个荒芜地区的一栋小房子里。我们所在的地方没有村落，人口很少，但有很多灰狐、狼、松鼠、野兔和其他野生动物。我们得知，由于灰狐很少与那里的人接触，我们可以在自然环境中观察它们。走过树林，泥泞的地面或沿着小路走向灰狐，真是让人惊讶！

非常幸运的是，我们看到了灰狐一家。我们得知当时正是灰狐幼崽成长的时候，在此期间，父亲为全家提供食物。小狐狸只有在四个月大的时候才能自己捕食。狐狸妈妈正在清理她的爪子，朝着我们的镜头眯着眼，幼崽们正在她的身边追逐打闹！我们没有靠得太近，生怕打扰了这温馨的一刻。

我们的两名导游，玛丽和比利，就如何在潮湿的森林环境中生存受过严格的训练。当我们离灰狐较近时，他们也让我们感到安心。他们教我们一种非常温和且尊重的方式，这样灰狐就不太会注意到我们在那里。尽管我们的导游并非来自哥伦比亚南部，但他们显然喜欢森林的环境，并与我们分享了很多东西。他们不仅要小心我们的安全，也关心灰狐的健康。

在这次旅行中，我们真的很幸运，因为有一位专业的摄影师和我们一起，她告诉我们拍出最好照片的方法。对我来说，我终于学会了如何使用我带来的一些复杂的设备。然而，当我们在那里的时候，我们不仅要应对刺眼的阳光，还要应对浓雾，所以遗憾的是，我们无法一直从她关于拍好照片的建议中获益，因为条件有时不太适合摄影。

至于我们的住宿，有点基础。虽然不够豪华，但工作人员提供了周到的服务和美味的当地食物。他们也在不断改进，他们刚建了一个新的接待区，十分漂亮，我们不出去找灰狐的时候，这里是享受时光的好地方！这是我多年来都会记得的一次旅行。

➢ 　词汇笔记

numerous /ˈnjuːmərəs/ *adj.* 众多的，许多的

例：This easeful apartment has attracted numerous people to live in.

这座舒适的公寓吸引了许多人前来居住。

近：many

muddy /ˈmʌdi/ *adj.* 泥泞的

例：Watch out! The path is a little muddy.

小心点！这条路有点泥泞。

cub /kʌb/ *n.* 幼崽

例：Raising a cat needs to follow several rules.

养育一只小猫需要遵循许多规则。

squint /skwɪnt/ *v.* 眯着眼睛看

搭：squint at 眯眼看

例：The bright sunlight made the boy squint.

强烈的阳光让男孩眯起了眼。

disturb /dɪˈstɜːb/ *v.* 打扰，干扰

例：It is common courtesy not to disturb others when they are resting.

不在其他人休息的时候去打扰是一种基本的礼貌。

派：disturbing *adj.* 令人不安的；烦扰的

近：bother

damp /dæmp/ *adj.* 潮湿的，微湿的

例：The damp and cold air made me uncomfortable.

湿冷的空气让我感到不舒服。

派：dampness *n.* 潮气

近：wet

moderate /ˈmɑːdərət/ *adj.* 温和的；中等的；不偏激的

例：The team enjoyed only moderate success last season.

上个赛季，这个队伍只取得了中等成绩。

regrettably /rɪˈɡretəbli/ *adv.* 遗憾地

例：Regrettably, crime has been increasing in this area.

令人遗憾的是，这一地区的犯罪率在不断上升。

accommodation /əˌkɒməˈdeɪʃn/ *n.* 住宿，食宿

搭：accommodation cost 住宿费

例：The accommodation is simple but spacious.

住宿环境虽然朴素，但宽敞。

Day 14　提分篇

1. 文章特点

　　此类文章往往语言风格较为平实，以真实记录为目的，作者通过文章，向人们展示自己的经历或见闻。

2. 例题及详解

Old Diaries

　　One afternoon I was looking through in a second-hand bookshop when I came across a boxful of notebooks—ancient diaries, possibly over 100 years old. I bargained with the owner, and left with my newly-discovered treasure. There was no name on the diaries, and only an address of a well-known college on the box.

　　As a writer, I was obsessive. Why didn't I write about the anonymous diarist? It would be the first ever biography in which the biographer was ignorant of whom his subject is. But when I got home, I slid the box into my study and shoved it under the table. Somehow I was loath to start reading in case the contents failed to correspond with what they'd already become in my mind. Anyway, I was deep at work on a biography and didn't thirst for being distracted by anything new.

　　Eventually, though, I did open the box. And I found that one of the oddities of reading the diaries of someone you know nothing about, not even their name or gender, is the huge significance than even the most trivial clues seem to assume. The writer had recorded the date in blunt, soft pencil at the top of each page, and made notes in the margins. That, together with the label on the box, was enough for me to conjure up a clear image of what I'd supposed was a youngish man, in his book-lined college rooms, bending over his desk, and annotating the diary with the same careful respect he'd given to his collection of scientifically significant seashells. But then as I read on, I made an important discovery. The writer was, in fact, much older than I'd thought.

At this stage, I also began to wonder whether he was someone famous. And as decisively as if the books had been dropped on my head, my attitude changed. The great excitement of an anonymous diary is that it might belong to absolutely anybody. This took away the vital thing that had made the books interesting. Imagining that he'd turn out to be a celebrity also brought back my initial guilty feelings that I hadn't tried harder to trace whoever the diaries might have belonged to.

However, it says a lot for the diarist that he managed to keep me reading. Throughout the guided tour he gave me of his mind, he remained honest and funny. I liked this man, whatever his name. I enjoyed his revelations about his clumsiness, his obsessions and his occasional outbursts of irritation. Nothing was hidden.

In fact, once I'd read the volumes from beginning to end. I began to think I recognized a lot of his qualities in myself, and it intensified my wish to understand him. Biographers often report that their task is made easier if they establish some kind of relationship with their subject. However, something about having got to know him also prevented me from proceeding further, and eventually the diaries made their way to a museum to be used in a history project there.

(1) Why didn't Martin start work immediately on the old diaries he bought?

A. He was obliged to complete another project first.

B. His initial enthusiasm for the task had begun to diminish.

C. He feared to become disillusioned by what he might discover.

D. He'd begun to realize it would be more time-consuming than he'd anticipated.

(2) When Martin finally began reading the diaries, he _____

A. became increasingly certain he knew the identity of the writer.

B. was impressed by the care given to the amount of detail that was recorded.

C. was grateful for the amount of chronological information included.

D. allowed his imagination to lead him to a false conclusion.

(3) When Martin began to suspect the diaries were written by someone famous, he_____

A. felt the mystery he'd been enjoying was suddenly disappeared.

B. began to wonder whether he might uncover important information.

C. realized the writer might be less approachable than he'd hoped.

D. began to feel a sense of guilt that he'd so far managed to avoid.

(4) What opinion of the diary writer's work did Martin form?

A. He found himself losing interest in some of the passages in the diary.

B. He admired the writer for revealing such an insight into his thinking.

C. He felt there was more potential in the style than he'd initially realized.

D. He was amused that the writer had depicted himself in a very positive light.

（5）Having got to the end of the diaries, Martin ＿＿＿＿＿＿

A. realized he actually had a lot in common with the writer.

B. fully understood the need for biographers to get close to their subjects.

C. started to wonder if the project had even been worth pursuing.

D. felt he was little closer to piecing together a complete picture of the writer.

➢ 试题详解

题号	出题类型	答案	解析
（1）	细节理解	C	题目：马丁为什么没有马上阅读他购买的旧日记? A 他不得不先完成其他任务。 B 他最初对这项任务的热情已经开始减弱。 **C 他害怕对他可能发现的东西感到幻灭。** D 他开始认识到这比他想象的更耗时间。 第二段第五句提到"Somehow I was loath to start reading in case the contents failed to correspond with what they'd already become in my mind.（不知怎么的，我不想开始阅读，生怕内容与我脑海中已经形成的内容不符。）"，可知作者害怕自己的愿望落空，所以 C 选项正确。 本段第六句确实提到了作者要完成另一部作品，但不是 A 选项中说的"不得不"，而是作者自己专心于写作，怕被分心，所以 A 选项错误。其余两个选项均未在文章中提及，可排除。
（2）	细节理解	D	题目：当马丁最终开始阅读，他 ＿＿＿＿＿＿ A 越来越确定他知道作者的身份。 B 对记录大量细节的关注印象深刻。 C 感激包含的大量时间信息。 **D 让自己的想象力得出了错误的结论。** 第三段第四句中提到"That, together with the label on the box, was enough for me to conjure up a clear image of what I'd supposed was a youngish man...（这一点，再加上盒子上的标签，足以让我清晰地联想到一个年轻男人的形象……）"。本段最后两句又提到"But then as I read on, I made an important discovery. The writer was, in fact, much older than I'd thought.（但当我继续读下去时，我有了一个重要的发现。事实上，这位作者比我想象的要老得多。）"可知作者在结合日记的内容进行了猜想，但最后发现猜想不正确，所以 D 选项正确。 本段第三句提到了日记的作者记录了日期，做了笔记，但本文作者并未提到自己对此的感受，所以 B 选项错误。其余两个选项均未在文中体现，可排除。

题号	出题类型	答案	解析
（3）	细节理解	D	题目：当马丁开始怀疑作者是名人后，他 _____ A 他一直享受的神秘感突然消失。 B 开始想要知道他能不能获得重要信息。 C 意识到作者不像他希望的那样平易近人。 **D 开始感到一种自己目前努力避免的罪恶感。** 第四段最后一句提到 "Imagining that he'd turn out to be a celebrity also brought back my initial guilty feelings that I hadn't tried harder to trace whoever the diaries might have belonged to.（想象他是一个名人，也让我回想起最初的罪恶感，因为我没有更努力地去追查那些日记的主人。）"，可知作者在这种情况下感到了罪恶感，所以D选项正确。其余选项均未在文中提及，可排除。
（4）	观点态度	B	题目：马丁对日记作者的作品有怎样的观点？ A 他发现自己对日记中的某些文章失去了兴趣。 **B 他钦佩日记作者对自己思想的洞察。** C 他觉得这本日记越来越像自己起初认为的风格。 D 作者把自己描绘得很正面，他觉得好笑。 第五段第二句提到 "Throughout the guided tour he gave me of his mind, he remained honest and funny.（在他带领我参观他思想的整个过程中，他始终保持着诚实和风趣。）"。本段第四句又提到 "I enjoyed his revelations about his clumsiness, his obsessions and his occasional outbursts of irritation.（我喜欢他对他的笨拙、他的执念和他偶尔爆发的愤怒的揭露。）"，可知日记的作者介绍了自己的思想，对自己的思想进行评价，马丁对此很欣赏，所以B选项正确。其余选项均未在文中提及，可排除。
（5）	细节理解	A	题目：读到日记的结尾，马丁 _____ **A 意识到自己实际上和作者有许多相像之处。** B 完全理解传记作者贴合主题的重要性。 C 开始想知道这个项目是否值得继续进行。 D 觉得自己拼凑的信息和作家的全貌相差不大。 根据文中最后一段第二句 "I began to think I recognized a lot of his qualities in myself, and it intensified my wish to understand him.（我开始认为我在自己身上发现了他的许多品质，这增强了我了解他的愿望。）" 可知，作者认为自己身上也有和日记作者一样的地方，所以A选项正确。 本段第三句虽然提到了建立与主题的关系，但随后作者认为这影响了自己的阅读，可知作者认为这一观点存在问题，所以B选项错误。其余两个选项均未在文中提及，可排除。

➤　全文翻译

旧日记

一天下午，我在一家二手书店浏览时，偶然发现了一箱笔记本——可能有100多年历史的古老日记。我和主人谈了价，带着我新发现的宝物离开了。日记上没有名字，箱子上只有一所知名大学的地址。

作为一名作家，我痴迷于此。我为什么不写那个匿名的日记作者的事呢？这将是有史以来第一部传记作者不知道他的主人公是谁的作品。但当我回到家时，我把盒子塞进了我的书房，并把它推到了桌子底下。不知怎么的，我不想开始阅读，生怕内容与我脑海中已经形成的内容不符。总之，我当时正埋头写传记，不希望被任何新事物分心。

但最终，我还是打开了盒子。我发现，读一个连名字和性别都不了解的人的日记的一个奇怪之处，是它的重要意义，甚至比最微不足道的线索都要重要。写信人在每一页的顶部用钝而软的铅笔记录了日期，并在空白处做了笔记。这一点，再加上盒子上的标签，足以让我清晰地联想到一个年轻男人的形象，他坐在摆满书的大学教室里，俯身在书桌上，用他在收藏有科学意义的贝壳时的认真态度在日记上做注释。但当我继续读下去时，我有了一个重要的发现。事实上，这位作者比我想象的要老得多。

在这个阶段，我也开始怀疑他是不是一个名人。我的态度改变了，就像书掉在我头上一样果断。匿名日记最令人兴奋的地方在于它可能属于任何一个人。这就剥夺了使这些书变得有趣的重要因素。想象他是一个名人，也让我回想起最初的罪恶感，因为我没有更努力地追查那些日记的主人。

他成功地让我一直读下去，日记作者的很多特点都展现了出来。在他带领我参观他思想的整个过程中，他始终保持着诚实和风趣。我喜欢这个人，不管他叫什么名字。我喜欢他对他的笨拙、他的执念和他偶尔爆发的愤怒的揭露。他很坦诚。

事实上，有一次我把书从头读到尾。我开始认为我在自己身上发现了他的许多品质，这增强了我了解他的愿望。传记作家经常说，如果他们与传记的主题建立某种关系，他们的任务就会更容易。然而，对他的一些了解也阻止了我继续下去，最终这些日记被送到了一个博物馆，用于那里的一个历史项目。

➤　词汇笔记

look through 浏览；逐一查看

例：She got the secret as she was looking through the data.

　　她在浏览资料时得到了那条秘密。

bargain /ˈbɑːgən/ *v.* 讨价还价

　　　　　　　　n. 便宜货

搭：bargain with 与……讨价还价

例：I picked up a few good bargains in the sale.

我在减价期间买了几样挺不错的便宜货。

treasure /ˈtreʒə(r)/ *n.* 珍宝，财富，宝藏

v. 珍视，珍爱

搭：priceless treasure 无价之宝

例：They were going to remove the treasure.

他们打算转移宝藏。

obsessive /əbˈsesɪv/ *adj.* 着迷的，迷恋的

搭：be obsessive about 对……着迷

例：Of course, obsessive attention to work can breed success.

当然，对工作的投入可以带来成功。

近：rapt

派：obsession *n.* 困扰；痴迷

anonymous /əˈnɒnɪməs/ *adj.* 匿名的

例：You can remain anonymous if you wish.

如果你愿意你可以保持匿名。

ignorant /ˈɪɡnərənt/ *adj.* 无知的，不了解的

例：He's ignorant about modern technology.

他对现代科技一无所知。

派：ignorance *n.* 无知，愚昧

loath /ləʊθ/ *adj.* 不情愿的，不愿意的

例：He was loath to tell the truth.

他不愿说出真相。

近：reluctant

distract /dɪˈstrækt/ *v.* 使分心，使转移注意力

搭：distract from 分心

例：It was another attempt to distract attention from the truth.

这又是企图分散人们对事实真相的注意力。

派：distraction *n.* 分心，让人分心的事物

oddity /ˈɒdəti/ *n.* 反常的人或事物

例：I was puzzled by the oddity of her behaviour.

她行为古怪，我对此感到莫名其妙。

近：anomaly

clue /kluː/ *n.* 线索；迹象

　　　　　 v. 给某人提供线索

例：The police followed the clue and finally caught the culprit.

　　警察根据线索，终于抓住了这个罪犯。

blunt /blʌnt/ *adj.* 钝的，迟钝的

　　　　　 n. 使变钝

例：The police said he had been hit with a blunt instrument.

　　警方说他遭到了钝器袭击。

近：dull

conjure up 使在脑海中浮现

例：I cannot but conjure up the memories of the good old days.

　　我不禁回忆起过去美好的日子。

annotate /ˈænəteɪt/ *v.* 注释，给……作注释

例：Historians annotate, check and interpret the diary selections.

　　历史学家们对这些日记选段进行注释、核对和阐释。

irritation /ˌɪrɪˈteɪʃn/ *n.* 恼怒；刺激

例：He was conscious of that vague feeling of irritation again.

　　他又一次感到微微有些恼火。

二、阐释说明类

1. 文章特点

　　这类文章内容通常具有一定的专业性，主题往往是日常生活中不常见的，可以是对某种复杂事物的说明，也可能是对某一领域的研究成果进行介绍。

2. 例题及详解

Brain Symphony

Scientists have found that professional musicians have more grey matter in a part of the brain involved in processing music. The discovery could explain why musical virtuosos tend to be born not made. But it fails to resolve the inveterate debate about what makes a potential Mozart. Repeated flexing of the brain by practising a musical instrument could account for the extra grey matter in the auditory cortex. Neurologists in

Germany played tones of varying frequencies to professional musicians, amateur musicians and non-musicians, and then recorded their brain responses.

The part of the brain they were looking at is a region called Heschl's gyrus. This structure—buried within the auditory cortex—is the area of the brain that responds to sound. The scientists found that professional musicians had 130% more grey matter in the part of the brain that makes sense of music. According to Peter Schneider, how much we have of this type of brain cell is associated with birth. So, there must be an inheritable component. He says that: "There must be a great influence of genetics to account for the great volume of grey matter in the professional musicians." But, as always, genes are not the whole story. Growing up in a musical family also played a role, allowing children to develop a "good ear" for music, said Schneider. He believes that musical talent, or an individual's potential for musical ability, is no longer plastic after the age of nine.

The recent research, published in the journal *Nature Neuroscience*, is unlikely to calm down the debate. According to Bob Carlyon, the problem with these types of studies is that you never know if the Heschl's gyrus has become larger and more responsive because of continued practice or whether people become musicians because they have large and responsive Heschl's gyrus. Whatever the implications, the study offers new insight into the way the brain responds to music.

Music-learning offers a huge impetuous for one's memory faculties. Trained musicians can create, encode and retrieve memories more rapidly and precisely than non-musicians, showing special improvement in verbal memory. In fact, children with one to five years of musical training were capable of remembering 20% more vocabulary words read to them off a list than children without such training. That's especially cogent because highly developed verbal memory skills have numerous applications in non-musical contexts, such as helping students learn new languages and remember more content from speeches and lectures.

No other art form, hobby or activity can bring the same level of lasting neurological benefits as music. And these benefits are never out of reach. Maintaining musical activity into adulthood, or picking up an instrument for the first time, can do wonders to stave off the effects of aging by slowing cognitive deterioration.

（1）What is the article writer trying to say in the first paragraph?

　　A. Musical geniuses need grey matter to develop their musical skills.

　　B. Scientists want to discover how Mozart was raised and repeat the process.

　　C. Grey matter might indicate who could become a highly skilled musician.

　　D. Mozart was a prodigy because he had more grey matter than his peers.

（2）Dr Schneider believes that _____

　　A. professional musicians are the only ones who have grey matter.

　　B. about 130% of a musician's grey matter makes sense of music.

　　C. grey matter can't be increased after the first nine years of life.

　　D. the first years of one's life can be crucial to brain development.

（3）What is Carlyon's view on Heschl's gyrus and musicians?

　　A. It isn't really possible to determine if an Heschl's gyrus has become larger.

　　B. Practice could be responsible for an enlargement of the Heschl's gyrus.

　　C. Successful musicians don't necessarily have a bigger Heschl's gyrus.

　　D. The Heschl's gyrus is what dictates whether someone can be a musician or not.

（4）How does the article writer feel about the research published in *Nature Neuro-science?*

　　A. It doesn't really add much to the already known facts.

　　B. It contains additional, albeit not decisive, information.

　　C. It analyses the matter from an unusual perspective.

　　D. Most scientists probably won't appreciate the content.

（5）Studies about the relationship between music and children show that _____

　　A. music-learning can be helpful for more than just music.

　　B. younger people can learn languages through music.

　　C. successful students are likely to excel in music too.

　　D. trying to remember words help with verbal memory.

（6）What does the article writer say in the last paragraph?

　　A. Music is the only recreational activity that has neurological benefits.

　　B. Studying music can significantly slow down cognitive processes.

　　C. Music can help delay or reduce the impact of ageing on the brain.

　　D. With time, adults can have the same neurological benefits as kids.

➢ 试题详解

题号	出题类型	答案	解析
(1)	细节理解	C	**题目：作者在第一段想要表达什么？** A 音乐天才需要灰质来发展他们的音乐技能。 B 科学家想要发现莫扎特是如何长大的，并重复这个过程。 **C 灰质可能表明谁可以成为一个技艺高超的音乐家。** D 莫扎特是一个天才，因为他比同龄人有更多的灰质。 文章第一段的第一句 "Scientists have found that professional musicians have more grey matter in a part of the brain involved in processing music.（科学家发现，专业音乐家大脑中处理音乐的部分有更多的灰质。）" 点明了文章的主题，即音乐家与灰质的关系。本段第三句提到 "But it fails to resolve the inveterate debate about what makes a potential Mozart.（但这并没有解决一个根深蒂固的争论，即怎样才能成为一名有潜力的莫扎特。）"，可知灰质并不是判断谁能成为音乐家的绝对标准，所以C选项正确。其余三个选项的说法均无法在本段的内容中得到印证，可排除。
(2)	观点态度	D	**题目：施耐德博士认为 _____** A 只有专业的音乐家才有灰质。 B 音乐家的脑中大约有130%的灰质帮助理解音乐。 C 灰质在出生九年后就不能增加。 **D 人生命的最初几年对大脑发育至关重要。** 根据题干中的 "施耐德博士"，可定位至第二段。本段第四句和第五句提到 "According to Peter Schneider, how much we have of this type of brain cell is associated with birth. So, there must be an inheritable component.（根据彼得·施耐德的说法，我们拥有多少这种类型的脑细胞与先天有关。因此，必须有一个可遗传的部分。）"，可知灰质与先天因素的关系密切，即先天因素是重要因素，所以D选项正确。 A选项的说法在文中没有体现。根据本段第三句可知，音乐家脑中的灰质比常人多出130%，而不是130%的灰质发挥作用，所以B选项错误。由本段最后一句可知，音乐潜能在九岁后不能再提升，而不是灰质，所以C选项错误。
(3)	观点态度	A	**题目：卡尔杨对颞横回和音乐家有什么看法？** **A 不太可能确定颞横回是否会变大。** B 颞横回的增大可能与训练有关。 C 成功的音乐家的颞横回不一定更大。 D 颞横回决定一个人能否成为音乐家。 根据关键词 "Dr Carlyon"，可定位至第三段。本段第二句提到 "According to Bob Carlyon, the problem with these types of studies is that you never know if the Heschl's gyrus has become larger and more responsive because of continued practice or whether people become

续表

题号	出题类型	答案	解析
（3）	观点态度	A	musicians because they have large and responsive Heschl's gyrus.（根据鲍勃·卡尔杨的说法，这些研究的问题是，你永远不知道是由于持续的练习，人们的颞横回变得更大、更有反应性，还是因为人们有更大、更有反应性的颞横回而成为音乐家。）。可知确定颞横回的增加存在困难，所以A选项正确。 定位句已经说到训练能否让颞横回增大、音乐家的颞横回是否较常人大这两个问题均无法得到确认，所以其余的三个选项均与文中的表述不符，为错误选项。
（4）	观点态度	B	题目：作者对发表在《自然神经科学》上的研究持怎样的观点？ A 并未在已知信息的基础上获得什么新信息。 **B 包含了一些新信息，虽然这不是决定性的。** C 从不同以往的角度进行分析。 D 大部分科学家可能不会接受这一内容。 根据关键词"Nature Neuroscience"将答案定位到第三段。本段最后一句指出"Whatever the implications, the study offers new insight into the way the brain responds to music.（无论结果如何，这项研究为大脑对音乐的反应提供了新的见解。）"。可知作者认为这一研究是具有一定价值的，首先可排除A和D两个选项，根据本段第二句的内容可知，该研究对一些问题并未得出确切的答案。C选项无法在文中找到依据，所以排除。B选项最能概括作者对此的观点，即有所进步，但并未得出根本结论，所以B选项正确。
（5）	细节理解	A	题目：有关音乐与儿童之间关系的研究说明了 _____ **A 音乐学习可能不仅仅对音乐有帮助。** B 年轻人可以通过音乐学习语言。 C 优秀的学生可能也精通音乐。 D 尝试记单词对语言记忆有帮助。 根据关键词"Studies about the relationship between music and children"可将答案定位至第四段。本段第三句提到 "In fact, children with one to five years of musical training were capable of remembering 20% more vocabulary words read to them off a list than children without such training.（事实上，接受过一到五年音乐训练的孩子比没有接受过这种训练的孩子能够多记住20%的单词。）"。可知通过音乐学习，可以使其他领域得到发展，A选项最能概括这一说法，所以A选项正确。 B选项是对原文的误解，学习音乐可以促进语言学习并不等同于可以通过音乐学习语言。C选项和D选项均未在文中提及，可排除。

题号	出题类型	答案	解析
(6)	细节理解	C	题目：作者在最后一段说了什么？ A 音乐是唯一对神经有益的娱乐活动。 B 学习音乐能够减缓认知过程。 **C 音乐可以帮助推迟或降低年龄对大脑的影响。** D 随着时间的推移，在神经方面成人可以获得和孩子一样的好处。 根据题干可以直接定位至最后一段，本段第三句说到"Maintaining musical activity into adulthood, or picking up an instrument for the first time, can do wonders to stave off the effects of aging by slowing cognitive deterioration.（成年后继续从事音乐活动，或者第一次接触乐器，可以通过减缓认知衰退来延缓衰老的影响。）"可知学习音乐能减少年龄对大脑的影响，所以C选项正确。 A选项是对本段第一句的误解，本句表明只有音乐给神经带来持久的好处，并不是说只有音乐能带来好处。B选项是对本段第三句的误解，本段第三句说的是减缓大脑衰老，而不是减缓认知过程。D选项未在文中提及，可排除。

➤ 全文翻译

大脑交响曲

科学家发现，专业音乐家大脑中处理音乐的部分有更多的灰质。这一发现可以解释为什么音乐大师往往是天生的，而不是后天培养的。但这并没有解决一个根深蒂固的争论，即怎样才能成为一名有潜力的莫扎特。练习乐器时大脑的反复弯曲可以解释听觉皮层中额外的灰质。德国的神经学家给专业音乐家、业余音乐家和非音乐家播放不同频率的音调，然后记录他们的大脑反应。

他们观察的大脑部分是一个叫作颞横回的区域。这个结构埋藏在听觉皮层中，是大脑对声音做出反应的区域。科学家们发现，专业音乐家大脑中负责音乐的灰质要高出130%。根据彼得·施耐德的说法，我们拥有多少这种类型的脑细胞与先天有关。因此，必须有一个可遗传的部分。他说："一定有很大的遗传影响，才能解释专业音乐家的大量灰质。"但是，一如既往，基因并不是全部。施耐德博士说，在一个音乐家庭中长大也起到了一定的作用，让孩子们对音乐有了"良好的耳朵"。他认为，音乐天赋或个人的音乐潜能在九岁后就不再具有可塑性。

最近发表在《自然神经科学》（*Nature Neuroscience*）杂志上的这项研究不可能平息这场争论。根据鲍勃·卡尔杨的说法，这些研究的问题是，你永远不知道是由于持续的练习，人们的颞横回变得更大、更有反应性，还是因为人们有更大、更有反应性的颞横回而成为音乐家。无论结果如何，这项研究为大脑对音乐的反应提供了新的见解。

学习音乐对一个人的记忆力有极大的促进作用。受过训练的音乐家可以比非音乐家更快更准确地创造、编码和检索记忆，在言语记忆方面表现出特殊的提高。事实上，接受过一到五年音乐训练的孩子比没有接受过这种训练的孩子能够多记住20%的单词。这一点特别有说服力，因为高度发达的言语记忆技能在非音乐环境中有很多应用，比如帮助学生学习新语言，记住更多演讲和讲座中的内容。

没有任何一种艺术形式、爱好或活动能像音乐一样给神经带来持久的益处。这些好处从来都不是遥不可及的。成年后继续从事音乐活动，或者第一次接触乐器，可以通过减缓认知衰退来延缓衰老的影响。

➢ 词汇笔记

musical virtuosos 音乐大师

例：Mozart is a genuine musical virtuosos.

莫扎特是一位真正的音乐大师。

inveterate /ɪnˈvetərət/ *adj.* 根深蒂固的，积习难改的

例：It is difficult to change the inveterate view in this issue.

在这一问题上，要改变这种根深蒂固的观念是很难的。

派：inveteracy *n.*根深蒂固，积习

近：ingrained

auditory cortex 听觉皮层

例：The auditory cortex is where a sound's acoustic features are processed.

听觉皮层是脑中处理声音特征的部分。

inheritable /ɪnˈherɪtəbl/ *adj.* 可继承的；会遗传的

例：Longevity is an inheritable characteristic.

长寿是一种可遗传的特性。

genetics /dʒəˈnetɪks/ *n.* 遗传学

搭：molecular genetics 分子遗传学

例：Genetics is also bringing about dramatic changes in our understanding of cancer.

遗传学也正使我们对癌症的理解发生巨大的变化。

派：genetic *adj.* 遗传学的，基因的

plastic /ˈplæstɪk/ *n.* 塑料，塑料学

adj. 塑料制成的；可塑的

搭：plastic bag 塑料袋

例：The pipes should be made of plastic.

153

这些管子应该是用塑料制作的。

impetus /ˈImpItəs/ *n.* 动力；推动

例：His articles provided the main impetus for change.

他的文章是促进变革的主要推动力。

派：impetuous *adj.* 冲动的，鲁莽的

近：momentum

retrieve /rɪˈtriːv/ *v.* 取回，找回；检索

搭：beyond retrieve 不可恢复，不可挽回

例：There was absolutely no way that we were going to be able to retrieve it.

我们将绝对不可能把它找回来。

派：retrievable *adj.* 可检索的；可找回的

cogent /ˈkəʊdʒənt/ *adj.* 有说服力的，让人信服的

例：He brought forward some very cogent arguments.

他提出了一些很有说服力的论据。

派：cogency *n.* 中肯，恳切

近：compelling

deterioration /dɪˌtɪəriəˈreɪʃn/ *n.* 恶化，劣化

搭：environmental deterioration 环境恶化

例：To avoid further deterioration, it is crucial to take prompt action.

为了避免进一步恶化，立即采取行动很重要。

近：exacerbation

三、观点评价类

1. 文章特点

此类文章通常从某一客观事物出发，对其进行评价或发表相关观点。客观事物可以是某一事件或现象，也可能是某一实物。

2. 例题及详解

Zoos—Positive or Negative?

Is there any reason, today, for breeding wild animals in captivity? Are zoos beneficial to the planet's endangered creatures—or are they reflection of past ruthless attitudes to wildlife? Zoos are, in fact, an indispensable part of culture in many countries. In Britain, for example, about 35 million visitors are attracted to zoos annually.

Some of these zoos are small and isolated—and are in dispute with local authorities for not abiding by stipulation of practice now and then. On the other hand, many larger institutions are certainly well-run and, according to supporters, justify their existence for three obvious reasons: education, research and conservation.

Supporters believe that exposing the world's wildlife to the public and investigating the biology of animals offer zoos cogent reasons to exist. In a world plagued by climate change, habitat loss and soaring human numbers, zoos provide protection for the world's endangered species. They educate visitors especially younger ones, about the wonders of the planet's wildlife. But people who are against keeping wild animals in captivity dissent. "Today, people get more from a TV nature documentary than they will ever get from seeing animals in a zoo. In captivity, a lion or a bear keeps away from its natural environment. Television or the Internet is a much better channel for comprehending animals than zoos," says one chief objector.

However, a prominent maker of wildlife documentaries disagrees and confesses that his programmes cannot be compared to seeing the real thing. "Only by seeing a creature in the flesh can we acquire an authentic understanding of its nature," he says. "People need to be able to see what an animal looks like. And sounds like. And smells like. This is education and certainly justifies a well-run zoo's existence." On the other hand, he does acknowledge that some animals in captivity fare better than others; polar bears, big raptors and large hunting mammals such as lions are not suitable for being kept in zoos unless they risk suffering from extinction in the wild.

He continues to say that breeding programmes for animals that are on the verge of extinction are of incontrovertible significance. If it were not for zoos, there would, for example, be no Arabian oryx left in the world. An opponent of zoos, though, would argue that it is a very small proportion of animals brought up by zoos that are on the verge of vanishing. Instead, zoos are saturated with non-endangered species put there purely to entertain the public: otters and meerkats are common examples.

In the end, these attempts at conservation may prove unavailing in a world threatened by climate change, habitat loss and population surge. Keeping alive a handful of the last of a sub-species starts to look meaningless because this puny population is bound either to a life in captivity or to extinction. This view, though, is queried by many scientists who still believe there is time to rescue species and who argue, arduously, that zoos have a role to play in saving endangered and threatened wildlife.

(1) In the first paragraph, what does the writer say about small zoos?

    A. They are situated mainly in remote places.

    B. They are visited by many people every year.

    C. They are normally not under the control of local authorities.

    D. They sometimes fail to follow official regulations.

(2) According to the second paragraph, people who are in favour of zoos think that ___

    A. animals in zoos prove to be better research subjects than those in the wild.

    B. zoos help visitors to come to a better understanding of the natural world.

    C. rising visitor numbers suggest that people think that zoos are important.

    D. animals live longer in zoos than in their natural habitat.

(3) What point is made by the documentary maker in the third paragraph?

    A. Zoos have well-organized educational programmes.

    B. People can best experience animals by seeing them up close on television.

    C. Most animals cope as well with life in zoos as they do in the wild.

    D. There are certain animals which ideally should not be put in zoos.

(4) What criticism is made of zoos in the fourth paragraph?

    A. Only a few of the species they house are endangered.

    B. Many of them are about to suspend breeding programmes.

    C. They look after far too many different species of animals.

    D. Few of them have the most interesting animals.

(5) According to the final paragraph, what do many scientists think?

    A. Over time most species will eventually become endangered.

    B. It is possible to prevent some species from becoming extinct.

    C. Endangered animals face fewer dangers in captivity than in the wild.

    D. Zoos should be better equipped to help save animals from extinction.

➢ 　试题详解

题号	出题类型	答案	解析
（1）	细节理解	D	题目：在第一段中，作者对小型动物园发表了怎样的看法？ A 它们多数都位于偏远的地方。 B 每年都有很多人参观。 C 它们通常不受地方当局的控制。 **D 它们有时不能遵守官方的规定。** 根据题干可直接定位至第一段。本段的第五句提到 "Some of these zoos are small and isolated—and are in dispute with local authorities for not abiding by stipulation of practice now and then.（这些动物园中有一些规模小，而且偏僻，并且有些动物园不遵守规定，时常与地方当局发生争执。）"，本句说明一些小动物园有时不能遵守规定，所以 D 选项正确。 本段第五句的确提到动物园的位置偏远，但并未说明是否大多数都如此，所以 A 选项错误。本段第四句的确表明了有很多人参观动物园，但这并不是针对小动物园来说的，所以 B 选项错误。其余选项均无法在文中找到依据，可排除。C 选项相关内容未在本段提及，可排除。
（2）	细节理解	B	题目：根据第二段，支持动物园的人认为 ＿＿＿＿ A 相较于在野外的动物，动物园中的动物是更好的研究课题。 **B 动物园帮助游客更好地了解自然世界。** C 游客人数的上涨说明人们认为动物园是重要的。 D 在动物园中生活的动物的寿命比自然环境中的长。 根据题干中的可直接定位至第二段。第二段第三句提到 "They educate visitors especially younger ones, about the wonders of the planet's wildlife.（他们向游客宣教这个星球上野生动物的奇迹，尤其是年轻的游客。）"，可知作者认为动物园具有教育意义。B 选项最能概括这一说法，所以 B 选项正确。 本段第一句的确说明动物园中的动物有助于进行研究，但并未比较动物园中的动物和自然环境中的动物明，所以 A 选项错误。其余两项均未在本段提及，可排除。
（3）	观点态度	D	题目：第三段中，纪录片制作人提出了怎样的观点？ A 动物园有组织良好的教育项目。 B 在电视上近距离观看动物是人们认识动物的最佳体验。 C 大多数动物在动物园里和在野外一样能适应生活。 **D 理想状态下，有些动物是不应该养在动物园的。** 根据题干可直接定位至第三段。本段的最后一句提到 "On the other hand, he does acknowledge that some animals in captivity fare better than others; polar bears, big raptors and large hunting mammals such as lions are not suitable for being kept in zoos unless they risk suffering from extinction in the wild.（另一方面，他承认有些动物在圈养状

题号	出题类型	答案	解析
（3）	观点态度	D	态下比其他动物过得好；北极熊、大型猛禽和像狮子这样的大型狩猎哺乳动物不适合被关在动物园里，除非它们在野外面临灭绝的危险。）"，可知作者认为并不是所有的动物都适合养在动物园中，所以D选项正确。 根据本段第一句可知，作者认为在影片中观看动物不如看真实的动物，所以B选项错误。其余两项均未在文中提及，可排除。
（4）	细节理解	A	题目：第四段中对动物园做了怎样的批评？ A 饲养的动物中只有少量的物种是濒危的。 B 许多动物都将暂停繁殖项目。 C 动物园要照顾太多不同种类的动物。 D 很少有动物园饲养最有趣的动物。 根据题干可直接定位至第四段。本段第三句提到"An opponent of zoos, though, would argue that it is a very small proportion of animals brought up by zoos that are on the verge of vanishing.（然而，反对动物园的人会争辩道，在动物园饲养的动物中，只有很小一部分濒临灭绝。）"，可知动物园中饲养的动物，濒危的物种很少，这与A选项的说法相符，所以A选项正确。其余选项均未在本段提及，可排除。
（5）	观点态度	B	题目：根据最后一段，科学家们持有怎样的观点？ A 随着时间的推移，多数物种将会最终濒临灭绝。 B 保护一些物种，防止它们灭绝是可能的。 C 和野外的动物相比，圈养的濒危动物面临的危险更少。 D 动物园应该提升自己的设施来保护动物免受灭绝。 由题干可直接定位至最后一段。本段的最后一句提到"This view, though, is queried by many scientists who still believe there is time to rescue species and who argue, arduously, that zoos have a role to play in saving endangered and threatened wildlife.（然而，这一观点受到了许多科学家的质疑，他们仍然认为有时间拯救物种，并坚决认为动物园在拯救濒危动物和受威胁的野生动物方面应该发挥作用。）"，可知科学家认为，动物是还有机会被拯救的，这与B选项的说法相符，所以B选项正确。 根据本段第二句可知，灭绝的只是一小部分动物，所以A选项错误，其余两项均未在文中提及，可排除。

➤ 全文翻译

动物园——积极还是消极？

现在，还有什么理由圈养野生动物吗？动物园对地球上濒临灭绝的动物有益吗？还是它们反映了过去对野生动物无情的态度？事实上，动物园是许多国家文化中不可或缺的一部分。例如，在英国，每年约有3500万名游客到动物园游玩。这些动物园中有一些规模小，而且偏僻，并且有些动物园不遵守规定，时常与地方当局发生争执。另一方面，许多大型动物园运营更良好，据支持者称，有三个显而易见的理由可以为动物园的存在提供支撑：教育、研究和保护。

支持者认为，向公众展示世界上的野生动物和研究动物的生物学，为动物园的存在提供了令人信服的理由。在一个饱受气候变化、栖息地丧失和人口激增困扰的世界，动物园保护了世界上的濒危物种。他们向游客宣教这个星球上野生动物的奇迹，尤其是年轻的游客。但是反对圈养野生动物的人持不同意见。一位主要反对者说："如今，人们从电视上的自然纪录片中得到的东西比在动物园里看动物得到的还要多。"被圈养的狮子或熊会远离自然环境。相较于动物园，电视或互联网是了解动物更好的渠道。"

然而，一位著名的野生动物纪录片制作人不同意这一观点，他坦言他的节目无法与看到真实的生物相提并论，"只有看到活生生的生物，我们才能真正了解它的本质，"他说。"人们需要能够看到动物长什么样，听起来什么样，闻起来什么样。这是一种对人的教育，当然也为一个管理良好的动物园的存在提供了理由。"另一方面，他承认有些动物在圈养状态下比其他动物过得好；北极熊、大型猛禽和像狮子这样的大型狩猎哺乳动物不适合被关在动物园里，除非它们在野外面临灭绝的危险。

他继续说，为濒临灭绝的动物进行繁殖的计划具有无可争辩的重要性。例如，如果没有动物园，世界上就不会有阿拉伯大羚羊了。然而，反对动物园的人会争辩道，在动物园饲养的动物中，只有很小一部分濒临灭绝。相反，动物园里满是纯粹为了娱乐公众而饲养的非濒危物种：水獭和猫鼬就是常见的例子。

最终，在一个受到气候变化、栖息地丧失和人类数量激增威胁的世界里，这些为保护而进行的尝试可能会证明是徒劳的。让最后几个亚种存活下来开始显得毫无意义，因为这个弱小的种群要么被圈养，要么灭绝。然而，这一观点受到了许多科学家的质疑，他们仍然认为有时间拯救物种，并坚决认为动物园在拯救濒危动物和受威胁的野生动物方面应该发挥作用。

➢　词汇笔记

breed /briːd/ *v.* 饲养，培育；交配繁殖

例：Many animals breed only at certain times of the year.

很多动物只在一年的某个时候交配繁殖。

captivity /kæpˈtɪvəti/ *n.* 囚禁，圈养

例：He was held in captivity for three years.

他被监禁了三年。

endangered /ɪnˈdeɪndʒəd/ *adj.* （动植物）濒危的

例：Pandas are an endangered species.

大熊猫是一种濒危物种。

ruthless /ˈruːθləs/ *adj.* 无情的，冷酷的

例：The way she behaved towards him was utterly ruthless.

她对待他真是无情至极。

近：relentless

indispensable /ˌɪndɪˈspensəbl/ *adj.* 不可或缺的；必不可少的

例：Cars have become an indispensable part of our lives.

汽车已成了我们生活中必不可少的一部分。

abide by 遵守，信守

例：It's crucial to abide by the safety regulations.

遵守安全规定是至关重要的。

近：comply with

stipulation /ˌstɪpjuˈleɪʃn/ *n.* 规定；条例

例：Both parties shall abide by the contractual stipulation.

双方都应遵守合同规定。

近：rule

now and then 偶尔，有时

例：He can work hard but he needs a nudge now and then.

他能够努力工作，但偶尔需要督促一下。

近：occasionally

cogent /ˈkəʊdʒənt/ *adj.* 有说服力的，令人信服的

例：She put forward some cogent reasons for abandoning the plan.

她为放弃这个计划提出了一些具有说服力的理由。

近：convincing

plague /pleɪg/ *v.* 困扰；折磨

　　　　　n. 瘟疫；传染病

例：The city is under threat from a plague of rats.

这座城市面临着鼠患的威胁。

habitat /ˈhæbɪtæt/ *n.* 栖息地

例：We destroyed that habitat of bees for our needs.

我们为了自己的需要毁坏了蜜蜂的栖息地。

派：habitant *n.* 居民

soaring /ˈsɔːrɪŋ/ *adj.* 高耸的；猛增的

例：They were protesting against soaring prices.

他们正在抗议不断飞涨的物价。

in the flesh 本人；亲自；以肉体形式

例：I saw him very much in the flesh only half an hour ago.

我在半小时以前还看见他活生生的。

mammal /ˈmæml/ *n.* 哺乳动物

例：A whale is a kind of mammal.

鲸是一种哺乳动物。

incontrovertible /ˌɪnkɒntrəˈvɜːtəbl/ *adj.* 无可争辩的

例：It is incontrovertible that the crime rate has been rising.

毫无疑问，犯罪率一直在上升。

近：indisputable

vanish /ˈvænɪʃ/ *v.* 突然不见，消失；灭绝

例：Some people believe that schools and libraries will vanish in the wake of the Internet.

一些人相信，在互联网出现之后，学校和图书馆将会消失。

saturated /ˈsætʃəreɪtɪd/ *adj.* 湿透的；饱和的；充满的

搭：be saturated with 充满

例：Snack food market is largely saturated，and to grow.

休闲食品市场基本饱和，并呈增长趋势。

unavailing /ˌʌnəˈveɪlɪŋ/ *adj.* 无效的，徒劳的

例：But all my efforts appeared unavailing.

但是，我所有的努力似乎是徒劳的。

近：futile

surge /sɜːdʒ/ *n.* 激增，猛增；涌起

v. 急剧上升；涌起

例：In contrast，the recent surge in world grain prices is trend-driven.

相比之下，最近的世界粮食价格上涨是由趋势造成的。

query /ˈkwɪəri/ *n.* 疑问，询问；问号

　　　　　　　v. 质疑，对……表示疑问

例：I'm not in a position to query their decision.

　　我无权怀疑他们的决定。

rescue /ˈreskjuː/ *v.* 营救，援救；拯救，挽救

　　　　　　n. 营救，救援；营救行动

例：The rescue operation began on Friday afternoon.

　　营救行动星期五下午展开。

arduously /ˈɑːdʒuəsli/ *adv.* 费力地

例：The company has arduously defended its decision to reduce the workforce.

　　公司竭力为其裁员的决定做辩护。

近：strenuously

Day 15 实战篇

1.

The Maijuna People's Sign Language
Linguist Grace Neveu discusses her field research in the Peruvian Amazon

I once spent five weeks in Nueva Vida, one of four Maijuna villages, to research Maijiki, the spoken language of the Maijuna, an indigenous people of the Peruvian Amazon. On my last night, at a village celebration, the communication between two men from different villages attracted my attention, so much so that my study transferred into something else entirely. One of the men, 27-year-old Raúl, was deaf, and the entire conversation was conducted in signs and gestures. I would return to the Maijuna communities three more times in the following years to study the gestural communication system I first observed at the party to see if this was an established sign language used by the Maijuna.

On my second field trip to the Maijuna, I began consulting about deaf people living in the community; however, everyone insisted Raúl was the only deaf person they knew. Six weeks later, a research participant showed me a photo of Simón, a 60-year-old man who lived in another Maijuna village, and said he was similar to Raúl. After I inquired specifically about Simón, everyone agreed that he signed. There was, however, some discussion about whether or not he was even deaf. I learned meaningful information about how the Maijuna define deafness—it's that you can't speak, not that you can't hear. I would have found more success if I asked about people who spoke with their hands, because the defect that needed to be solved was a communicative one rather than a physical one.

Simón, Raúl and others like them growing up without a spoken language yet are truly functioning community members. This is because they have formed what is called a "home sign system"—an invented system of gestures with language like structures such as consistent word order. In the Maijuna community life, there is no expectation that Simón and Raúl will lip-read. Those who communicate with Simón and Raúl—primarily their families and Maijuna men, on account of the separation of labour by gender—learn to sign and never use their voices when signing, even when other hearing people are nearby.

The complicated signing system that has developed around Simón and Raúl is remarkable for several reasons. Their home sign system spans at least two different villages and three generations. It has a relatively stable vocabulary with about 80 percent overlap between Raúl and Simón even though the two men have never lived in the same village and seldom met.

What became obvious is Simón and Raúl grew up in a community that supports the innovation of an unexpectedly complex signing system that wasn't affected by any recognized sign languages, including Peruvian Sign Language（PSL）. The Maijuna show the significance of community in the evolution of language. Though home sign systems aren't perfect—they don't possess sound language features, and communication breakdowns frequently occur—they are still conspicuous examples of human creativity.

（1）What do we learn about Grace Neveu in the first paragraph?

    A. She took part in a discussion that greatly influenced her work.

    B. She traveled to Peru originally to study a particular sign language.

    C. She faced challenges of communicating with the Maijuna.

    D. She decided to alter the focus of her research.

（2）What became evident during Grace's second trip?

    A. If she wanted to continue her research, she needed to get the Maijuna's trust.

    B. The Maijuna kept trying to prevent her from locating more deaf people.

    C. She would need to adapt the way she was making inquiries with the Maijuna.

    D. The Maijuna tend not to discuss anyone's differences out of respect.

（3）In the third paragraph, what is Grace doing?

    A. Underlining how Simón and Raúl persuaded others to learn a signing system

    B. Explaining the conditions that led to a unique signing system

    C. Comparing the benefits of lip-reading and signing

    D. Describing the barriers to studying the unique signing system

（4）What does Grace say is remarkable about the Maijuna's "home sign system"？

A. It has not changed much over a period of time.

B. It involves close collaboration between Simón and Raúl.

C. It was not until recently that it was widely used in several villages.

D. It has trivial variations which reflect each village's culture.

（5）In the final paragraph, what is Grace's main point?

A. The Maijuna constantly try to improve their home signing system.

B. The Maijuna realize the importance of preserving their home signing system.

C. The case of the Maijuna illustrates a key factor in how language develops.

D. The Maijuna home signing system would benefit from adopting some elements of PSL.

2.

A Competition Between Scientists

The Serbian-American scientist Nikola Tesla was an outstanding and odd genius whose inventions enabled modern-day power and mass communication systems. His biggest rival and former boss, Thomas Edison, was the widely known American inventor of the light bulb, the phonograph and the moving picture. The two feuding geniuses waged a "War of Currents" in the 1880s over whose electrical system would power the world—Tesla's alternating-current (AC) system or Edison's direct current (DC) electric power. Amongst science nerds, few disputes are more than the ones that compare Nikola Tesla and Thomas Edison. So, who was the superior inventor?

"They're different inventors, but you can't really say who is greater, because American society calls for some Edisons and it calls for some Teslas," said W. Bernard Carlson, a famous author and professor. From their obviously different personalities to their abiding gifts to the humanity, here's how the two duelling inventors compete against each other.

Tesla possessed a clear memory, which meant he could very accurately recall images and objects. This helps him to accurately visualize complicated 3D objects, and as a result, he could construct working prototypes using just a few simple drawings. "He really worked out his inventions in his imagination," Carlson says. On the contrary, Edison obsessively tried things out making gradual adjustments. "If you were going to the laboratory and watching him at work, you'd find he'd have stuff all over the table: wires, coils and various parts of inventions," Carlson said. In the end, however, Edison sold 1,093 patents to use his inventions. Tesla, who never had much wealth, acquired less than 300 worldwide. It is worth noticing that, since he could afford it, Edison had employed more assistants helping him design inventions, and also bought some of his own licenses.

Though the light bulb, the phonograph and moving pictures are regarded as Edison's most important inventions, other people were already working on similar technologies, said Leonard DeGraaf, an archivist and author. "If Edison hadn't invented those things, other people would have," DeGraaf declared. In a not so wise move, Edison considered Tesla's idea of an AC system of electric power transmission "impractical", instead promoting his simpler, but less efficient, the DC system. By contrast, Tesla's ideas were often more revolutionary technologies that didn't have a definite market demand. And his alternating-current motor and hydroelectric plant at Niagara Falls—a first-of-its-kind power plant—truly electrified the world.

（1）What was the "War of Currents"?

A. A conflict between those who used an AC system and those who preferred the DC system.

B. A battle between Tesla and Edison to determine who created more inventions.

C. A discussion to establish who between Tesla and Edison should be the other scientist's boss.

D. A competition in which both Tesla and Edison are believed to have invented the best electrical system.

（2）W. Bernard Carlson believes that _____

A. Tesla and Edison were equally skilled.

B. The two scientists were, after all, quite similar.

C. Modern society would benefit from both Edison and Tesla.

D. Scientists should challenge each other like Tesla and Edison did.

（3）According to the third paragraph, _____

A. Edison didn't have Tesla's ability to imagine a finished prototype.

B. Tesla had an exceptional talent for drawing and copying objects.

C. Edison generally lacked tidiness and method.

D. Tesla was more precise and much faster in his work than Edison.

(4) What does the article writer say about the two scientists'success?

A. Tesla wasn't as good as Edison at selling his inventions.

B. Edison sold more patents, but he cheated.

C. Tesla struggled to find people who would work for him.

D. Edison had more financial resources than Tesla.

(5) Leonard DeGraaf believes that _____

A. Edison didn't really invent anything new and maybe he stole other people's ideas.

B. There were scientists much smarter than Edison in the past.

C. If Edison hadn't existed, things like the light bulb would still have been invented.

D. The light bulb and the phonograph aren't Edison's most important inventions.

(6) According to the article writer, what was Edison's mistake?

A. His inventions were far too simple.

B. He underestimated Tesla's AC system.

C. He didn't consider working with electricity at the Niagara Falls.

D. He was too concerned about promoting his creations.

3.

An Artistic Eyesight

Can you sketch a landscape, or even a convincing piece of fruit? If not, chances are that your brain is getting in the way, says painting teacher David Dunlop. "People don't see like a camera," he says, "We go through life expecting what we are going to see and miss—which is why so many wedding invitations go out with the wrong date." In his art classes, one of the first things Dunlop demands from students is to stop identifying objects and instead regard scenes as collections of lines, shadows, shapes and contours.

In fact, artists'special way of seeing translates into eye scan patterns that are relatively different from those of non-artists, according to Stine Vogt, PhD. In her study, she asked nine mathematics students and nine art students to view a series of images while a camera and computer monitored where their focus fell. She found that artists' eyes are inclined to scan the whole picture, including apparently empty expanses of ocean or sky, while the non-artists'eyes focus on objects, especially people. This finding indicates that while non-artists were busy turning images into concepts, artists were noticing colours and contours, Vogt says.

While it takes years of training to grasp to see the world like an artist, a common visual disability may give some people an aid, says Bevil Conway, PhD. In one of his studies, he analyzed 36 Rembrandt self-portraits, and found that the artist described himself as wall-eyed, with one eye looking straight ahead and the other wandering outward. This condition, called strabismus, affects 10% of the population and leads to stereoblindness—an inability to use both eyes to construct a full view of the world. Stereoblind people also have limited depth perception and must resort to other clues, such as shadows and occlusion, to navigate the world. Rembrandt's stereoblindness, says Conway, may have given him an advantage in seeing the world like an artist. It's no accident that art teachers frequently tell their students to close one eye before sketching a scene, he says. "Rembrandt had a whole lifetime of honing the ability to render three-dimensional images in two-dimensional space," he says. A new and yet-unpublished study by Conway and Livingstone finds that the art students are far more likely to have the visual disability than non-artists.

Vogt, a painter as well as a scientist, says that stereoblindness and concept-blindness help artists see the world as it really is, as a mass of shapes, colours and forms. As a result, artists can and ought to paint pictures that jar regular people out of our well-worn habits of seeing. "As artists, our job is to get people to enjoy their vision, instead of just using it to get around." she says.

To sum things up, visual artists live in the same world as everyone else, but they experience it fairly differently. Artists view the world as raw material that can enroll into works of art, and they may notice things that others neglect. A painter might be enthralled by the colour of a shadow cast by one building onto another, or marvel at the intricate chevron shapes of a dandelion's leaf. To the trained eyes of an artist, these seemingly mediocre sights might be as fascinating as a cascading waterfall or a majestic mountain peak.

(1) Which of the following is the actual link between wedding invitations and drawings?

A. Mistakes in drawings and wedding invitations prove that people don't correctly visualize reality.

B. Both drawings and wedding invitations have a strong and distracting graphic component.

C. Drawings, just like wedding invitations, are the result of an artistic effort to capture reality.

D. Wedding invitations represent one of the many distractions that can interfere with drawing.

(2) What did the experiment involving artists and non-artists prove?

A. Artists have the ability to be faster at eye-scanning a picture.

B. Non-artists are more attracted to people rather than objects.

C. Non-artists tend to interpret a picture whereas artists analyze it.

D. Both categories can fully scan a picture, albeit having different methods.

(3) Rembrandt is mentioned as an example of _____

A. artistic talent being immune to sight problems.

B. a stereoblind person who documented his struggles.

C. an exception to what studies say about art and vision.

D. a person artistically benefiting from a sight problem.

(4) What has Conway recently determined?

A. Rembrandt was a masterful painter because he had time to practice.

B. People without a visual disability are less likely to find art interesting.

C. Rembrandt used to perceive reality as being two-dimensional.

D. Individuals without stereoblindness are less likely to become artists.

(5) According to the fourth paragraph, Vogt believes that _____

A. true artists are those who deliver a familiar view of reality.

B. an artist's vision of the world is distorted, but also valuable.

C. all artists should steer clear of ordinary visions of reality.

D. an audience should find artists' view of the world disturbing.

(6) Which of the following statements reflect what is written in the final paragraph?

A. Simple things can be more valuable than complicated ones.

B. Artists have the ability to simplify what they see.

C. Complex and simple sights can be equally inspiring.

D. Painters tend not to focus too much on details.

4.

Film Review: *The Village at the End of the World*, directed by Sarah Gavron

Niaqornat is a miniature settlement in north-west Greenland. Accessible only by boat (when the sea isn't frozen) and helicopter (when the weather permits), Niaqornat is home to 36 people. It is decorated by snow for the majority of the year, and is especially deserving of the title *The Village at the End of the World*. For this documentary film, British director Sarah Gavron, who had previously specialized only in fictional pieces, and her husband, the Danish cinematographer David Katznelson, followed a year in the life of the isolated village. What they have created is an inspiring figure of a community fighting against the adversity.

The landscapes are fascinating but have harsh climate, and although there are astonishing shots of the icy wilderness, the film isn't indulged in this environment. Nevertheless, the lasting impression, as it arguably should be, is of the inhabitants: Martin, the town's only teenager who thirst for moving away; and Billy, the oldest resident, who describes a time when seal fat was used for lighting. This isn't a documentary occupied by the high drama, but there're plenty of things for thought. For example, seeing how the locals treat the arrival of tourists, who stop off as part of a cruise, is particularly charming and reveals a side of tourism most of us never witness.

Gavron and Katznelson shot the film over the course of three years—the whole project from start to end took four years—and Gavron admits she had no idea of the consequence of the story in her camera until the material was translated. Only one person in the town spoke English, so Gavron used her own instincts during filming. She attended a town meeting but during it she had no idea what was being discussed—afterwards she discovered the fish factory, on which almost the whole town depended for their livelihoods, had been shut down. In the film, the mayor Luke struggles to get the factory re-opened as a co-operative.

Although being so isolated from the outside world, the town's residents were surprisingly welcoming to Gavron and her cameras. She felt this was due to the fact that she was often accompanied by her two young children. She also thought that because they received so few visitors, everyone was open to the idea of being documented on camera, although obviously a few did opt not to, out of shyness.

The Village at the End of the World is comparable to other documentaries and, while its content and style aren't pioneering, it offers a glimpse of a life that we wouldn't otherwise know about. Gavron is full of admiration for the community, which comes across clearly in her work: "You can go somewhere, on the face of it so alien and remote, and find connections. Coming from a city, it was modest to remind myself about the power of nature. I was moved by their energy and determination, as they set about changing their lot, and by the fact that they felt they could. We feel powerless a lot of the time, and they very much didn't take that attitude. It was enlightening," she says.

(1) What information about the film is given in the first paragraph?

　　A. The title of the film is not the most proper.

　　B. The film represents Gavron's first attempt at a documentary.

　　C. The film is a new collaboration between Gavron and Katznelson.

　　D. The subject of the film has not been documented by any other directors.

(2) In the second paragraph, the writer makes the point that, by focusing on the town's inhabitants, the film _____

　　A. gives us much to reflect on.

　　B. ignores the beautiful landscape.

　　C. shows a less attractive aspect of tourism.

　　D. reveals tensions between different generations.

(3) In the third paragaph, what is reported about Sarah Gavron's experience during filming?

　　A. She was unsure whether the translator was reliable.

　　B. She was unaware of the impact of the work she filmed.

　　C. She was doubtful the project could be finished so quickly.

　　D. She was dispirited by not being able to speak directly to local people.

(4) Gavron found that bringing her children to Niaqornat during filming was beneficial because _____

　　A. it might promote more visitors to travel there.

　　B. she could film the residents interacting with her children.

　　C. it meant the locals were more hospitable to her.

　　D. this encouraged even the shiest residents to appear on camera.

（5）According to the final paragraph, what does Gavron's film convey successfully?

A. her resistance of life in big cities

B. her passion for innovative cinema

C. her respect for the people of Niaqornat

D. her fears for people living in remote areas

考前冲刺——全真模拟题

Day 16 考前冲刺篇

1. For this question, choose the correct answer.

> **Movie Tickets**
> Buy these on the cinema website, and then collect them from the agency.

    A. Pay for tickets online before picking them up from the agency.

    B. Check the website for information about the price of the tickets.

    C. Let the agency know soon if you are planning to buy tickets.

2. For this question, choose the correct answer.

> Hi Sam,
> The pet exhibition will start tomorrow. If you fancy going, come to my flat at 2:30. Danny will pick us up from there.
> Jim

    A. Sam should tell Jim if he wants to go to the exhibition.

    B. Jim has already arranged a vehicle to the exhibition.

    C. Sam must meet Jim at the exhibition.

3. For this question, choose the correct answer.

    Special attention should be_____to correct grammar.

    A. granted   B. paid   C. set   D. used

4. For these questions, type the correct answer in each gap.

    Type only one word in each gap.

Multi-tasking

    At home, are you someone who mops the floor while cooking the soup? At home, do you pride (1) _____ on your capacity to cope with more than one task simultaneously? (2) _____ so, you ought to look at how you tackle your to-do list in more detail.

The problem lies in that the majority of people think they're multi-tasking when actually they are just allowing themselves to become distracted. Students finishing homework on computers, on average, wander every 12 minutes. Audiences who bring electronics with the Internet access to lectures aren't performing very (3) _____ better, since 58% of the web pages they click during lectures have (4) _____ relation to the topic.

Research also reveals that paying attention to more than one thing reduces your IQ by 8 points, and it almost goes without saying (5) _____ hazardous it is to multi-task while cutting up vegetables.

5. For these questions, choose the correct answer.

Chinese Tea Culture

Tea drinking was popular in ancient China as tea was deemed to be one of the seven daily necessities, the others being firewood, rice, oil, salt, soy sauce, and vinegar. Tea culture in China diverges from that of Europe, Britain or Japan in such things as preparation methods, tasting methods and the occasions for which it is consumed. Even now, on both casual and formal Chinese occasions, tea is consumed frequently. In addition to being a drink, Chinese tea is used in herbal medicine and in cooking.

There are several special circumstances in which tea is prepared and consumed. Formerly, lower class people would have served tea to higher-class people. At present, as Chinese society becomes more liberal, parents may pour a cup of tea for their children, or a boss may even pour tea for subordinates at restaurants. The lower-class person should not expect the higher-class person to serve him or her tea on serious occasions.

In the traditional Chinese marriage ceremony, both the bride and groom kneel in front of their parents and serve them tea as if they were saying "Thank you for bringing us up. We owe it all to you". The parents will usually drink a small portion of the tea and then give the couple a red envelope, which represents good luck. The tea ceremony during weddings also serves as a means for both parties in the wedding to meet with members of the other family. As Chinese families can be rather extended, it is entirely possible during a courtship not to have been introduced to someone. This was especially true in older generations where the family leader may have had more than one wife and not all family members got along well. As such, during the tea ceremony, the couple would serve tea to all family members and call them by their official title.

After a person's cup was filled, that person might knock his bent index and middle fingers on the table to thank the person who served the tea. This custom was derived from the Qing Dynasty. Emperor Qianlong would sometimes travel in disguise through the empire. Servants were told not to expose his identity. One day in a restaurant, the emperor, after pouring himself a cup of tea, filled a servant's cup as well. To that servant it was a huge glory to have the emperor pour him a cup of tea. As a reflex he wanted to kneel and express his thanks, but he couldn't do that since it would reveal the emperor's identity so he bent his fingers on the table and knocked to express his respect to the emperor.

(1) According to the first paragraph, which of these facts about tea is true?

A. Tea is now as popular in Europe as it is in China.

B. Tea used to be the most demanded product in the world.

C. Tea still has many different uses in China.

D. Tea is consumed following strict rules.

(2) What can be said about tea and society?

A. The practice of drinking tea erased the social class system.

B. Nowadays tea is only present on important occasions.

C. Lower-class people can now be served tea at their own risk.

D. There have been some changes in the traditional social customs.

(3) During a marriage, the bride and groom pour tea for their parents _____

A. as a sign of submission.

B. as a sign of respect.

C. as a sign of gratitude.

D. as a sign of good luck.

(4) According to the third paragraph, the fact that some family members don't know each other _____

A. still characterizes every Chinese marriage.

B. used to be much more common in the past.

C. is an excuse not to drink tea at marriages.

D. used to happen between two or more wives.

（5）Why did the emperor's servant knock his fingers on the table?

A. To express his admiration.

B. To express his loyalty to the Dynasty.

C. To hide his own identity.

D. To show appreciation to the emperor.

（6）An appropriate subtitle for this article would be _____

A. origins and meanings.

B. how family members.

C. tea and power relationships.

D. the reason for celebrations.

6. For this question, choose the correct answer.

She ought _____ more time to review before the test.

A. have had   B. to do   C. to have had   D. have

7. For this question, choose the correct answer.

CANCELLED

We regret to notice you that the concert planned for this evening won't be taking place. An eleventh-hour decision of the Organizing Committee deemed appropriate to put off the concert to a future date. All pre-sold tickets will still be valid until further notice.

A. The Committee decided to cancel the concert during a night meeting.

B. The location for the scheduled event has been changed.

C. Pre-sold tickets might eventually lose their validity.

8. For this question, choose the correct answer.

> ### French Literature (Prof. Peter)
>
> The lessons for this course will all take place in the next semester. Meanwhile, I can share with you some of the slides I used last year, so that you can get an insight into the essence of my course. If you have trouble downloading the files, send me an email or come talk to me after my History of the French Language classes every Monday.

A. Professor Peter tells his students that they can attend his classes online.

B. Professor Peter will provide some of the material he used for his classes for students.

C. Professor Peter is not teaching any courses this semester.

9. Click on each gap then choose the correct answer.

What do people in the Western countries eat currently? And how is this different from our eldership? In the past, mealtimes (1) _____ be more stable, with breakfast at 8 a.m., lunch at 12 p.m. and dinner at 6 p.m..

(2) _____, nowadays we snack often and mealtimes are variable. People were accustomed to feeding on dishes (3) _____ meat and two vegetables, and fried chicken and burger are common midweek dinners today. Ready-made meals and eating out are the substitute for the home-cooked dishes. But what is the future like? Will this be composed of even more fast food, instead of cooking? Or we (4) _____ go in another direction, and return to growing and eating our own food? I can't wait to (5) _____ out!

(1) A. didn't use to   B. often   C. used   D. used to

(2) A. Despite   B. Lest   C. However   D. Hence

(3) A. contain   B. containing   C. contains   D. contained

(4) A. would   B. will   C. shall   D. are

(5) A. turn   B. lay   C. find   D. break

全真模拟题二

1. For this question, choose the correct answer.

> For a door-to-door service from the repairman please phone the maintenance point by 16:00.

    A. The service of repairman is available before 16:00.

    B. If you plan to meet the repairman, call the maintenance point after 16:00.

    C. Phone before 16:00 if you want the repairman to solve the problem in your home.

2. For this question, choose the correct answer.

> **From:** Moon Travel Agency
>
> **To:** Peter Obama
>
> **Subject:** Vacation in Iceland
>
> Dear Mr. Obama,
>
> Thank you for consulting information about our nobility vacation in Iceland. The quota is completely reserved until the last day of April, but it's available after that.
>
> Kind regards,
>
> Martin Emmons

    The purpose of this email is _____

    A. to ask for information about different destinations.

    B. to give information about vacation dates.

    C. to ask for the experience about a vacation in Iceland.

3. For this question, choose the correct answer.

    My grandpa often described me as a _____ young gentleman.

    A. definitive   B. modified   C. recurrent   D. refined

4. For this question, choose the correct answer.

    I applied for an interesting club but was turned _____.

    A. out   B. down   C. in   D. back

5. For these questions, type the correct answer in each gap.

Type only one word in each gap.

Films with Subtitles

I haven't (1) _____ fond of films with subtitles all the time. When I was younger, the idea of having to watch a scene while reading (2) _____ the characters said made me feel uncomfortable. It all changed when I started to study French at university. I realized that, thanks to subtitles, I could enjoy French movies and, in the meanwhile, I could improve my language skills. Since (3) _____, I have often bought DVDs that included the original audio and subtitles. A friend of (4) _____ has invited me to his house to watch a Dutch film with subtitles. I am really looking (5) _____ to it, since I don't even know what Dutch sounds like.

6. For these questions, choose the correct answer.

It's a few minutes before the class starts. At first glance, the activity on the playground seems typical of any elementary school, with energetic children intimately interacting with each other. But if you expected to hear where you might expect a lot of noise, you would be dispirited. There is only silence, accompanied by the rapid movements the children make with their fingers, arms and face as they use fluent sign language to communicate. I am at the Edward Deaf Education Centre and Residential School, launched in 1905, which has recently been in the media. A large group of past and present pupils and parents are striving for the school's future as, despite its remarkable success, the Department of Education is considering removing its financial support and moving all deaf education to the regular 'hearing' school system.

Parents of deaf children are naturally upset about ensuring that their children will be able to communicate with the wider community. Majority of them feel that attending a regular school and learning to lip read, that is, following the movements of people's mouths as they speak, is the best solution for their children. Some, such as the Houstons, have taken this a step further: they are preventing their child from learning sign language. "We're thinking about the future here," says Mrs. Houston. "If we don't want Cathy to be cut off from a normal life or to limit her options, then she'll need to learn to read fluently and get a good education in spite of her disability. So, we are enrolling her at our local school."

Those efforts to save Edward School would be in line with the Houston's aims, but feel that these will be better served in an environment where sign language is used, as this provides a better language input. "Although lip reading is certainly a tough skill to learn, that is not the main problem here." says Edward Principal Donald Davis. "If a child isn't adept at it, the speaker has to be facing them for the child to understand. In regular, so-called mainstream schools, many situations providing language input cannot offer this type of support. In a normal classroom, children may move around, call out answers from the back of the room, or shout to each other across the playground. In all these situations, a lip-reader would find communication difficult."

Davis adds that, while lucky children will have a full-time aide, the majority will have only definite help. They end up missing out on so much due to this shortage of support. The studies are inclined to support this view. Fewer deaf children in mainstream schools are admitted to university than their hearing classmates, and many report feeling neglected in school. A deaf school, besides, provides a broader social circumstance along with the academic one. Most significantly, there is the opportunity to use complex communication to develop deep friendships, something that deaf children often lack in mainstream schools.

Of course, deaf schools face a dilemma, too. Many of their graduates struggle to deal with the demands of the hearing world after years spent in a deaf-only school, and it is undoubtedly true that using only sign language is limiting. But closing the schools altogether seems an overreaction to these difficulties. Perhaps combining residential schooling with periods in mainstream schools could provide the best of both worlds.

（1）Why has Edward School been in the news?

　　A. Its students might be forced to move to other schools.

　　B. It has reached a meaningful anniversary.

　　C. It is trying to raise more funds for running costs.

　　D. It's striving for approval by the Department of Education.

（2）What do the Hustons think about lip reading?

　　A. Deaf schools should teach lip reading exclusively.

　　B. Deaf children who acquire lip reading are disadvantaged.

　　C. Lip reading is much more useful than sign language.

　　D. Lip reading should be used along with sign language.

（3）What does Donald Davis regard as the biggest challenge to deaf children in regular schools?

A. Lip reading is too difficult for most deaf students.

B. There are lots of difficulties in which lip reading is infeasible.

C. Deaf children have barriers socializing with other students.

D. Deaf children need more language input than other students.

（4）What is the main idea of paragraph 4?

A. Deaf schools emphasize social interaction above academic study.

B. Deaf students fail academically in mainstream schools.

C. Deaf schools provide students with more academic opportunities.

D. Deaf students'social needs are better met in deaf schools.

（5）What is the writer's conclusion about separate education for the deaf?

A. It prevent deaf children from reaching their potential.

B. It has disadvantages, but we needn't pay attention to.

C. It should be supplemented with mainstream education.

D. It is likely the ideal solution for some, but not for deaf children.

（6）What is the best title for this article?

A. Who Best Serves the Needs of Deaf Students?

B. Can Deaf Schools Meet Needs of the Future?

C. Edward: The Case Against Deaf Schools

D. Mainstream Schools Prepare to Accept Deaf Students

7. For this question, choose the correct answer.

This practical course provides students with chances to _____ their skills in real-life situations.

A. pursue   B. practice   C. know   D. train

8. For this question, choose the correct answer.

Spring reciting challenge for library members aged 10~18. Choose from the attached word list. You'll get a certificate for every 100 words you recite and a prize if you recite 500 words.

A. People can recite any word as part of the reciting challenge.

B. Only certain people can take part in the reciting challenge.

C. Everyone who takes part in the reciting challenge will receive a prize.

9. Click on each gap then choose the correct answer.

The Implications of Becoming an Architect

Architects don't only design structures; they create a thorough experience for the users and the coming generations. They are taught about the various impacts that their designs can exert on the mindset and the mental health of the users. They also hold the power to (1) _____ the current state of the environment as their techniques and design strategies can make the structures more (2) _____ and environment-friendly. The architectural (3) _____ or the monuments in a region make it unique and (4) _____. Furthermore, architects can attempt to safeguard whatever is left of this planet by designing a harmonious object—spatial environment in which the architectural elements represent an attempt to neutralize the adverse consequence that the (5) _____ urbanization brings.

(1) A. embellish　　B. beautify　　C. ameliorate　　D. bedeck

(2) A. supportable　　B. sustainable　　C. pliable　　D. bendable

(3) A. marvels　　B. senses　　C. utensils　　D. liabilities

(4) A. observable　　B. perceptible　　C. comparable　　D. distinguishable

(5) A. sprinting　　B. limping　　C. galloping　　D. propelling

参考答案与解析

Day 1　同义改写练习

1. big/sizeable

   is going to build

   will be constructed by the neighbourhood committee soon

2. because of

   As a result of the diligence and good luck

   without the diligence and good luck

3. display

   will open

   won't open until

4. Numerous/A lot of

   adept at/proficient in

   Dealing with the urgent task

5. capacity

   very/fairly

   great importance/great significance

6. proposal

   facilitates

   the impetus for the implement of the project

7. as well as

   takes charge of

   teaching and the management; the responsibilities of the class teacher

8. imperative

   requires

   required to enter this area

9. the way to

   have no idea about

makes us confused

10. unreliable

　　don't believe his testimony

Day 3   实战篇

1. 【答案】B

   【材料类型】邮件

   【题目翻译】

   杰弗里发邮件是为了 _____

   【选项翻译】

   A 抱怨丽莉提供的餐厅地址是错误的。

   B 为在丽莉的生日聚会上迟到而道歉。

   C 询问丽莉生日聚会的餐厅是否更换。

   【解析】邮件中第一句说到"很抱歉，我昨天缺席了你的生日聚会"，后文又对原因进行了解释，即没有找到餐厅，所以B选项正确。

   邮件中最后一句说到"我最后确实到了餐厅，但是你的聚会已经结束"，可知杰弗里找到了聚会地点并到达，所以餐厅的地址并没有错误，所以A选项错误。邮件中并未询问餐厅是否更换，所以C选项错误。

2. 【答案】A

   【材料类型】标识

   【选项翻译】

   A 电池应放入黑色垃圾桶。

   B 塑料瓶可以扔入任意的一个垃圾桶。

   C 纸张应扔入黄色垃圾桶。

   【解析】本则标识中说到"可回收物要放入绿色垃圾桶，不可回收物要放入黄色垃圾桶，有毒垃圾要放入黑色垃圾桶"。电池属于有毒垃圾，应该放入黑色垃圾桶，所以A选项正确。

   塑料瓶属于可回收物，应该扔入绿色垃圾桶，而不是仍入任意的一个垃圾桶，所以B选项错误。纸张属于可回收物，也应该扔进绿色垃圾桶，所以C选项错误。

3. 【答案】C

   【材料类型】通知

【选项翻译】

A 午餐前乘客要将随身物品放到大巴车上。

B 随身物品必须准备好，以便午餐后装上大巴车。

C 午餐期间司机会将乘客的随身物品放到大巴车上。

【解析】通知中说到"上午十一点半前把随身物品放在门外，司机会把其放到大巴车上。午餐十一点半开始，大巴车十三点出发"，可知大巴车出发前，随身物品的运送工作应该结束，所以C选项正确。

午餐前乘客需要做的是把随身物品放到门外，不需要放到车上，所以A选项错误。通知中并未提及午餐结束的时间，所以无法判断随身物品的运送工作是否在午餐结束后完成，所以B选项错误。

4. 【答案】B

【材料类型】广告

【选项翻译】

未来职业服务中心 ＿＿＿＿＿＿＿

A 给员工提供丰厚的报酬。

B 是渴望更好职业发展者的理想场所。

C 想为自己招聘几位员工。

【解析】广告的第一句说到"未来职业服务中心，致力于职业培训和职业介绍"，可以看出，未来职业服务中心能够为职场人士提供职业培训和介绍服务，所以B选项正确。

材料中主要介绍的是未来职业服务中心的服务项目，并未提到未来职业服务中心员工的报酬问题，也没有提到想为自己招聘员工，所以A选项和C选项错误。

5. 【答案】C

【材料类型】通知

【选项翻译】

A 新俱乐部一周有三次网球课。

B 新网球俱乐部只能接纳15位成员。

C 有意加入俱乐部的申请者需尽快报名。

【解析】材料的第一句话说到"如果想要加入新网球俱乐部，需在周二（明天）之前报名"，可知考虑的时间很短，要尽快行动，所以C选项正确。

根据材料最后一句话"俱乐部的训练时间是周一、周三晚上，有时周五晚上也会训练"可知并不是每周都会训练三天，所以A选项错误。根据材料的第二句话，可知俱乐部还有15个席位，并不是只能容纳15人，所以B选项错误。

6. 【答案】A

【材料类型】邮件

【选项翻译】

A 游客在旅行前一周或更早时间取消，可收到全额退款。

B 七月三日，游客可更换原始日期为七月四日的票。

C 至少要在旅行的七天前进行网络订票。

【解析】根据材料中的第一句和第二句可知，网络渠道订购的博物馆门票现在可以免费取消。但至少需要在参观的七天前，所以A选项正确。

材料中第三句说到"在原始日期48小时内，不可更换门票"，所以原始日期为七月四日的门票，应该在七月二日及之前更换，所以B选项错误。材料说的是退票及换票的时间限制，并未说明订票的时间限制，所以C选项错误。

7. 【答案】C

【材料类型】标识

【选项翻译】

A 一名12岁的男孩可以独自进入这片水域。

B 成年人可以不受限制地进入深水区。

C 此标识可能是为水上乐园设计的。

【解析】材料中第一句提到"深水区危险"，可知此标识可能应用于有水的场所，所以C选项正确。

根据材料第二句可知只有成人和在成人陪同下的十岁以上儿童可以进入，所以 A选项错误。材料中第三句话说到"对于所有进入者，都要求做好防护措施"，可知成年人也不应例外，所以B选项错误。

8. 【答案】C

【材料类型】邮件

【选项翻译】

A 苏珊不能频繁给比利写邮件，因为苏珊把电话弄丢了。

B 在森林时，苏珊的身体一直很好。

C 比利明天可能会收到另一封来自苏珊的邮件。

【解析】根据邮件最后一句话"明天我会详细讲述我的经历"，可知苏珊和比利明天还会联系，所以C选项正确。

邮件的第二句说到"我们最近的时间安排很紧凑，这也是我没有像以往那样给你写邮件的原因"，可知苏珊没给比利写邮件是时间问题，所以A选项错误。材料中第四句提到"我的胳膊受伤了，还得了感冒"，可知苏珊在森林里身体出现了一些问题，所以B选项错误。

9. 【答案】A

【材料类型】通知

【选项翻译】

A 图书馆的读者几乎可以在大楼的任何地方连接无线网络。

B 图书馆无线网络的个人密码在总台分发给读者。

C 读者可以连接图书馆无线网络做任何用途。

【解析】根据材料的第一句话"大楼内的所有房间都安装了路由器，所有人都能享受最好的体验"，可知大楼内每个地方都能连接无线网络，所以A选项正确。

根据材料第二句话"我们欢迎所有使用者向一楼总台报告出现的任何问题"，可知总台并不负责分发个人密码，所以B选项错误。材料中第三句和第四句说到"我们还提示您，不允许进行不当用途。服务器持续进行监测，我们有权中断任何异常的网络活动"，所以C选项错误。

10. 【答案】B

【材料类型】广告

【选项翻译】

A 该课程只关注如何应对逆境。

B 参加这一课程后，逆境可能不再像之前那样可怕。

C 课程结束后，你将不会遇到逆境。

【解析】广告中的第二句提到"从这一课程毕业后，面对逆境，你会变得更冷静，也更能在压力下取得进步"，可知这一课程能提高人们应对逆境的能力，所以B选项正确。

广告中的第三句话提到"我们的课程包括从多角度去应对和预防逆境的方法"，可知课程包含两部分，所以A选项错误。广告中并没有说到参加这一课程能让你从此不会遇到逆境，所以C选项错误。

Day 6 实战篇

1. 【答案】C

【出题类型】词义辨析

【解析】A选项意为"推翻，颠覆"；B选项意为"考虑"；C选项意为"维护；证明……无辜；证明……正确"；D选项意为"怀疑，不信任"，正确选项应该要与空格后的"his conjecture"进行搭配。由逗号后的内容可知，逗号前的内容表达积极含义，将选项代入后，C选项最符合语境，所以C选项正确。句意为"专家的新研究成果将会证实他的猜想，这是个好消息"。

2. 【答案】D

【出题类型】词义辨析

【解析】A选项意为"后悔的"；B选项意为"忠诚的"；C选项意为"有成果的"；D选项意为"健忘的"。根据句中that后的内容，可知D选项最符合语境，所以D选项正确。句意为"他特别健忘，以至于汤姆提醒了他三遍要检查个人物品"。

3. 【答案】C

【出题类型】语法基础

【解析】本题考查shall疑问句的回答方式，这类疑问句的回答方式很多，基本的回答方式为Yes，we shall/No，we shan't。表示请求时还可以用Good idea/Sorry等回答。由材料可知，此处shall表请求，可以用C选项进行回答，所以C选项正确。对话内容为"我太饿了，要不我们吃个热狗吧"，"好的"。其余三个选项均错误，shall开头的疑问句不能用这些表达进行回答。

4. 【答案】B

【出题类型】固定搭配

【解析】本题从选项上看，容易误认为是对词义辨析的考查。结合题干和选项可知，空格后的内容应表示"受关注"之意。A选项意为"视觉；景象"；B选项意为"眼睛"；C选项意为"重点；焦点"；D选项意为"注意；注意力"。B选项可与空格前内容构成固定搭配"in the public eye"，表示"广为人知；受公众瞩目"之意，符合题意，所以B选项正确。其余三个选项迷惑性较大，但均无法构成固定搭配。句意为"名人的烦恼之一就是持续受公众关注"。

5. 【答案】B

【出题类型】固定搭配

【解析】A选项、B选项和D选项均意为"乞求，恳求"；C选项意为"催促"；根据逗号后的内容可知，C选项与语境不符，可排除。其他的三个选项虽然符合语境，但空格后出现了"with"，只有B选项可以与其构成搭配，所以B选项正确。句意为"露西的父母求她不要去另一个城市工作，但没人能说服她"。

6. 【答案】C

【出题类型】词义辨析

【解析】A选项意为"代替品"；B选项意为"补充物"；C选项意为"职位相当的人"；D选项意为"复制品"。空格前的"his"相当于"France's education minister"，所以C选项正确。句意为"法国教育部部长和意大利教育部部长在意大利政府进行了友好的会谈。"

7. 【答案】A

【出题类型】固定搭配

【解析】本题考查固定搭配，空格处后出现"all accounts"，所以正确选项能够与之构成固定搭配。A选项与"all accounts"搭配意为"无论如何；总的来说"；B选项与"all accounts"搭配意为"根据大家的说法"；C选项与"all accounts"搭配意为"在所有账户上"；D选项与"all accounts"无法构成搭配。结合句首的内容可知，A选项最符合语境，所以A选项正确。句意为"尽管有些小瑕疵，但总的来说，莎莉在学校的个人音乐会还是圆满的"。

8. 【答案】C

【出题类型】固定搭配

【解析】A选项意为"放；布置"；B选项意为"发动；发起"；C选项意为"投射；抛"；D选项意为"运送；移交"。C选项可以构成固定搭配"cast doubt on"，意为"使人怀疑"，符合语境，所以C选项正确。句意为"学生对口头测试的模糊回答使人怀疑他对这个问题的理解方式"。

9. 【答案】C

【出题类型】词义辨析

【解析】本题考查词义辨析。A选项意为"利润"；B选项意为"交换"；C选项意为"透支"；D选项意为"预算"。由逗号后的内容可知，这种功能使消费金额高于实际金额，C选项符合这一表达，所以C选项正确，句意为"我的信用卡能开通透支功能了，所以我可以花比实际更多的钱"。

10.【答案】D

【出题类型】词义辨析

【解析】A选项意为"借给"；B选项意为"节省"；C选项意为"出租，租借"；D选项意为"借入"。C选项无法与句中的"money"搭配，首先排除。本题易错选A和B两项，A选项虽然也表示借的含义，但表达的是借出，由句子可知，借钱才能买车，所以需要的是向他人借，而不是借给别人，排除A选项。由材料中的后半句"她的朋友都很贫穷"，可知玛丽应该是想向别人借钱，而不是自己省钱，排除B选项，所以D选项正确，句意为"为了买车，她不得不借钱，但是她的朋友都很贫穷"。

11.【答案】C

【出题类型】语法基础

【解析】本题考查语法基础知识。原句中的空格前出现了"ought"，这一单词与介词"to"连用表示"应该"，所以A和D两个选项可以排除。根据句中的"before the test"，可知这是对过去的行为进行评价。情态动词对过去的行为进行评价时，采用"情态动词+have done"的结构，意为"本来……"，所以C选项正确。句意为"考试前她本应该有更多的时间去复习，但她管不住自己，去看电影了"。

12.【答案】B

【出题类型】词义辨析

【解析】A选项意为"理解，弄清楚"；B选项意为"错过；不理解"；C选项意为"使变钝"；D选项意为"获得；习得"。根据句中的已知信息，可排除A选项和D选项。C选项代入原句中与空格后的内容无法搭配，所以B选项正确。句意为"丹尼尔没有理解我所讲的，他完全没抓到要点"。

13.【答案】C

【出题类型】词义辨析

【解析】本题考查词义辨析。四个选项都有"结果"的含义。所以要注意区分它们之间的区别。A选项和D选项泛指结果。B选项多指受到某种影响后产生的结果。C选项侧重指不好的结果。结合句中的已知信息，C选项最为恰当，所以C选项正确。句意为"如果公民不遵守既有的法规，那么以后会有严重的法律后果"。

14.【答案】C

【出题类型】固定搭配

【解析】本题考查固定搭配。空格前为"name"，结合句中的信息可知，我的名字和我祖父的名字相同。name与C选项搭配可表示"以……命名"的含义，符合语境，所以 C 选项正确。句意为"我的父母用我祖父的名字给我起名，他也叫比尔"。

15. 【答案】A

【出题类型】固定搭配

【解析】空格前出现了动词"come"，可知本题考查由 come 构成的动词短语。A 选项与 come 搭配意为"走近；发生；上来"；B 选项与 come 搭配意为"开始；赶快"；C 选项与 come 搭配意为"偶遇，碰到"；D 选项与 come 搭配意为"突然感到"，结合句中的已知信息，A 选项最符合语境，所以 A 选项正确。句意为"我真的很抱歉在这么短时间内就让你失望了，但是发生了一些事情，所以我不能赴约了"。

16. 【答案】B

【出题类型】词义辨析

【解析】本题的四个选项均可表示内容间存在的关系。空格位于两个句子之间，所以要充分理解句子含义，判断它们间的关系。A 选项意为"因此"，表示因果关系；B 选项意为"随即"，可表递进关系；C 选项意为"除……以外"；D 选项意为"尽管"，表让步关系。原句前半部分说到怀特食品集团开始的状态，后半句说到其后来的状态，B 选项最符合语境，所以 B 选项正确。句意为"怀特食品集团在成立之初是一家小烘焙店，后来成了世界上最知名的食品品牌之一"。

17. 【答案】A

【出题类型】固定搭配

【解析】本题考查固定搭配。结合逗号后的内容可知，本句话想表达凭密码进入的含义。A 选项意为"进入"；B 选项意为"来"；C 选项意为"移动"；D 选项意为"记录"。A 选项可以构成固定搭配"enter a password"，意为"输入密码"，符合语境，所以 A 选项正确。句意为"这片居民区很安全，因此所有人进入都需要输入密码"。

18. 【答案】C

【出题类型】词义辨析

【解析】本题考查词义辨析。A 选项意为"极度的；最大的"；B 选项意为"最接近的"；C 选项意为"仅仅"；D 选项意为"最纯的"。将以上四个选项代入句中，C 选项最符合语境，所以 C 选项正确。句意为"专家发现的化石数量对于存于地下的总数来说，可能仅仅是很小的一部分"。

19. 【答案】B

【出题类型】固定搭配

【解析】本题考查固定搭配。A 选项意为"核实；证实"；B 选项意为"拿，取"；C 选项意为"出现，呈现"；D 选项意为"表明；指出"。B 选项可与句中的"pride in"构成固定搭配，意为"为……自豪"，所以D选项正确。句意为"教授为他的学生在世界级难题上的研究成果而自豪"。

20.【答案】D

【出题类型】词义辨析

【解析】本题考查词义辨析。A选项意为"与……作战，斗争"；B选项意为"奋斗；斗争"；C选项意为"持续；坚持"；D选项意为"承受"。四个选项的差异较大，我们需要结合句意进行判断。将四个选项代入原句中，D选项最符合语境，所以D选项正确。句意为"一个工程师团队花了三年的时间发明了一种相机，它重量轻，可以承受不利的自然条件"。

Day 9 实战篇

1.

➤ **试题详解**

(1)【答案】A

【出题类型】固定搭配

【解析】A选项意为"角色；作用"；B选项意为"功能"；C选项意为"位置；状态"；D选项意为"地位；状况"。本句中出现了"play"和"in"，A选项能够与其构成搭配"play a role in"，意为"扮演……角色，发挥……作用"，所以A选项正确。本句意为"近年来，人们越来越关注音乐在生活中所发挥的作用"。

(2)【答案】B

【出题类型】词义辨析

【解析】A选项意为"改善"；B选项意为"发展；进步；成长"；C选项意为"结果，后果"；D选项意为"改变，变化"。将四个选项代入句中，B选项最符合语境，所以B选项正确。句意为"关于它如何影响儿童发育的研究也得以开展"。

(3)【答案】D

【出题类型】固定搭配

【解析】A选项意为"连续；系列"；B选项意为"区域"；C选项意为"程度；范围"；D选项意为"范围；界限"。"a wide range of"为固定搭配，意为"广泛的，各式各样的"，符合语境，所以 D选项正确。本句意为"市场上到处是益智玩具、录像带和各种播放流行歌曲或古典音乐的娱乐设备"。

(4)【答案】C

【出题类型】固定搭配

【解析】A选项意为"发送，邮寄"；B选项意为"展示；表明"；C选项意为"暴露，显露"；D选项意为"展示；陈列"。C选项能够与句中的"to"构成搭配，意为"暴露于；处于……的影响下"，符合语境，所以C选项正确。句意为"让儿童听音乐有利于他们的整体智力和大脑的发育"。

（5）【答案】A

【出题类型】词义辨析

【解析】四个选项均表示"增加，变大"的含义。A选项意为"增加；提升"，侧重表示在原有基础上增加；B选项意为"增加；提高"，为不及物动词；C选项意为"扩大，增大"，侧重表示范围变大；D选项意为"增加，添加"，侧重表示将某物加到……中。正确选项应能与"self-confidence"搭配，所以A选项正确。句意为"鼓励孩子们听不同风格的音乐也会提高他们的自信，同时培养创造和探索的能力"。

➤ 全文翻译

青少年与音乐

近年来，人们越来越关注音乐在生活中所发挥的作用。关于它如何影响儿童发育的研究也得以开展。市场上到处是益智玩具、录像带和各种播放流行歌曲或古典音乐的娱乐设备。为什么？音乐让人感到愉快，也充满趣味，最新的研究已经证明，让儿童听音乐有利于他们的整体智力和大脑的发育。鼓励孩子们听不同风格的音乐也会提高他们的自信，同时培养创造和探索的能力。

➤ 词汇笔记

deluge /ˈdeljuːdʒ/ *v.* 泛滥；使充满

n. 暴雨；洪水

搭：be deluged with 充满

例：About a dozen homes were damaged in the deluge.

在这场暴雨中大约有十几家房屋被毁。

近：inundate

recreation /ˌrekriˈeɪʃn/ *n.* 娱乐，消遣

例：Saturday afternoon is for recreation and outings.

周六下午是娱乐和外出的时间。

派：recreational *adj.* 娱乐的，消遣的

近：entertainment

conducive /kənˈdjuːsɪv/ *adj.* 有助益的

搭：be conducive to 对……有助益的

例：Make your bedroom as conducive to sleep as possible.

把你的卧室尽可能地布置得有助于睡眠。

近：helpful

disparate /ˈdɪspərət/ *adj.* 不同的

例：Scientists are trying to pull together disparate ideas in astronomy.

科学家正试图把天文学界各种不同的观点汇集起来。

近：different

nurture /ˈnɜːtʃə(r)/ *v.* 养育，培养

例：Parents want to know the best way to nurture and raise their child to adulthood.

父母们想了解把他们的孩子养育成人的最好方法。

近：foster

2.

➢ **试题详解**

（1）【答案】C

【出题类型】词义辨析

【解析】A选项意为"目标"；B选项意为"原因"；C选项意为"想法，主意"；D选项意为"含义；价值"。根据本句逗号前的内容可知，谁首先制造了滑板是无法确定的。后半句中的空格前出现"come up with"，将四个选项代入原句中，C选项最为恰当，所以C选项正确。句意为"似乎有几个人在同一时间有了类似的想法"。

（2）【答案】A

【出题类型】固定搭配

【解析】本题考查与start相关的动词短语。A选项与start搭配意为"从……开始"；B选项与start搭配意为"出发，动身去"；C选项与start搭配意为"重新开始"；D选项与start搭配意为"出发；开始进行"。结合句中的已知信息，本句想表达是滑板起初的形态，所以A选项正确。句意为"滑板最早时是木盒或木板，底部固定着轮滑轮"。

（3）【答案】C

【出题类型】词义辨析

【解析】A选项意为"出售，销售"；B选项意为"商业，生意"；C选项意为"交易"；D选项意为"工作"。C选项置于句中最符合语境，所以C选项正确。句意为"当时一个有野心的冲浪商店老板与一家轮滑公司合作"。

（4）【答案】B

【出题类型】固定搭配

【解析】A选项意为"度数；程度"；B选项意为"规模；刻度"；C选项意为"大小，尺寸"；D选项意为"数量；金额"。B选项与空格前的"on a large"构成搭配，意为"大规模地"，符合语境，所以B选项正确。句意为"到20世纪60年代，南加州的冲浪设备制造商大规模制造滑板"。

（5）【答案】A

【出题类型】词义辨析

【解析】四个选项均为动词。A选项意为"证明；表露；演示"；B选项意为"建议；提出"；C选项意为"通知，告发"；D选项意为"指示；指导"。将四个选项代入原句中，A选项最符合语境，所以A选项正确。句意为"并雇佣一批又一批的滑板手在运动场和公园里展示他们的产品"。

➤ 全文翻译

滑板

制造出第一块滑板的人尚未明确，似乎有几个人在同一时间有了类似的想法。滑板最早时是木盒或木板，底部固定着轮滑轮。最早的人造滑板是冲浪者在休息时使用的，当时一个有野心的冲浪商店老板与一家轮滑公司合作，用轮滑轮和方形木板制造一种设备。到20世纪60年代，南加州的冲浪设备制造商大规模制造滑板，并雇佣一批又一批的滑板手在运动场和公园里展示他们的产品。

➤ 词汇笔记

in the meanwhile 同时，在此期间

例：In the meanwhile, more and more people start to pay attention to this problem.

同时，越来越多的人开始关注这个问题。

roller /ˈrəʊlə(r)/ *n.* 滚筒；滚轴

例：We need to move the piano on rollers.

我们需要用滚轮来移动钢琴。

ambitious /æmˈbɪʃəs/ *adj.* 有抱负的，雄心勃勃的

例：Tom is an ambitious young man.

汤姆是一个有雄心的年轻人。

派：ambition *n.* 雄心，抱负

近：aspiring

3.

➤ 试题详解

（1）【答案】B

【出题类型】词义辨析

【解析】本题的四个选项均为动词的分词形式。其中前三个选项均表示"变化，变更"的含义。D选项意为"生长，长大"。将它们代入原文后，D选项明显与语境不符，首先排除。其余三个选项含义相近，解题的关键在于区分它们之间的细微差别。A选项

表示的变化侧重于不规则的变化，B选项表示的变化往往是较为彻底的，与之前有着明显的不同。C选项常表示的变化是在保持原有总体状态下的轻微变化。原文中发生变化的是"季节"，B选项最符合语境，所以B选项正确。句意为"希波克拉底认为季节的变化与健康有关"。

（2）【答案】C

【出题类型】词义辨析

【解析】A选项意为"捏造的"；B选项意为"精心制作的"；C选项意为"人造的；人工的"；D选项意为"错误的；伪造的"。空格处内容在句中与"light"进行搭配，结合空格前的内容，C选项最符合语境，所以C选项正确。句意为"有人推断，我们现代的生活方式让人们长时间待在室内的人造光下"。

（3）【答案】B

【出题类型】词义辨析

【解析】A选项意为"使困惑，使迷惑"；B选项意为"中断；扰乱"；C选项意为"毁坏，破坏"；D选项意为"阻止；防止"。空格处与句中的"metabolism"搭配，将选项代入句中，B选项最为恰当，所以B选项正确。句意为"白天睡觉，晚上醒着，打乱了正常的光照和黑暗周期，这会扰乱身体的新陈代谢"。

（4）【答案】A

【出题类型】词义辨析

【解析】本题的四个选项均为形容词。A选项意为"强壮的，结实的"；B选项意为"坚固的；困难的"；C选项意为"坚硬的；固体的"；D选项意为"坚固的，结实的"。空格处内容修饰句中的"immune systems"，将四个选项代入原句，A选项最恰当，所以A选项正确。句意为"这几乎可以影响一切：我们如何从食物中分解能量，我们的免疫有多强大，以及几种影响情绪和体重的物质"。

（5）【答案】B

【出题类型】固定搭配

【解析】A选项意为"证据；证明"；B选项意为"例子，实例"；C选项意为"证据；证明"；D选项意为"样本，样品"。空格处所在句将上一句的内容具体化，B选项与空格前的"for"搭配，意为"例如"，符合语境，所以B选项正确。句意为"例如，经常上夜班的人往往比不上夜班的人体重更重"。

➤ 全文翻译

阳光的力量

希波克拉底认为季节的变化与健康有关，关键是在一年中的不同时间里有多少可以摄取的阳光。有人推断，我们现代的生活方式让人们长时间待在室内的人造光下，这可能会导致悲伤和绝望的情绪。白天睡觉，晚上醒着，打乱了正常的光照和黑暗周期，这会扰乱身体的新陈代谢。这几乎可以影响一切：我们如何从食物中分解能量，我们的免疫有多强大，以及几种影响情绪和体重的物质。例如，经常上夜班的人往往比不上夜班的人体重更重。

> ➤ 词汇笔记

associated /əˈsəʊʃieɪtɪd / *adj.* 相关的；联合的

搭：be associated with 与……相关

例：The result is associated with several factors.

　　这一结果与多个因素相关。

派：associate *v.* 联想；联系

近：relevant

induce /ɪnˈdjuːs/ *v.* 引诱，诱发

例：Nothing would induce me to take the job.

　　没有什么能诱使我接受这份工作。

派：induction *n.* 归纳法；感应；诱导

近：trigger

metabolism /məˈtæbəlɪzəm/ *n.* 新陈代谢

搭：metabolism disorder 新陈代谢紊乱

例：The body's metabolism is slowed down by extreme cold.

　　严寒可以使身体新陈代谢的速度下降。

派：metabolic *adj.* 新陈代谢的

immune /ɪˈmjuːn/ *adj.* 免疫的；不受影响的

搭：immune system 免疫系统

例：Adults are often immune to this disease.

　　成人往往对这种疾病有免疫力。

派：immunity *n.* 免疫力

substance /ˈsʌbstəns/ *n.* 物质；实质

搭：in substance 实质上

例：It's questionable whether anything of substance has been achieved.

　　是否已取得任何实质性的进展值得质疑。

派：substantial *adj.* 实质的；大量的；牢固的

shift /ʃɪft/ *v.* 移动；改变

                n. 转变；偏移；（工作的）班次

搭：night shift 夜班

例：That shift affected only one segment of the population.

    这种转变只影响了一部分人口。

4.

> **试题详解**

（1）【答案】D

【出题类型】词义辨析

【解析】本题的四个选项均为形容词。A选项意为"切实的；可行的"；B选项意为"多产的"；C选项意为"盈利的，有利可图的"；D选项意为"精通的，熟练的"。空格处的内容与其后的"in their second language"搭配。将四个选项代入原句中，D选项最为恰当，所以D选项正确。句意为"心理学家和认知神经学家梅根·齐恩斯坦发起的一项研究表明，精通第二语言的双语者……"。

（2）【答案】B

【出题类型】词义辨析

【解析】本题的四个选项均为动词。A选项意为"监管，监督"；B选项意为"追求，追逐"；C选项意为"烦扰；纠缠不清"；D选项意为"出没；困扰"。正确选项应该能与空格后的"higher education"搭配，将四个选项代入原句中，B选项最恰当，所以B选项正确。句意为"比如来美国追求高等教育的国际学生……"。

（3）【答案】C

【出题类型】固定搭配

【解析】A选项意为"认为；相信"；B选项意为"判断，评判"；C选项意为"解释，说明；占……的比例"；D选项意为"向往"。空格处出现了"for"，所以正确选项应该能与其构成搭配。C和D两项能够与for构成搭配。结合句中的已知信息以及下一句中的"evidence"，可知C选项更恰当，account for意为"对……负有责任；解释原因；占……比例"，所以C选项正确。句意为"由于懂得不止一种语言和接触到不同的语言输入，熟练使用双语的人必须面对挑战，当对其进行考虑时……"。

（4）【答案】A

【出题类型】固定搭配

【解析】A选项为形容词，意为"内在的；固有的"；B选项为动词envelop的过去式，意为"包围，盖住"；C选项为动词wedge的过去式，意为"挤入，楔入"；D选项为动词shatter的过去式，意为"使破碎，破坏"。空格后出现了介词in，A选项与in搭配表示"内在的；固有的"含义，符合语境，所以A选项正确。句意为"这项研究强调了承认可变性和多样性是双语群体内在特征的必要性"。

（5）【答案】B

【出题类型】词义辨析

【解析】四个选项均为动词。A选项意为"乞求；援引"；B选项意为"改变，改动"；C选项意为"减去，扣除"；D选项意为"放气；使泄气"。将四个选项代入句中，B选项最符合语境，所以B选项正确。句意为"这种方法有可能显著地改变使用语言的意义"。

➤ 全文翻译

探索双语思维

心理学家和认知神经学家梅根·齐恩斯坦发起的一项研究表明，精通第二语言的双语者，比如来美国追求高等教育的国际学生，不仅可以克服发生在非母语环境中的困难，而且还可以像只掌握一种语言的同龄人一样使用第二语言的阅读策略。"由于懂得不止一种语言和接触到不同的语言输入，熟练使用双语的人必须面对挑战，当对其进行考虑时，我们从大脑活动中看到证据，一些第二语言读者可以主动预测接下来单词的意思。为了研究双语如何影响晚年的认知和大脑健康，我们首先需要了解双语者在每天使用语言时面临的认知和环境压力。"这项研究强调了承认可变性和多样性是双语群体内在特征的必要性——这种方法有可能显著地改变使用语言的意义。

➤ 词汇笔记

bilingual /ˌbaɪˈlɪŋgwəl/ *adj.* 会两种语言的，使用两种语言的

搭：bilingual teaching 双语教学

例：I want to buy a bilingual dictionary.

我想买一本双语字典。

psychologist /saɪˈkɒlədʒɪst/ *n.* 心理学家

例：She has an appointment with a psychologist.

她约了一位心理学家。

派：psychology *n.* 心理学

psychological *adj.* 心理学的

neuroscientist /ˈnjʊərəʊsaɪəntɪst/ *n.* 神经科学家

例：We recruited a computational neuroscientist last week.

　　我们上周招聘了一位计算神经科学家。

派：neuroscientific *adj.* 神经科学的

immerse /ɪˈmɜːs/ *v.* 沉浸于，深陷于

搭：immerse in 全神贯注于，专心于

例：They all immerse in the beautiful music.

　　他们都沉浸在动听的音乐中。

派：immersion *n.* 专心；投入；浸泡

monolingual /ˌmɒnəˈlɪŋɡwəl/ *adj.* 单语的；只会一种语言的

例：Here is the monolingual edition of this book.

　　这本书的单语版本在这里。

peer /pɪə(r)/ *n.* 同龄人；地位相同的人

　　　　　　　 v. 凝视

搭：peer pressure 同辈压力

例：Most of them can get in well with peers.

　　他们中的大部分都能和同龄人融洽相处。

近：fellow

on account of 由于，因为

例：The flight was postponed on account of bad weather.

　　因为恶劣天气，航班延期了。

underline /ˌʌndəˈlaɪn/ *v.* 强调；突出

例：Underline the following part that applies to you.

　　在以下适用于你的部分下面画线。

近：emphasize；stress；highlight

Day 12   实战篇

1.

> ➤   参考答案

（1）【参考答案】up

【出题类型】固定搭配

【解析】观察可知空格处为谓语，空格前的"pick"与"up"搭配表示"捡起，拾起"，符合语境，所以本题应填"up"。句意为"这只幼年海鸥捡起了一台摄像机，这台机器本来计划拍摄鲸鱼"。

（2）【参考答案】been

【出题类型】语法基础

【解析】观察句子可知，空格所在处为定语从句，引导词在句中做主语，从句中的主语"摄像机"与谓语"计划拍摄"间应是被动关系，应使用被动语态，所以本题应填"been"。本句意为"这只幼年海鸥捡起了一台摄像机，这台机器本来计划拍摄鲸鱼"。

（3）【参考答案】After

【出题类型】内容理解

【解析】观察本句可知，本句中涉及了两个动作，一个是幼鹰打开了相机，二是拍摄短片，结合句意可知，拍摄短片应在打开相机之后。同时注意由于空格处位于句首，所以首字母要大写，所以本题应填"After"。本句意为"在这只海鸥意外打开了摄像机的开关后，摄像机在海鸥飞过上空的时候拍摄了一段野生动物短片"。

（4）【参考答案】in

【出题类型】语法基础

【解析】空格处所在句为定语从句，结合句意可知逗号后的从句部分中，引导词在句中充当地点状语，但which无法充当状语，所以本题应填"in"。本句意为"然后它快飞到自己的窝了，这时它对摄像机失去了兴趣"。

（5）【参考答案】a

【出题类型】语法基础

【解析】空格位于名词"birdwatcher"前，该名词为可数名词，且为单数形式，需使用冠词。由于这里并没有特指，所以本题应填 "a"。句意为 "最后，一位当地的护鸟人捡到了摄像机"。

> 全文翻译

前所未有的电影——由非人类摄影师摄制

野生动物拍电影会有多难？事实上，加拿大北部的一只海鸥最近就做到了。这只幼年海鸥捡起了一台摄像机，这台机器本来计划拍摄鲸鱼。在这只海鸥意外打开了摄像机的开关后，摄像机在海鸥飞过上空的时候拍摄了一段野生动物短片。这只海鸥带着相机飞行了150千米，这让人称奇。然后它快飞到自己的窝了，这时它对摄像机失去了兴趣。这只鸟直接把摄像扔在了地上。最后，一位当地的护鸟人捡到了摄像机。

> 词汇笔记

juvenile /ˈdʒuːvənaɪl/ *adj.* 未成年的，幼年的

例：We should pay attention to the juvenile crime.

我们应该关注未成年人犯罪。

近：infantile

documentary /ˌdɒkjuˈmentri/ *adj.* 书面的；文件的

n. 纪实节目，纪录片

例：A documentary about African wildlife is being produced.

一部关于非洲野生动物的纪录片正在制作中。

派：documentation *n.* 证明材料，文献记载

grab /græb/ *v.* 攫取；抓住

n. 攫取；赚取

例：I managed to grab a couple of hours' sleep on the plane.

我在飞机上抓紧时间睡了几个钟头。

近：grasp

discard /dɪˈskɑːd/ *v.* 扔掉，抛弃

n. 被抛弃物

例：Take the information that you can use and discard the rest.

吸取你能用上的部分，抛弃其余的信息。

近：abandon

2.

> 参考答案

（1）【参考答案】who/that

【出题类型】语法基础

【解析】观察句子可知，空格后的内容为定语从句，修饰之前的"designer"，空格处应该是从句的引导词。引导词在从句中做主语，且指代人，所以本题应填"who/that"。句意为"我设法弄到了为我装饰房子的设计师的电话号码"。

（2）【参考答案】up

【出题类型】固定搭配

【解析】结合句中的已知信息，作者整个晚上都在翻阅合同和旧收据，并且空格前出现了"stayed"，所以本题应填"up"，二者构成的搭配表示"不睡觉，熬夜"。句意为"我整晚都没睡，翻看了我的联系人和旧收据"。

（3）【参考答案】after

【出题类型】固定搭配

【解析】根据句中的已知信息，可知作者忘记了设计师公司的名字，后来通过设计师母亲的名字回忆起来了。空格前的"name"与"after"搭配，意为"以……命名"，符合语境，所以本题应填"after"。句意为"但后来我想起来她的公司是根据她母亲命名的"。

（4）【参考答案】mine

【出题类型】内容理解

【解析】根据语境可知，发件人与收件人为朋友关系，空格处想表达"我的朋友"的含义。名词+of+名词性物主代词与形容词性物主代词+名词均表示"……的"，空格前出现了"of"，所以本题应填"mine"。本句句意为"当你给她打电话时，告诉她你是我的朋友，我相信她会好好为你服务"。

（5）【参考答案】Let

【出题类型】内容理解

【解析】根据句中的已知信息，本句作者表达的是想知道事情的进展，且空格处位于句首，首字母要大写，所以本题应填"Let"，句意为"如有后续进展，请告诉我"。

➤ 全文翻译

发件人：汤姆·布莱克
收件人：迈克尔·比斯利
主题：装饰设计师

你好，比斯利，
我有一些让人激动的消息。我设法弄到了为我装饰房子的设计师的电话号码。她的名字叫南希。我整晚都没睡，翻看了我的联系人和旧收据。一开始，我找不到她公司的名字，但后来我想起来她的公司是根据她母亲命名的，所以我大致花了两个小时，却找错了姓！当你给她打电话时，告诉她你是我的朋友，我相信她会好好为你服务。
如有后续进展，请告诉我。

照顾好自己，
布莱克

➤ 词汇笔记

look up 查找

例：Can you look up the opening times on the website?
你可以在网站上查一下开放的时间吗?

近：search

receipt /rɪˈsiːt/ *n.* 发票；收据

例：Can I have a receipt, please?
请给我开个收据，好吗?

派：receiptor *n.* 收受人

近：quittance

surname /ˈsɜːneɪm/ *n.* 姓；别名

例：May I have your surname, please?
请问您贵姓?

近：family name

3.

> **参考答案**

（1）【参考答案】as

【出题类型】内容理解

【解析】空格前说到多种好处，空格后表达的是一种锻炼的方式，所以填入的内容应该将这两部分连接在一起。as可以表示"作为"，符合语境，所以本题应填"as"。句意为"作为一种锻炼的方式，它有很多优点"。

（2）【参考答案】not

【出题类型】固定搭配

【解析】空格前出现了"whether or"，"whether or not"为固定搭配，意为"是否，无论"，所以本题应填"not"。句意为"但是对于不同个体来说，这是否是最佳的锻炼方式，取决于你的需求和喜好"。

（3）【参考答案】is

【出题类型】语法基础

【解析】观察本句可知，空格前为名词短语，空格后为that引导的从句，根据这两部分的内容，可以推断出空格处应表示"是"的含义，应填入be动词。空格前的内容为单数，所以本题应填"is"。句意为"人们普遍认为游泳锻炼你的全身"。

（4）【参考答案】at

【出题类型】固定搭配

【解析】根据句中的信息可知，本句表达的是有些游泳方式不需要消耗太多能量。空格后出现了"all"，可推断出空格处应该能与其构成搭配。"at all"这一搭配常在表否定含义的句子中使用，意为"完全，丝毫"，符合语境，所以本题应填"at"。本句意为"在游泳池里仰面游泳，可能根本不用消耗太多能量"。

（5）【参考答案】if

【出题类型】内容理解

【解析】根据前文的内容，可以推断出句中的"that"指代"强健骨骼和增肌"，明确这一点后，可以推断出逗号前的内容为条件，逗号后的内容为结果，所以本题应填"if"。句意为"所以如果这是你的愿望，你最好去健身房"。

> **全文翻译**

长久以来，人们都认为游泳对身体有益。作为一种锻炼的方式，它有很多优点：它能保持心脏健康，增强肺部功能。但是对于不同个体来说，这是否是最佳的锻炼方式，取决于你的需求和喜好。人们普遍认为游泳锻炼你的全身，但这的确取决于你游泳的方式。在游泳池里仰面游泳，可能根本不用消耗太多能量。这一切都意味着你无法获得快速游泳所带来的对健康的益处。游泳不能强健骨骼，也不能练出大块肌肉。所以如果这是你的愿望，你最好去健身房。

➤ 词汇笔记

workout /ˈwɜːkaʊt/ *n.* 锻炼，训练

例：She does a 20-minute workout every morning.

她每天早晨做20分钟的运动。

近：exercise/practice

consensus /kənˈsensəs/ *n.* 一致同意，共识

搭：reach a consensus 达成共识

例：There is a growing consensus of opinion on this issue.

对这个问题的看法日趋一致。

派：consensual *adj.* 一致同意的

近：agreement

lean on 依赖，靠在……上

例：You may need a good friend to lean on.

你可能需要依靠好友。

miss out on 错过机会，错失

例：Then we will miss out on a lot of fun.

那样的话，我们就会失去很多乐趣。

better off 更富裕的；更好的

例：The weather was so bad that we'd have been better off staying at home.

天气非常恶劣，我们还不如待在家里舒服。

4.

➤ 参考答案

（1）【参考答案】from

【出题类型】固定搭配

【解析】本题考查固定搭配，由语境可知，本句应表达的是"掌握这些文化方面的小建议，能让人受益"的含义，benefit与from搭配，表示从……中获益，符合语境，所以本题应填"from"。本句意为"去美国旅游的游客可能会从掌握这些文化技巧中受益，帮助他们与当地人进行沟通"。

（2）【参考答案】will

【出题类型】语法基础

【解析】本题考查语法基础知识，空格处之前，出现了if条件句，空格处所在句为主句，所以应使用一般将来时，所以本句应填"will"。本句意为"如果你站得太近，有可能让他们感到焦躁或不安"。

（3）【参考答案】despite

【出题类型】内容理解

【解析】本题考查内容理解。观察空格处前后内容可知，这两部分内容存在对比关系，此题极易误填though，但观察这两部分内容的结构可知，空格前为完整句子，而空格后则为先行词加定语从句的结构，并不是完整的句子，所以不能在空格处填入连词。despite一词做介词使用时，表示"尽管，不管"，且与词或词组连用。符合语境及语法要求，所以本题应填"despite"。本题的易错点在于，空格后内容中的定语从句省略了引导词，极易被误认为完整的句子。本句意为"尽管初次见面时他们给予你热情欢迎"。

（4）【参考答案】point

【出题类型】固定搭配

【解析】本题考查固定搭配。结合句意可知，坦诚是美国人的特点。空格处与坦诚并列，所以空格处内容表达的意思应与其相近。get straight to the point为固定搭配，表示"开门见山"。符合语境，所以本题应填"point"。本句意为"他们的坦率和开门见山表明了他们'时间就是金钱'的态度"。

（5）【参考答案】on

【出题类型】固定搭配

【解析】本题考查固定搭配，结合句意可知，本处表达的应是"在……上浪费时间的含义"，waste表达这一含义时，与介词on连用，所以本题应填"on"。本句意为"他们通常不会浪费时间去闲谈"。

> 全文翻译

去美国旅游的游客可能会从掌握这些文化技巧中受益，帮助他们与当地人进行沟通。初见面，美国人可能看起来很友好，见到你的时候会微笑并称呼你的名字。然而，他们有很强的个人空间感，如果你站得太近，有可能让他们感到焦躁或不安。他们一开始时的友好可能不会持续太久，尽管初次见面时他们给予你热情欢迎。美国人觉得没必要快速建立亲密的私人关系。他们认为应该建立联系的是老朋友，而不是初次见面的人。他们的坦率和开门见山表明了他们"时间就是金钱"的态度，他们通常不会浪费时间去闲谈。

> 词汇笔记

amicable /ˈæmɪkəbl/ *adj.* 心平气和的，友善的

例：I believe we can solve disputes through an amicable negotiation.

我认为我们可以通过友好协商的方式解决争议。

近：friendly

restless /ˈrestləs/ *adj.* 坐立不安的，烦躁的

例：My father seemed very restless and excited.

我父亲看起来非常坐立不安和兴奋。

派：restlessness *n.* 坐立不安，不安定

近：uneasy

acquaintance /əˈkweɪntəns/ *n.* 认识的人；相识

例：We are the casual acquaintance of a long railway journey.

我们是在铁路长途旅行中偶然结识的。

Day 15 实战篇

1.

> 试题详解

题号	出题类型	答案	解析
（1）	细节理解	D	题目：在第一段中，我们能获取格蕾丝·奈芙的什么信息？ A 她参加了一场对她的研究有重大影响的讨论。 B 她去秘鲁旅行最初是为了学习一种特殊的手语。 C 她面临着与迈朱纳人交流的挑战。 **D 她决定转变研究的重点。** 根据题干可直接定位至第一段。本段的第二句说到 "On my last night, at a village celebration, the communication between two men from different villages attracted my attention, so much so that my study transferred into something else entirely.（在我在那的最后一个晚上，在一个村庄的庆典上，两个来自不同村庄的人之间的交流吸引了我的注意力，我甚至完全改变了研究的主题。）"，可知主人公的研究主题发生了改变，所以 D 选项正确。 同时由本句也可知，作者参加的是庆祝活动，所以 A 选项错误。由本段第一句可知，作者前往秘鲁是为了研究一种口头语言，所以 B 选项错误。C 选项没有在原文中提及，所以排除。
（2）	细节理解	C	题目：格蕾丝第二次前往时，什么是显而易见的？ A 如果她想继续研究，需要取得迈朱纳人的信任。 B 迈朱纳人试图不想让她知道更多的聋人。 **C 她需要改变询问迈朱纳人的方式。** D 出于尊重，迈朱纳人不倾向讨论他人的不同。 根据关键词 "Grace's second trip" 可定位至第二段。本段第一句提到 "I began consulting about deaf people living in the community; however, everyone insisted Raúl was the only deaf person they knew.（我开始咨询住在社区里的聋人；然而，每个人都坚持说劳尔是他们认识的唯一的聋人）"。本段第五句提到 "I learned meaningful information about how the Maijuna define deafness—it's that you can't speak, not that you can't hear.（我了解到迈朱纳人如何定义聋人的重要信息——不能说话，而不是听不见。）"，可知作者认为的聋人与当地人认为的聋人并非同一概念。本段第六句又提到 "I would have found more

题号	出题类型	答案	解析
(2)	细节理解	C	success if I asked about people who spoke with their hands...（如果我问谁用手说话，我会获得更大的成功……）"，可知作者认为换一种说法会有更多收获。C选项最符合这一说法，所以C选项正确。其余三个选项均与文中表述不符。
(3)	主旨大意	B	题目：第三段中，格蕾丝做了什么？ A 强调了西蒙和劳尔是如何说服其他人学习手语体系。 **B 解释了形成独特手语体系的条件。** C 比较唇语阅读和手语的好处。 D 描述学习独特手语体系的障碍。 根据题干可直接定位至第三段。本段最后一句提到"Those who communicate with Simón and Raúl—primarily their families and Maijuna men, on account of the separation of labour by gender—learn to sign and never use their voices when signing, even when other hearing people are nearby.（那些与西蒙和劳尔交流的人——主要是他们的家人和迈朱纳的男人，因为性别的分工——学习手语，在使用手语时从不使用口头语言，即使周围有其他听力正常的人。）"，可知这一部分内容介绍了这种语言体系是以什么样的方式发挥作用的，所以B选项正确。其余三个选项均与文中的表述不符。
(4)	细节理解	B	题目：格蕾丝在说到迈朱纳"家庭手语体系"引人关注时，说了什么？ A 一段时间内没有什么变化。 **B 这包含了西蒙和劳尔的亲密合作。** C 直到最近才在几个村庄广泛运用。 D 存在细微的差异，反映各个村庄的文化。 根据关键词"remarkable"和"home sign system"可定位至第四段。本段第三句提到"It has a relatively stable vocabulary with about 80 percent overlap between Raúl and Simón even though the two men have never lived in the same village and seldom met.（家庭手势体系有相对稳定的词汇量，尽管劳尔和西蒙从来没有住在同一个村子里，也很少见面，但他们之间有大约80%的词汇重合。）"，即二者在没有交集的情况下，使用的手势大部分是相同的，B选项的说法最为恰当，所以B选项正确。其余三个选项的内容均未在文中体现，可排除。
(5)	观点态度	C	题目：最后一段中，格蕾丝的主要观点是什么？ A 迈朱纳人一直尝试改进家庭手语体系。 B 迈朱纳人意识到保护家庭手语体系的重要性。 **C 迈朱纳的例子阐释了语言发展中的重要因素。** D 运用秘鲁手语的要素，会让迈朱纳家庭手语体系获益。

题号	出题类型	答案	解析
(5)	观点态度	C	根据题干可直接定位至最后一段。本段第二句提到"The Maijuna show the significance of community in the evolution of language.（迈朱纳人展示了社区在语言进化中的重要意义。）"，可知迈朱纳手语反映出了语言发展中的重要因素，所以C选项正确。 本段的第一句虽然提到了"Peruvian Sign Language（秘鲁手语）"，但说的是迈朱纳手语体系不受其影响，所以D选项错误。其余两个选项均未在文中提及，可排除。

➤ 全文翻译

迈朱纳人的手语

语言学家格蕾丝·奈芙讨论了她在秘鲁亚马孙开展的实地研究

我曾经在纽瓦维达待了五周，那里是迈朱纳民族的四个村庄之一，我研究了迈朱纳人说的迈朱纳语，迈朱纳是秘鲁亚马孙地区的一个土著民族。在我在那的最后一个晚上，在一个村庄的庆典上，两个来自不同村庄的人之间的交流吸引了我的注意力，我甚至完全改变了研究的主题。其中一名27岁的男子劳尔是位聋人，整个对话都是用手势进行的。在接下来的几年里，我又三次回到迈朱纳社区，研究我第一次在聚会上观察到的手势交流体系，看看这是否是迈朱纳人使用的一种既定的手语。

在我第二次去迈朱纳实地考察时，我开始咨询住在社区里的聋人；然而，每个人都坚持说劳尔是他们认识的唯一的聋人。六周后，一位研究参与者给我看了一张西蒙的照片，他是一位60岁的男人，住在迈朱纳的另一个村庄，他说他和劳尔很像。在我详细询问了西蒙之后，大家都说他用手势交流。然而，也有一些关于他是不是聋人的讨论。我了解到迈朱纳人如何定义聋人的重要信息——不能说话，而不是听不见。如果我问谁用手说话，我会获得更大的成功，因为需要解决的缺陷是交流的问题，而不是身体上的问题。

西蒙、劳尔以及其他像他们一样的人在没有口头语言的情况下长大，但他们是真正发挥作用的社区成员。这是因为他们形成了所谓的"家庭手势体系"——这是一种人造的手势体系，具有类似语言的结构，如连贯的语序。在迈朱纳的社区生活中，没有人期望西蒙和劳尔会读唇语。那些与西蒙和劳尔交流的人——主要是他们的家人和迈朱纳的男人，因为性别的分工——学习手语，在使用手语时从不使用口头语言，即使周围有其他听力正常的人。

围绕西蒙和劳尔形成的复杂手势体系之所以引人注目，有几个原因。他们的家庭手势体系至少跨越了两个不同的村庄和三代人。家庭手势体系有相对稳定的词汇量，尽管劳尔和西蒙从来没有住在同一个村子里，也很少见面，但他们之间有大约80%的词汇重合。

显而易见的是，西蒙和劳尔成长的社区支持一种意想不到的复杂手语体系的创新，这种体系不受任何公认的手语的影响，包括秘鲁手语（PSL）。迈朱纳人展示了社区在语言进化中的重要意义。尽管家庭手势体系并不完美——它们不具备语音语言特征，而且经常发生沟通障碍——但它们仍然是人类创造力的范例。

➤ 词汇笔记

indigenous /ɪnˈdɪdʒənəs/ *adj.* 本土的

例：The kangaroo is indigenous to Australia.

袋鼠原产于澳大利亚。

近：native

consistent /kənˈsɪstənt/ *adj.* 始终如一的，持续的；连贯的

例：That has been our consistent stand.

这是我们一贯的主张。

近：constant

on account of 由于，因为

例：She retired early on account of ill health.

她体弱多病，所以提前退休。

近：due to/thanks to

overlap /ˌəʊvəˈlæp/ *v.* 重叠；互搭

例：The needs of students invariably overlap.

学生们的各种需求是相互重合的。

span /spæn/ *v.* 持续；贯穿；横跨

　　　　　 n. 时间跨度；跨距；范围

例：Small children have a short attention span.

幼儿注意力持续时间短。

breakdown /ˈbreɪkdaʊn/ *n.* 损坏；故障

例：My car had a breakdown on the motorway.

我的车在高速公路上出了故障。

近：malfunction

conspicuous /kənˈspɪkjuəs/ *adj.* 引人注目的，显眼的

例：Attitudes to conspicuous consumption are changing.

人们对于炫耀性消费的看法正在改变。

近：showy

2.

> 试题详解

题号	出题类型	答案	解析
（1）	细节理解	D	题目：什么是"电流之战"？ A 使用交流电和喜欢直流电人群的冲突。 B 特斯拉和爱迪生之间关于谁的发明更多的争论。 C 关于特斯拉和爱迪生之间谁是其他科学家的老板的争论。 **D 关于特斯拉和爱迪生谁发明了最好的电力系统的争论。** 根据题干中的关键词"War of Currents"可定位至第一段。本段第三句提到"The two feuding geniuses waged a "War of Currents" in the 1880s over whose electrical system would power the world...（这两位长期不和的天才在19世纪80年代发动了一场"电流之战"，争论谁的电力系统将为世界提供动力……）"，这与D选项的说法相符，所以D选项正确。 由本句也可知竞争的双方为爱迪生和特斯拉，所以排除A选项。根据本段第二句可知，爱迪生是特斯拉之前的老板，所以C选项错误。B选项未在本段提及，可排除。
（2）	细节理解	C	题目：W·伯纳德·卡尔森认为_____ A 特斯拉和爱迪生在技术水平上相当。 B 不管怎样，这两位科学家很相像。 **C 现代社会从爱迪生和特斯拉身上获益。** D 科学家应该像特斯拉和爱迪生那样相互挑战。 由题干中的关键词"W·Bernard Carlson"可定位至第二段。本段第二句说到"From their obviously different personalities to their abiding gifts to the humanity...（从他们明显不同的个性到他们对人类持久的贡献……）"，可知这两位科学家个性不同，但都为人们带来了益处，所以B选项错误。C选项的说法与文中相对应，所以C选项正确。其余选项的说法无法在文中得到印证。
（3）	细节理解	A	题目：根据第三段可知，_____ **A 爱迪生没有像特斯拉那样想象成品原型的能力。** B 特斯拉在绘画和复制物体方面有非凡的天赋。 C 总体上看，爱迪生缺乏条理和方法。 D 与爱迪生相比，特斯拉在工作上更精确、更迅速。 根据题干可直接定位至第三段，本段第一句说到"Tesla possessed a clear memory, which meant he could very accurately recall images and objects.（特斯拉有清晰的记忆力，这意味着他可以非常精确地回忆起图像和物体。）"，本段的第四句提到"On the contrary, Edison obsessively tried things out making gradual adjustments.（相比之下，爱迪生痴迷于不断尝试，逐步调整。）"，可知这两位科学家的工作风

题号	出题类型	答案	解析
(3)	细节理解	A	格不一样，一位擅长在脑海中构思，一位则擅长动手实操，所以A选项正确。 由A选项的定位句可知，特斯拉的长处在于在脑海中进行构思，并不是绘画和复制物体，所以B选项错误。第三段第五句说到"'If you were going to the laboratory and watching him at work, you'd find he'd have stuff all over the table: wires, coils and various parts of inventions.'Carlson said.（卡尔森说："如果你去实验室看他工作，你会发现他的工作台上到处都是东西：电线、线圈和各种各样的发明部件。"）"，可知这里只说了爱迪生的工作台上堆满了东西，但不能就此说明爱迪生缺乏条理，C选项错误。D选项的内容无法在本段得到印证，可排除。
(4)	细节理解	D	**题目：本文作者怎样描述二位科学家的成功？** A 特斯拉不如爱迪生善于销售自己发明。 B 爱迪生出售了更多专利，但是欺骗他人。 C 特斯拉很费力地寻找为他工作的人。 **D 爱迪生的财力比特斯拉强。** 根据题干中的"success"可定位至第三段，第三段第六句、第七句提到"In the end, however, Edison sold 1, 093 patents to use his inventions. Tesla, who never had much wealth, acquired less than 300 worldwide.（然而，爱迪生最终售出了1093个他的发明专利。特斯拉则没有这么多财富，他在全球的专利不到300个。）"，可知爱迪生出售的专利多于特斯拉，这与D选项的说法相符，所以D选项正确。 本段的相关内容展示的是两位主人公售卖专利的结果，并不是谁更擅长做这件事，所以A选项错误。文中并未说爱迪生欺骗他人，所以B选项错误。C选项的内容未在文中提及，可排除。
(5)	细节理解	C	**题目：伦纳德·迪格拉夫认为_____** A 爱迪生并没有真正地发明什么新的东西，可能窃取了他人的想法。 B 过去还有比爱迪生更聪明的科学家。 **C 如果爱迪生没有来到世上，还会有其他人发明像灯泡这样的东西。** D 灯泡和留声机并不是爱迪生最重要的发明。 根据题干中的"Leonard DeGraaf"可定位至第四段，本段第二句说到"'If Edison hadn't invented those things, other people would have,'DeGraaf declared.（"如果爱迪生没有发明这些东西，其他人也会发明的。"迪格拉夫宣称。）"，可知这与C选项的说法相符，所以C选项正确。 本段第一句说到"'Though the light bulb, the phonograph and moving pictures are regarded as Edison's most important inventions, other people were already working on similar technologies,'said Leonard DeGraaf, an archivist and author.（档案保管员兼作家伦纳德·迪格拉夫说："尽管灯泡、留声机和电影被认为是爱迪生最重要的发明，但其他人已经在研究类似的技术了。"）"，可知A和D两个选项与此说法不符，所以A选项和D选项错误。B选项未在文中提及，可排除。

题号	出题类型	答案	解析
(6)	细节理解	B	题目：本文作者认为，爱迪生的错误是什么？ A 他的发明太简单了。 **B 他低估了特斯拉的交流电系统。** C 他没有考虑过在尼亚加拉大瀑布从事电力工作。 D 他太在意推销自己的发明了。 文章第四段第三句提到 "In a not so wise move, Edison considered Tesla's idea of an AC system of electric power transmission "impractical", instead promoting his simpler, but less efficient, the DC system.（一个不太明智的举动使爱迪生认为特斯拉的交流电力传输系统的想法"不切实际"，而推广了他更简单但效率更低的直流电系统。）"，可知爱迪生对特斯拉交流电的评价不佳，所以B选项正确。 A选项未在文中提及，可排除。文中的确提到了尼亚加拉大瀑布，但并未提到在此工作，所以C选项错误。D选项也未在文中提及，可排除。

➤ **全文翻译**

一场科学家之间的竞争

塞尔维亚裔美国科学家尼古拉·特斯拉是一位杰出而古怪的天才，他的发明使现代电力和大众通信系统得以实现。他最大的竞争对手和前老板托马斯·爱迪生是美国著名的灯泡、留声机和电影的发明家。这两位长期不和的天才在19世纪80年代发动了一场"电流之战"，争论谁的电力系统将为世界提供动力——特斯拉的交流电系统还是爱迪生的直流电系统。在科学书呆子中，很少有争论比尼古拉·特斯拉和托马斯·爱迪生之间的比较更频繁的了。那么，谁是更优秀的发明家呢？

"他们是不同的发明家，但你真的不能说谁更伟大，因为美国社会需要一些爱迪生，也需要一些特斯拉"，知名作家兼教授W·伯纳德·卡尔森说。从他们明显不同的个性到他们对人类持久的贡献，下面来说说这两位争斗的发明家是如何相互竞争的。

特斯拉有清晰的记忆力，这意味着他可以非常精确地回忆起图像和物体。这使他能够准确地可视化复杂的3D物体，因此，他只需要几张简单的图纸就能构建工作原型。卡尔森说："他真的是在想象中完成了他的发明。"相比之下，爱迪生痴迷于不断尝试，逐步调整。卡尔森说："如果你去实验室看他工作，你会发现他的工作台上到处都是东西：电线、线圈和各种各样的发明部件。"然而，爱迪生最终售出了1093个他的发明专利。特斯拉则没有这么多财富，他在全球的专利不到300个。值得一提的是，由于爱迪生可以负担得起，他请了更多的助手来帮助他设计发明，还买了他自己的一些专利。

档案保管员兼作家伦纳德·迪格拉夫说："尽管灯泡、留声机和电影被认为是爱迪生最重要的发明，但其他人已经在研究类似的技术了。""如果爱迪生没有发明这些东西，其他人也会发明的。"德格拉夫宣称。一个不太明智的举动使爱迪生认为特斯拉的交流电力传输系统的想法"不切实际"，而推广了他更简单但效率更低的直流电系统。相比之下，特斯拉的想法往往是没有明确的市场需求，但更具革命性的技术。他在尼亚加拉大瀑布建造的交流电机和水力发电厂——这是一个史无前例的发电厂——真正为世界供电。

➤ 词汇笔记

odd /ɒd/ *adj.* 古怪的，反常的

例：There's something odd about that man.

那个人有点古怪。

近：strange

feud /fjuːd/ *v.* 长期争斗，长期不和

例：He has been feuding with Bill for decades.

几十年来，他一直与比尔不和。

wage /weɪdʒ/ *n.* 工资，报酬

　　　　　　　v. 发动（战争，运动）

例：His wages have gone up.

他的工资涨了。

近：salary

call for 要求，提倡

例：Air pollution calls for our special concern.

空气污染需要我们的特别关注。

duel /ˈdjuːəl/ *v.* 决斗，竞争

例：Men are more concerned with displaying their strength by dueling.

男性更在意通过决斗的方式展现自己的力量。

prototype /ˈprəʊtətaɪp/ *n.* 原型，雏形；范例

例：What's the prototype of a function?

什么是一个函数的原型呢？

近：archetype

archivist /ˈɑːkɪvɪst/ *n.* 档案保管员

例：Archivist manages all documents collected and created by the team.

档案管理员管理小组收集和创作的所有文件。

revolutionary /ˌrevəˈluːʃənəri/ *adj.* 革命的，革命性的

例：This was a pretty revolutionary finding.

这是一个极具革命性的发现。

hydroelectric /ˌhaɪdrəʊɪˈlektrɪk/ *adj.* 水力发电的

例：The hydroelectric station is nearing completion.

水电站即将竣工。

3.

➤ **试题详解**

题号	出题类型	答案	解析
（1）	细节理解	A	题目：下面哪一项是婚礼请柬和绘画之间存在的真正联系？ A 绘画和婚礼请柬中的错误证明了人们不会正确地设想现实。 B 绘画和婚礼请柬都含有极大分散注意力的图像成分。 C 绘画如同婚礼请柬，都是艺术家努力捕捉现实的成果。 D 婚礼请柬是干扰绘画的因素之一。 根据题干中的 "wedding invitations and drawings" 可定位至第一段第三句，本句说到 "We go through life expecting what we are going to see and miss—which is why so many wedding invitations go out with the wrong date.（我们在生活中期待着我们将要看到的东西和错过的东西——这就是为什么那么多婚礼请柬在错误的日期发出。）"，可知婚礼请柬中的错误说明人们在认识事物方面会出现错误，这与A选项的说法相符，所以A选项正确。 B选项和C选项均未在原文中提及，可排除。根据本段第二句的内容可知，不能正确地进行绘画是大脑在起阻碍作用，所以D选项错误。
（2）	细节理解	C	题目：包含艺术家和非艺术家的实验说明了什么？ A 艺术家具备较快扫视图片的能力。 B 非艺术家更容易被人吸引而不是物。 C 非艺术家倾向于解释一幅画，而艺术家则对其进行分析。 D 尽管采用的方法不同，这两个群体都能充分扫视图片。 根据题干中的 "experiment involving artists and non-artists" 可定位至第二段。本段最后一句说到 "This finding indicates that while non-artists were busy turning images into concepts, artists were noticing colours and contours...（这一发现表明，当非艺术家忙于将图像转化为概念时，艺术家则在注意颜色和轮廓……）"，可知艺术家和非艺术家之间的行为存在不同，非艺术家关注图画的意义，而艺术家关注图画的特性。这与C选项的说法相符，所以C选项正确。 第二段第三句提到 "...while the non-artists' eyes focus on objects, especially people.（……而非艺术家的眼睛则专注于物体，尤其是人。）"，可知图画上的人和物都会吸引非艺术家，这与B选项的说法不符，所以B选项错误。A选项和D选项均未在原文中提及，可排除。

题号	出题类型	答案	解析
(3)	细节理解	D	题目：伦博朗作为_____的例子被提及。 A 艺术天才不会出现视力问题 B 一个记录他挣扎的立体失明患者 C 艺术与视觉研究的特例 **D 视力有问题的人却在艺术方面获益** 根据题干中的"Rembrandt"可定位至第三段，本段第五句说到"Rembrandt's stereoblindness, says Conway, may have given him an advantage in seeing the world like an artist.（康威说，伦勃朗的立体失明可能给了他一个优势，让他可以像艺术家一样看待世界。）"，可知视力问题能提升艺术能力，这与D选项的说法相符，所以D选项正确。 本段最后一句提到"A new and yet-unpublished study by Conway and Livingstone finds that the art students are far more likely to have the visual disability than non-artists.（康威和利文斯通的一项尚未发表的新研究发现，艺术专业的学生比非艺术专业的学生更有可能出现视觉障碍。）"，可知在艺术上有造诣的人出现视力问题的概率更大，所以A选项错误。这一段侧重说明视力问题对艺术方面的帮助，并不是视力问题给人造成的困难，所以B选项错误。文章并未提及与C选项相关的内容，可排除。
(4)	细节理解	D	题目：康威最近得出了什么结论? A 伦博朗是一位技艺高超的画家，因为他有时间练习。 B 没有视觉障碍的人对艺术感兴趣的可能性更低。 C 伦博朗曾认为现实是二维的。 **D 拥有立体视觉的人成为艺术家的可能性更低。** 根据题干中的"Conway"可定位至第三段，第三段最后一句话"A new and yet-unpublished study by Conway and Livingstone finds that the art students are far more likely to have the visual disability than non-artists.（康威和利文斯通的一项尚未发表的新研究发现，艺术专业的学生比非艺术专业的学生更有可能出现视觉障碍。）"与D选项说法相符，所以D选项正确。其余三个选项均与文中表述不符，可排除。
(5)	细节理解	C	题目：根据第四段，沃格特认为_____ A 真正的艺术家是那些传递人们熟悉的现实观点的人。 B 艺术家眼中的世界是扭曲的，但也是有价值的。 **C 所有艺术家都应该避免对现实的平凡幻想。** D 观众应该会发现艺术家对世界的看法让人不安。 根据题干可直接定位至第四段，本段第二句说到"As a result, artists can and ought to paint pictures that jar regular people out of our well-worn habits of seeing.（因此，艺术家能够并且应该画出让普通人摆脱以往视觉习惯的画。）"，可知这与C选项说法相符，所以C选项正确。 A选项的说法与定位句表述相反，所以A选项错误。B选项和D选项均未在本段提及，可排除。

题号	出题类型	答案	解析
(6)	细节理解	C	题目：下面哪一项反映了最后一段的内容？ A 简单的事物比复杂的事物更有价值。 B 艺术家有能力把看到的事物简化。 **C 复杂的景象和简单的景象都具有启发性。** D 画家往往不会太关注细节。 根据题干可直接定位至最后一段，本段最后一句说到"To the trained eyes of an artist, these seemingly mediocre sights might be as fascinating as a cascading waterfall or a majestic mountain peak.（在训练有素的艺术家眼中，这些看似平庸的景象可能像落下的瀑布或雄伟的山峰一样迷人。）"，可知艺术家善于发现生活中微小的事物，这也具有很大的价值，这与C选项的说法相符，所以C选项正确。 A选项是对定位句的错误理解，文章并未将复杂事物和简单事物进行比较，而是说明二者同样重要，所以A选项错误。B选项和D选项的内容均未在本段提及，可排除。

➤ 全文翻译

艺术家的眼光

你能勾勒出一幅风景画，甚至是一幅令人信服的水果画吗？如果不能，很可能是你的大脑在妨碍你，绘画老师大卫·邓洛普说。他还说："人们不像照相机那样看东西。我们在生活中期待着我们将要看到的东西和错过的东西——这就是为什么那么多婚礼请柬在错误的日期发出。"在他的艺术课上，邓洛普要求学生做的第一件事就是停止识别物体，而是将场景视为线条、阴影、形状和轮廓的集合。

事实上，根据斯汀·沃格特博士的说法，艺术家特殊的观察方式转化为眼睛扫描模式，与非艺术家的眼睛扫描模式相对不同。在她的研究中，她让9名数学系学生和9名艺术系学生观看一系列图像，同时有一台摄像机和电脑监控他们的目光锁定在哪里。她发现，艺术家的眼睛倾向于扫描整个画面，包括空旷的海洋或天空，而非艺术家的眼睛则专注于物体，尤其是人。沃格特说，这一发现表明，当非艺术家忙于将图像转化为概念时，艺术家则在注意颜色和轮廓。

贝维尔·康威博士说，虽然需要多年的训练才能掌握像艺术家一样观察世界的方法，但常见的视觉障碍可能会对一些人有所帮助。在他的一项研究中，他分析了伦勃朗的36幅自画像，发现这位艺术家称自己的眼睛很迟钝，一只眼睛直视前方，另一只眼睛向外张望。这种情况被称为斜视，影响了10%的人口，并导致立体失明——无法用两只眼睛构建一个完整的世界。立体失明患者的深度感知能力也很有限，他们必须借助像阴影和遮挡等其他线索来探索世界。康威说，伦勃朗的立体失明可能给了他一个优势，让他可以像艺术家一样看待世界。他还说，美术老师经常让学生在画一个场景之前闭上一只眼睛，这并非偶然。"伦勃朗一生都在磨炼在二维空间中渲染三维图像的能力，"他说，康威和利文斯通的一项尚未发表的新研究发现，艺术专业的学生比非艺术专业的学生更有可能出现视觉障碍。

身为画家和科学家的沃格特说，立体失明和概念失明帮助艺术家们看到世界的真实面貌，将其视为一大堆形状、颜色和形式。因此，艺术家能够并且应该画出让普通人摆脱以往视觉习惯的画。她说："作为艺术家，我们的工作是让人们享受他们的视觉，而不仅仅是用它来四处乱看。"

总而言之，视觉艺术家和其他人生活在同一个世界，但他们的体验却截然不同。艺术家将世界视为可以加入艺术作品的原材料，他们可能会注意到其他人忽略的东西。画家可能会被一栋建筑物投在另一栋建筑物上的阴影颜色所吸引，或者为蒲公英叶子错综复杂的 V 形图案而感叹。在训练有素的艺术家眼中，这些看似平庸的景象可能像落下的瀑布或雄伟的山峰一样迷人。

➤ 词汇笔记

get in the way 妨碍，阻碍

例：Life and all its pressures get in the way for all of us.

生活及其压力妨碍了我们每一个人。

contour /ˈkɒntʊə(r)/ *n.* 轮廓；外形

搭：contour line 等高线

例：The road follows the natural contours of the coastline.

这条路沿着海岸线的自然轮廓延伸。

近：outline

disability /ˌdɪsəˈbɪləti/ *n.* 残疾；无能力

搭：intellectual disability 智力障碍

例：Facilities for people with disabilities are still insufficient.

供残疾人使用的设施仍然不足。

portrait /ˈpɔːtreɪt/ *n.* 肖像，画像

搭：self-portrait 自画像

例：We hung her portrait above the fireplace.

我们把她的画像挂在壁炉上方。

wander /ˈwɒndə(r)/ *v.* 漫游，游荡

n. 漫步

搭：wander about 闲逛，漫步

例：I went to the park and had a wander around.

我去公园转了一圈。

近：stroll

resort /rɪˈzɔːt/ *v.* 诉诸，求助于

搭：resort to 诉诸，求助于

例：To save face, they may even resort to lying.

为了挽回面子，他们甚至可能会采取撒谎的手段。

occlusion /əˈkluːʒn/ *n.* 闭塞；遮蔽；吸收

例：He was diagnosed as the arterial occlusion.

他被诊断为动脉闭塞。

navigate /ˈnævɪɡeɪt/ *v.* 导航；穿过；操纵

例：The river became too narrow and shallow to navigate.

河道变得又窄又浅，无法航行。

hone /həʊn/ *v.* 磨炼；训练；把……磨快

例：Using the bulleted methods above will definitely help hone your focus.

使用以上项目符号方法一定能够帮你训练专注力。

近：whet

render /ˈrendə(r)/ *v.* 使成为，使处于某种状态；给予，提供

例：It contained so many errors as to render it worthless.

太多的错误使之变得毫无价值。

dimensional /daɪˈmenʃənl/ *adj.* 维度的

例：Architecture is a three-dimensional form.

建筑设计是三维形式的。

jar /dʒɑː(r)/ *v.* 震动；刺激；不相配

搭：jar with 与……不一致

例：Their opinions jar with ours.

他们的意见和我们不一致。

well-worn 无新意的；用旧的

例：Most British visitors beat a well-worn path to the same tourist areas of the US.

大多数英国游客沿着一条老路线参观相同的美国旅游景点。

enthrall /ɪnˈθrɔːl/ *v.* 迷住，使着迷

例：The sculptures enthrall tourists with their ingenious construction.

这些雕塑以其精妙的构造使很多游客着迷。

近：obsess

mediocre /ˌmiːdiˈəʊkə(r)/ *adj.* 平庸的

例：You should see yourself as a mediocre person.

你应该把自己看作是一个平庸的人。

近：mundane

majestic /məˈdʒestɪk/ *adj.* 雄伟的，壮丽的

例：The setting, at the foot of the Alps, is majestic.

阿尔卑斯山脚的风景雄伟壮丽。

近：magnificent

4.

➤ 试题详解

题号	出题题型	答案	解析
(1)	细节理解	B	题目：第一段中可以得知关于电影的什么信息？ A 电影的片名并不是最合适的。 **B 这部电影代表加龙首次尝试拍摄纪录片。** C 这部电影是加龙和卡兹尼尔森的全新合作。 D 这部电影的题材没有被其他导演拍摄过。 根据题目要求定位至第一段。第一段的第四句提到"For this documentary film, British director Sarah Gavron, who had previously specialized only in fictional pieces...（在这部纪录片中，此前只专注于拍摄虚构作品的英国导演莎拉·加龙……）"，可知，加龙之前专攻虚构作品的拍摄，而这部电影是对真实场景的记录，由此可知，加龙第一次尝试拍摄这类电影，所以B选项正确。其余三个选项的内容均未在第一段中体现，可排除。
(2)	细节理解	A	题目：在第二段中，通过关注小镇上的居民，作者认为这部电影_____ **A 让我们有了更多的思考。** B 忽视了美丽的景色。 C 展示了旅游业不那么吸引人的一面。 D 反映了不同代人之间的矛盾。 根据题目要求定位至第二段。第二段第三句提到"This isn't a documentary occupied by the high drama, but there're plenty of things for thought."即"这不是一部充满戏剧性的纪录片，但有很多值得思考的东西。"，所以A选项正确。 本段首句提到"The landscapes are fascinating but have harsh climate, and although there are astonishing shots of the icy wilderness, the film isn't indulged in this environment.（这里的景色迷人，但气候恶劣。尽

绕表

题号	出题题型	答案	解析
			管有令人惊叹的冰雪荒野镜头，但影片并没有只展示这种环境。）"，可以得知电影中出现了关于景色的镜头，所以B选项错误。C选项的内容在文中没有体现，可排除。本段第二句提到了一位年轻人马丁和一位老人比利，但并未涉及二者间的矛盾，所以D选项错误。
(3)	细节理解	B	**题目：** 第三段中，提到了莎拉·加龙在拍摄过程中的哪项经历？ A 她不确定翻译是否可靠。 **B 她并没有意识到自己拍摄的作品的影响力。** C 她不确定项目能否这么快就完成。 D 她为不能直接与当地人对话而沮丧。 根据题目要求定位至第三段，本段第一句提到 "...and Gavron admits she had no idea of the consequence of the story in her camera until the material was translated. （……加龙承认，直到素材被翻译出来，她才知道镜头里的故事会有什么结果。）"，可知加龙当时没有意识到自己的作品会产生怎样的影响，所以B选项正确。其余三个选项的内容均未在第三段提及，可排除。
(4)	细节理解	C	**题目：** 加龙发现在拍摄期间把孩子带到尼亚科纳特有好处，因为_____ A 能够促使更多的游客来此游玩。 B 她能够拍摄居民与孩子的互动。 **C 这意味着当地居民对她更热情。** D 这甚至鼓励了最害羞的居民出镜。 根据题目内容，首先在文章中寻找与"孩子"相关的内容。在第四段第二句 "She felt this was due to the fact that she was often accompanied by her two young children." 中，出现与孩子相关的内容。本句想要表达她觉得这是因为经常有两个年幼的孩子陪着她，可知带孩子是某事的原因，其之前的句子 "Although being so isolated from the outside world, the town's residents were surprisingly welcoming to Gavron and her cameras. （尽管与外界隔绝，小镇上的居民却出人意料地欢迎加龙和她的相机。）"，说明带孩子让当地人更热情，所以C选项正确。A和B两项均未在原文中提及，可排除。根据本段最后一句可知，有些居民很害羞，还是选择不出镜，所以D选项错误。
(5)	细节理解	C	**题目：** 根据最后一段，加龙的电影成功地传递了什么？ A 她抵触在大城市生活 B 她对创新性电影的热情 **C 她对尼亚科纳特人的敬意** D 她担心居住在偏远地区的人们 根据题目要求定位至最后一段。最后一段第二句提到 "Gavron is full of admiration for the community, which comes across clearly in her work... （加龙对这个群体充满了钦佩，这在她的作品中表现得很明显……）"，所以C选项正确。其余选项均未在最后一段中提及，可排除。

> 全文翻译

电影评论：《世界尽头的村庄》，莎拉·加龙执导

尼亚科纳特是格陵兰岛西北部的一个小型村落。这里有36位居民，只能乘船（当海面没有结冰时）和直升机（当天气允许时）前往。它一年中大部分时间都被雪覆盖，是名副其实的"世界尽头的村庄"。为了这部纪录片，此前只专注于拍摄虚构作品的英国导演莎拉·加龙和她的丈夫——丹麦摄影师大卫·卡兹尼尔森在这个与世隔绝的村庄里生活了一年。他们创造了一个与逆境抗争的鼓舞人心的群体形象。

这里的景色迷人，但气候恶劣。尽管有令人惊叹的冰雪荒野镜头，但影片并没有只展示这种环境。然而，人们对这里的居民留下了深刻的印象：马丁是镇上唯一渴望离开的青年；还有最年长的居民比利，他描述了海豹脂肪被用来照明的时代。这不是一部充满戏剧性的纪录片，但有很多值得思考的东西。例如，看到当地人如何对待乘坐游轮在中途停留的游客，这特别迷人，揭示了我们大多数人从未见过的旅游业的一面。

加龙和卡兹尼尔森花了三年时间拍摄这部电影——整个项目从头到尾花了四年时间——加龙承认，直到素材被翻译出来，她才知道镜头里的故事会有什么结果。镇上只有一个人会说英语，所以加龙在拍摄时凭直觉行事。她参加过一次城镇会议，但在会议期间，她不知道在讨论什么——后来她发现，几乎整个城镇的人都赖以为生的养鱼场已经关闭了。在电影中，市长卢克努力让工厂以合作社的形式重新开业。

尽管与外界隔绝，小镇上的居民却出人意料地欢迎加龙和她的相机。她觉得这是因为经常有两个年幼的孩子陪着她。她还认为，因为他们接待的游客很少，所以每个人都愿意接受被镜头记录的想法，尽管显然有一些人因为害羞而选择不这样做。

《世界尽头的村庄》可以与其他纪录片相媲美，虽然它的内容和风格并不具有开创性，但它让我们得以了解我们原本不知道的生活。加龙对这个群体充满了钦佩，这在她的作品中表现得很明显："你可以去某个地方，表面上看起来如此陌生和遥远，但你可以找到联系。来自城市的我谦虚地提醒自己自然的力量。我被他们开始改变命运的能量和决心所感动，也被他们认为自己能够改变的事实所感动。很多时候，我们感到无能为力，而他们却没有采取那种态度。这很有启发性"，她说。

> 词汇笔记

miniature /ˈmɪnɪtʃə(r)/ *adj.* 微型的，小型的

n. 微缩模型

例：Paris is France in miniature.

巴黎是法国的缩影。

近：tiny

specialize /ˈspeʃəlaɪz/ *v.* 专门从事（或从事），专攻

例：Certain publishers specialize in specific markets.

某些出版商擅长于特定的市场。

isolated /ˈaɪsəleɪtɪd/ *adj.* 偏僻的；与世隔绝的

例：Some patients may become very isolated and depressed.

有些病人可能变得非常孤独和抑郁。

近：remote

adversity /ədˈvɜːsəti/ *n.* 逆境，厄运

例：They had to struggle against all kinds of adversity.

他们不得不同与各种困境做斗争。

近：plight

harsh /hɑːʃ/ *adj.* （环境）恶劣的；残酷的，严厉的

例：He said many harsh and unkind things about his opponents.

他说了许多关于他对手的严厉且残酷的话。

近：tough

indulge /ɪnˈdʌldʒ/ *v.* 沉湎，沉溺；纵容

搭：indulge in 沉湎于，沉溺于

例：Don't let yourself indulge in vain wishes.

不要让自己沉溺于空虚的希望中。

opt /ɒpt/ *v.* 选择

搭：opt to do sth. 选择做某事

例：Depending on your circumstances, you can opt for a method.

根据自己的情况，你可以选择一种方法。

派：option *n.* 选择，选择权

pioneering /ˌpaɪəˈnɪərɪŋ/ *adj.* 首创的，先驱的

例：However, although he takes credit for discovering it, his achievement was not pioneering.

然而，他因这个发现而得到好评，但他的成就并非首创。

近：original

alien /ˈeɪliən/ *adj.* 陌生的；外国的，异域的

搭：alien to 不相容，相抵触

例：The idea is alien to our religion.

这种思想与我们的宗教不相容。

enlightening /ɪnˈlaɪtnɪŋ/ *adj.* 启迪的，使人获得启发的

例：Travel for business or pleasure will be enlightening.

无论是商务旅行还是休闲旅行都将为你带来灵感。

近：illuminating

Day 16 考前冲刺篇

全真模拟题一

1. 【答案】A

   【材料类型】通知

   【选项翻译】

   A 网上支付票款后，从代售点取票。

   B 在网站上查询票价信息。

   C 如果你打算购票，要尽快通知代售点。

   【解析】由本通知的正文内容 "Buy these on the cinema website, and then collect them from the agency.（在电影院网站上购票，然后在代售点取票。）" 可知A选项说法与此相符，所以A选项正确。

   通知中并未涉及票价的相关信息，所以B选项错误。通知中也没有说明购票需要通知代售点，所以C选项错误。

2. 【答案】B

   【材料类型】信件

   【选项翻译】

   A 山姆如果想去看展览，应该告诉吉姆。

   B 吉姆已经安排好了去展览的车。

   C 山姆一定会在展览上见到吉姆。

   【解析】根据信件的第三句 "Danny will pick us up from there.（丹尼会在那里接我们。）"，可知B选项说法与此相符，所以B选项正确。

   信件中第二句说到 "If you fancy going, come to my flat at 2:30.（如果你想去，两点半到我的公寓来）"，这说明山姆如果想去看展览，直接去吉姆家即可，无须告知，所以A选项错误。这封信件的目的是询问山姆是否去看展览，山姆是否会去看展览还不能确定，所以C选项错误。

3. 【答案】B

【出题类型】固定搭配

【解析】A选项意为"授予；给予"；B选项意为"支付；缴纳"；C选项意为"放置；设置"；D选项意为"使用；利用"。其中B选项可以和句中的"attention"和"to"构成固定搭配"pay attention to"，意为"关注"，其他选项均无法进行搭配，所以B选项正确。句意为"要在纠正语法上特别注意"。

4.

➤ 试题详解

（1）【参考答案】yourself

【出题类型】固定搭配

【解析】本句的前一句说到能同时完成多项任务，再结合本句中"pride"和"on"，可知本句表达为此自豪的含义。"pride oneself on"为固定搭配，意为"引以为傲，感到自豪"，符合语境，所以本题应填"yourself"。本句意为"在家里，你是否为自己同时处理多项任务的能力而感到自豪"。

（2）【参考答案】If

【出题类型】内容理解

【解析】本题考查对文章内容的理解。观察本句可知，逗号前为本句的条件，且空格位于句首，单词的首字母要大写，所以本题应填"If"，表示条件关系。本句意为"如果是的话，你应该更详细地看看如何处理你的待办事项清单"。

（3）【参考答案】much

【出题类型】内容理解

【解析】本题考查对文章内容的理解。本句的前一句说到学生注意力不集中的问题，本句是将其与针对听众的研究进行比较，目的在于说明听众的表现也不尽如人意，所以本题应填"much"，修饰后面的"better"。本句意为"带着能上网的电子设备的听众在讲座上的表现也没好到哪去"。

（4）【参考答案】no

【出题类型】内容理解

【解析】本题考查对文章内容的理解，根据本句内容可知，听众也会像学生那样分心，填入的内容应体现出听众关注的内容与讲座主题不相干的含义，所以本题应填"no"。本句意为"因为他们在讲座中点击的网页有58%与讲座的主题无关"。

（5）【参考答案】how

【出题类型】语法基础

【解析】本题所在句存在感叹句结构，旨在说明一心多用的危险性，感叹句的基本结构为"How+形容词（副词）+主语+谓语"，符合本句中的结构，所以本题应填"how"。本句意为"而且切菜时一心多用多么危险啊！这几乎是显而易见的"。

➤ 全文翻译

多面手

在家里，你是那种一边煲汤一边拖地的人吗？在家里，你是否为自己同时处理多项任务的能力而感到自豪？如果是的话，你应该更详细地看看如何处理你的待办事项清单。

问题在于，大多数人认为他们能同时处理多项任务，而实际上他们只是让自己分心。在电脑上完成作业的学生平均每12分钟就会走神一次。带着能上网的电子设备的听众在讲座上的表现也没好到哪去，因为他们在讲座中点击的网页有58%与讲座的主题无关。

研究还表明，把注意力集中在多件事情上会使你的智商降低8个百分点，而且切菜时一心多用多么危险啊！这几乎是显而易见的。

➤ 词汇笔记

mop /mɒp/ *v.* 用拖把拖；擦拭

n. 拖把

例：I mop the kitchen floor twice a week.

我每周拖两次厨房的地板。

simultaneously /ˌsɪmlˈteɪniəsli/ *adv.* 同时地

例：Simultaneously, the liberal arts become more important than ever.

与此同时，文科变得比以往任何时候都更重要。

lie in 存在于

例：The biggest problem lies in the labour market.

最大的问题就是劳动力市场。

distract /dɪˈstrækt/ *v.* 使分心，使转移注意力

搭：distract from 转移，使从……分心

例：The noise out of window makes me distract from my reading.

窗外的喧闹声使我不能专心看书。

wander /ˈwɒndə(r)/ *v.* 漫游；走神；偏离

例：I jumped to my feet so my thoughts wouldn't start to wander.

我猛地站了起来，这样我就不会走神了。

hazardous /ˈhæzədəs/ *adj.* 危险的；有危害的

例：German law forbids the dumping of hazardous waste on German soil.

德国法律禁止在德国国土上倾倒危险废弃物。

近：dangerous

go without saying 不用说；显而易见

例：This should go without saying, but make sure you have a secure password.

这一点是不用说的，但要确保你有一个安全的密码。

5.

➢ **试题详解**

题号	出题类型	答案	解析
(1)	细节理解	C	**题目：根据第一段，哪项关于茶的事实是正确的？** A 如今，茶在中国和在欧洲一样受欢迎。 B 茶曾是世界上需求量最大的产品。 **C 茶在中国依然有很多用途。** D 茶的饮用有着严格的规定。 根据题干可直接定位至第一段，本段最后一句说到 "In addition to being a drink, Chinese tea is used in herbal medicine and in cooking.（除做饮品外，中国茶还用于草药和烹饪。）"，可知茶的用途广泛，这与C选项说法相符，所以C选项正确。 本段第二句提到 "Tea culture in China diverges from that of Europe, Britain or Japan in such things as preparation methods, tasting methods and the occasions for which it is consumed.（中国的茶文化与欧洲、英国或日本在制作方法、品尝方法和饮用场合等方面有所不同。）"，可知这里只说明了不同国家茶文化的不同，并未说明受欢迎程度，所以A选项错误。B选项和D选项的内容均未在本段提及，可排除。
(2)	细节理解	D	**题目：关于茶和社会的哪项说法正确？** A 饮茶的习惯抹去了社会等级制度。 B 如今，茶只会在重要场合出现。 C 下层阶级的人现在可以自担风险被人奉茶。 **D 传统的社会习俗已经发生了一些变化。**

题号	出题类型	答案	解析
(2)	细节理解	D	根据题干中的"茶和社会"，可定位至第二段，本段第二句和第三句提到"Formerly, lower class people would have served tea to higher-class people. At present, as Chinese society becomes more liberal, parents may pour a cup of tea for their children, or a boss may even pour tea for subordinates at restaurants.（以前，下层阶级的人会给上层阶级的人沏茶。目前，随着中国社会变得更加自由，父母可能会给他们的孩子倒一杯茶，老板甚至可能会在餐馆给下属倒茶。）"，由此可知饮茶时的行为发生了变化，也反映出了社会风俗的变化，所以D选项正确。A选项说法过于绝对，风俗的变化并不能说明社会等级的消失，所以A选项错误。B选项和C选项的内容均未在文中提及，可排除。
(3)	细节理解	C	题目：在婚姻中，新郎和新娘给父母倒茶_____ A 是屈服的象征。 B 是尊敬的象征。 **C 是感激的象征。** D 是好运的象征。 根据题干中的"marriage"，可定位至第三段，本段第一句提到"In the traditional Chinese marriage ceremony, both the bride and groom kneel in front of their parents and serve them tea as if they were saying 'Thank you for bringing us up. We owe it all to you'.（在传统的中国婚礼仪式上，新娘和新郎都跪在他们的父母面前，给他们奉茶，好像在说：'谢谢你们把我们养大。这都是你们的功劳。'）"，可知给父母倒茶表示的是对父母养育之恩的感激，所以C选项正确。 本段第二句说到"The parents will usually drink a small portion of the tea and then give the couple a red envelope, which represents good luck.（父母通常会喝一点茶，然后给新人一个红包，代表好运。）"，可知父母饮茶、给红包是好运的象征，不是倒茶，所以D选项错误。A选项和B选项内容均未在文中提及，可排除。
(4)	细节理解	B	题目：根据第三段，一些家庭成员互相不认识的事实_____。 A 仍是每个中国婚姻的特征。 **B 在过去尤为常见。** C 是婚礼中不喝茶的借口。 D 过去发生在两个或更多的妻子中。 根据题干可直接定位至第三段，本段第三句和第四句提到"As Chinese families can be rather extended, it is entirely possible during a courtship to not have been introduced to someone. This was especially true in older generations where the family leader may have had more than one wife and not all family members got along well.（由于中国的

题号	出题类型	答案	解析
（4）	细节理解	B	家庭是相当庞大的，在求爱期间完全有可能没有被介绍给某人。这在老一辈中尤为真实，家主可能有多个妻子，并不是所有的家庭成员都相处得很好。）"，可知这种情况在过去较为常见，所以B选项正确。 由上述定位句可知，有两个及以上配偶且成员关系不好的家庭会出现成员互相不认识的情况，所以D选项错误。A选项和C选项的内容均未在文中提及，可排除。
（5）	细节理解	D	题目：为什么皇帝的仆人用手指敲桌子？ A 表达敬意。 B 表达对王朝的忠诚。 C 隐藏自己的身份。 **D 表达对皇帝的感谢。** 根据关键词"servant"可定位至最后一段。本段第六句和第七句提到"To that servant it was a huge glory to have the emperor pour him a cup of tea. As a reflex he wanted to kneel and express his thanks, but he couldn't do that since it would reveal the emperor's identity so he bent his fingers on the table and knocked to express his respect to the emperor.（对那个仆人来说，皇帝为他倒一杯茶是一种莫大的荣耀。作为一种条件反射，他想跪下来表示感谢，但他不能这样做，因为这会暴露皇帝的身份，所以他把手指弯曲在桌子上，敲了敲以示对皇帝的尊敬。）"，可知仆人用手指敲桌子是为了表示感谢，所以D选项正确。 上述定位句也表明，仆人这样做是为了隐藏皇上的身份，而并非自己的身份，所以C选项错误。A选项和B选项的内容均未在文中提及，可排除。
（6）	主旨大意	A	题目：这篇文章最合适的副标题是_____ **A 起源和意义。** B 家庭成员如何交往。 C 茶和权力的关系。 D 进行庆祝的原因。 这一问题需要结合整篇文章的内容进行分析。文章分别介绍了茶文化的发展、在一些场合的用途以及饮茶时的礼仪，所以A选项最能概括文章的内容，所以A选项正确。 B选项和D选项明显与本文的内容不符，可排除。C选项的内容虽然在文中有所提及，但不能对整篇文章进行概括，所以也可排除。

➢ 全文翻译

中国茶文化

在古代中国，饮茶很受欢迎，因为茶被认为是七种日常生活必需品之一，其他的是柴、米、油、盐、酱油和醋。中国的茶文化与欧洲、英国或日本在制作方法、品尝方法和饮用场合等方面有所不同。即使是现在，在中国休闲和正式的场合，人们也经常饮茶。除做饮品外，中国茶还用于草药和烹饪。

制茶和饮茶有几种特殊情况。以前，下层阶级的人会给上层阶级的人沏茶。目前，随着中国社会变得更加自由，父母可能会给他们的孩子倒一杯茶，老板甚至可能会在餐馆给下属倒茶。在严肃的场合，下层阶级的人不应指望上层阶级的人为他或她奉茶。

在传统的中国婚礼仪式上，新娘和新郎都跪在他们的父母面前，给他们奉茶，好像在说："谢谢你们把我们养大。这都是你们的功劳。"父母通常会喝一点茶，然后给新人一个红包，代表好运。婚礼期间的茶道也是婚礼双方与对方家庭成员见面的一种方式。由于中国的家庭是相当庞大的，在求爱期间完全有可能没有被介绍给某人。这在老一辈中尤为真实，家主可能有多个妻子，并不是所有的家庭成员都相处得好。因此，在茶道中，新婚夫妇会向所有家庭成员奉茶，并称呼他们的官方头衔。

当一个人的杯子倒满后，他可能会用弯曲的食指和中指敲打桌子，以感谢上茶的人。这个习俗起源于清朝。乾隆皇帝有时会乔装在全国各地旅行。仆人们被告知不要暴露他的身份。一天，在一家餐馆里，皇帝给自己倒了一杯茶后，又给仆人倒了一杯。对那个仆人来说，皇帝为他倒一杯茶是一种莫大的荣耀。作为一种条件反射，他想跪下来表示感谢，但他不能这样做，因为这会暴露皇帝的身份，所以他把手指弯曲在桌子上，敲了敲以示对皇帝的尊敬。

➢ 词汇笔记

diverge /daɪˈvɜːdʒ/ *v.* 相异；出现分歧；分开

搭：diverge from 与……相异；背离

例：Opinions diverge in a series of articles around this issue.

围绕这个问题，一系列文章中出现了不同的观点。

派：divergent *adj.* 不同的；分歧的；发散的

divergence *n.* 差异；不同

近：differ

herbal /ˈhɜːbl/ *adj.* 草药的

搭：herbal medicine 草药

例：On the other hand, they can try herbal teas to relax.

另一方面，他们可以尝试让人放松的草本茶。

subordinate /sə'bɔːdɪnət/ *n.* 下级；从属

　　　　　　　　　v. 使从属于；使处于次要地位；使隶属；使服从

　　　　　　　　　adj. 从属的；下级的；次要的

搭：be subordinate to　从属于……

例：Sixty of his subordinate officers followed his example.

　　他的60个下级官员都以他为榜样。

近：affiliate

bride /braɪd/ *n.* 新娘

例：That day, I became your bride.

　　那天，我成了你的新娘。

groom /gruːm/ *n.* 新郎；马夫

　　　　　　v.（给动物）刷毛

例：The groom enters the church from a side door.

　　新郎要从侧门进入教堂。

kneel /niːl/ *v.* 跪下

例：At church people kneel when they pray.

　　人们在教堂祈祷时要下跪。

courtship /'kɔːtʃɪp/ *n.* 求婚；求爱；追求

例：After a short courtship, she accepted his proposal.

　　在短暂追求之后，她接受了他的求婚。

disguise /dɪs'gaɪz/ *v.* 伪装；假扮

　　　　　　　　n. 伪装

例：She wore glasses and a wig as a disguise.

　　她戴着眼镜和假发作为伪装。

reflex /'riːfleks/ *n.* 本能反应；反射；反映物

例：Almost as a reflex action, I grab my pen as the phone rings.

　　几乎是一种下意识的动作，电话铃一响，我就抓起笔。

6.【答案】C

【出题类型】语法基础

【解析】本题考查情态动词表示推测的用法，首先空格前的 "ought" 与 "to" 搭配，表示 "应该"，所以排除A选项和D选项。句中的 "before the test" 表明本句是对过去事件的评价。情态动词+have+过去分词的结构，意为"本来"，表示对过去发生事情的评价，所以C选项正确。句意为"考试前，她本来有更多的时间复习"。

7. 【答案】C

【材料类型】通知

【选项翻译】

A 在晚间进行的会议中，组委会决定取消音乐会。

B 举办音乐会的地点发生了变化。

C 预售的票最终可能失效。

【解析】通知的最后一句提到"All pre-sold tickets will still be valid until further notice.（所有预售票在下次通知前依然有效。）"，这说明下一次通知后，预售票可能失效，所以C选项正确。

通知的第二句提到"An eleventh-hour decision of the Organizing Committee deemed appropriate to put off the concert to a future date.（组委会在最后一刻做出决定，认为应该将音乐会推迟到以后举行。）"，可知音乐会的举办时间发生了变化，并不是举办地点变化，所以B选项错误。通知中并未说明会议在什么时间举办，所以A选项错误。

8. 【答案】B

【材料类型】通知

【选项翻译】

A 彼得教授告诉他的学生可以在网上上课。

B 彼得教授将给学生提供一些课上使用的资料。

C 彼得教授这学期不教任何课程。

【解析】通知的第二句提到"Meanwhile, I can share with you some of the slides I used last year, so that you can get an insight into the essence of my course.（同时，我可以给你们分享一些我去年用过的幻灯片，这样你们能领悟我课程的要义）"，这与B选项的说法相符，所以B选项正确。

通知中并未提到可以在网上上课，所以A选项错误。通知中也未说明彼得教授这学期是否需要教授课程，所以C选项错误。

9.

➤ 试题详解

（1）【答案】D

【出题类型】内容理解

【解析】A选项表示"过去不经常……"；B选项意为"经常"；C选项是use的过去式；D选项意为"过去常常……"。本句中列出了每餐的时间，可知本句想表达的是以前每一餐的时间较为固定，所以D选项正确。本句意为"在过去，用餐时间常常比较固定，早餐在上午8点，午餐在下午12点，晚餐在下午6点"。

（2）【答案】C

【出题类型】内容理解

【解析】A选项意为"尽管"；B选项意为"以防，唯恐"；C选项意为"然而"；D选项意为"因此"。第一段最后一句中说到了用餐时间固定，而本句说的是就餐的时间变得多样，可知前后存在转折关系，所以C选项正确。本句意为"然而，现在我们经常吃零食，而且用餐时间变得更多样"。

（3）【答案】B

【出题类型】语法基础

【解析】本题的四个选项为contain的各种形式，观察本句可知，句中已经有谓语且句中无连词，所以空格处的内容不能充当谓语，所以排除A选项和C选项。此空格位于dishes之后，做后置定语，所以B选项正确。本句意为"人们习惯吃的菜肴包含肉和两种蔬菜"。

（4）【答案】B

【出题类型】语法基础

【解析】根据前一句可知，本句应是对未来情况的设想，所以应该用一般将来时，所以B选项正确。本句意为"或者我们将遵循另一种模式"。

（5）【答案】C

【出题类型】固定搭配

【解析】观察本句可知，空格处内容要能与句中的"out"搭配，A选项与"out"搭配意为"结果是；熄灭"；B选项与"out"搭配意为"安排；展开"；C选项与"out"搭配意为"找出，查明"；D选项与"out"搭配意为"爆发"。前一句提出了问题，所以本句表达的是弄清楚这个问题，所以C选项正确。本句意为"我等不及要查清楚这个问题了"。

➤ **全文翻译**

现在西方国家的人吃什么？这和我们的长辈有什么不同？在过去，用餐时间常常比较固定，早餐在上午8点，午餐在下午12点，晚餐在下午6点。

然而，现在我们经常吃零食，而且用餐时间变得更多样。人们习惯吃的菜肴包含肉和两种蔬菜，炸鸡和汉堡是现在常见的周中晚餐。现成的饭菜和外出就餐代替了家常菜。但未来会是什么样子？是更多地吃快餐，而不是自己烹饪？或者我们将遵循另一种模式，回到吃自己种植的食物的时代？我等不及要查清楚这个问题了！

➤ 词汇笔记

eldership /ˈeldəʃɪp/ *n.* 长辈，前辈

例：Please speak mannerly with the eldership.

跟长辈讲话请有礼貌。

stable /ˈsteɪbl/ *adj.* 稳定的；牢固的；沉稳的

例：Conditions were set fair for stable economic development.

形势适合经济稳定发展。

派：stability *n.* 稳定性；坚定

近：steady

variable /ˈveəriəbl/ *adj.* 易变的，多变的

例：The temperature remained constant while pressure was variable in the experiment.

做这实验时温度保持不变，但压力可变。

近：volatile

accustomed /əˈkʌstəmd/ *adj.* 习惯的，适应的

搭：be accustomed to 习惯于

例：You have to train hard to be accustomed to the arrangements.

你要努力训练以适应安排。

feed on 以……为食；以……为能源

例：Insects feed on plants.

昆虫吃植物。

substitute /ˈsʌbstɪtjuːt/ *v.* 用……替代

n. 替代物

搭：substitute for 替代

例：The course teaches you the theory, but there's no substitute for practical experience.

这门课教你理论，但没有任何东西能代替实践经验。

近：replace

全真模拟题二

1. 【答案】C

【材料类型】通知

【选项翻译】

A 维修工在16点前提供服务。

B 如果你计划见修理工，16点后给维修点打电话。

C 如果你想让修理工上门解决问题，在16点前打电话。

【解析】本则通知意为"如果想让修理工上门服务，请在16点前给维修点打电话"，C选项的说法与此相符，所以C选项正确。

通知中的时间"16点前"是打电话的时间，并不是服务截止的时间，且通知中说的是"上门服务"，所以A选项错误。B选项中的时间"16点后"显然与通知中不符，所以B选项错误。

2. 【答案】B

【材料类型】邮件

【题目翻译】这封邮件的目的是

【选项翻译】

A 询问关于不同目的地的信息。

B 提供关于度假日期的信息。

C 询问在冰岛度假的经历。

【解析】 根据邮件正文第二句"The quota is completely reserved until the last day of April, but it's available after that.（截至4月30日的名额已全部预订，但之后还有剩余名额。）"，可知发送这封邮件的目的是回复对方询问某一日期是否有余票，与时间相关，所以B选项正确。

邮件中并未出现不同的目的地，所以A选项错误。邮件中也并未提及度假的经历，所以C选项错误。

3. 【答案】D

【出题类型】词义辨析

【解析】A选项意为"明确的；最终的"；B选项意为"修改的，改良的"；C选项意为"经常发生的；循环的"；D选项意为"精炼的；文雅的"。选项均为形容词，且修饰句中的"young gentleman"，所以D选项正确。句意为"我的祖父经常说我是个优雅的年轻绅士"。

4.【答案】B

【出题类型】固定搭配

【解析】结合选项和空格前出现的"turned"，可知本题考查 turn 组成的固定搭配。A 选项与 turn 搭配意为"结果是；关掉"；B 选项与 turn 搭配意为"调小；拒绝"；C 选项与 turn 搭配意为"上交，交还"；D 选项与 turn 搭配意为"往回走"。B 选项最符合语境，所以 B 选项正确。本句意为"我申请了一个有趣的俱乐部，但被拒绝了"。

5.

➢ 试题详解

（1）【参考答案】been

【出题类型】语法基础

【解析】本题考查语法基础知识。观察句子可知，空格前出现 haven't，这是现在完成时的标志，因此空格处应填入动词过去分词形式，固定搭配 be fond of 表示"喜欢"，be 的过去分词形式为 been，所以本题应填"been"，句意为"我并不总是喜欢看有字幕的电影"。

（2）【参考答案】what

【出题类型】内容理解

【解析】本题考查对文章内容的理解，本句话要表达"一想到要一边看电影一边读角色说的话，我就感到不舒服"，空格处表达"角色说了什么"，所以填入的内容应表示"什么"，所以本题应填"what"。本句意为"当我还小的时候，一想到要一边看电影一边读角色说的话，我就感到不舒服"。

（3）【参考答案】then

【出题类型】固定搭配

【解析】本题考查固定搭配。since then 是固定搭配，意为"从那以后，自从那时起"，一般用于现在完成时，所以本题应填"then"。本句意为"从那时起，我经常购买包含原始音频和字幕的 DVD"。

（4）【参考答案】mine

【出题类型】内容理解

【解析】本题考查对文章内容的理解，本句话要表达"我的一个朋友邀请我去他家看一部有字幕的荷兰电影"，名词+of+名词性物主代词表示"……的……"，空格处应填入第一人称的名词性物主代词，所以本题应填"mine"。本句意为"我的一个朋友邀请我去他家看一部有字幕的荷兰电影"。

（5）【参考答案】forward

【出题类型】固定搭配

【解析】本题考查固定搭配。look forward to 是固定搭配，意为"期待"，所以本题应填"forward"。本句意为"我真的很期待，因为我甚至不知道荷兰语听起来是什么样"。

➤ 全文翻译

带字幕的电影

我并不总是喜欢看有字幕的电影。当我还小的时候，一想到要一边看电影一边读角色说的话，我就感到不舒服。当我在大学开始学习法语时，一切都变了。我意识到，多亏了字幕，我可以欣赏法语电影，同时，我可以提高我的语言技能。从那时起，我经常购买包含原始音频和字幕的DVD。我的一个朋友邀请我去他家看一部有字幕的荷兰电影。我真的很期待，因为我甚至不知道荷兰语听起来是什么样。

➤ 词汇笔记

subtitle /ˈsʌbtaɪtl/ *n.* 字幕；副标题

　　　　　　　v. 为（电影）提供字幕

例：The dialogue is in Spanish, with English subtitles.

　　这段对话是西班牙语，配有英语字幕。

character /ˈkærəktə(r)/ *n.* 性格；品质；人物，角色

　　　　　　　　v. 使具有特征

例：He reveals his true character to very few people.

　　他很少向人显露过他的真实性格。

audio /ˈɔːdiəʊ/ *n.* 声音；音频

　　　　　　adj. 声音的；音频的

例：This digital audio player supports multiple formats.

　　这台数字音频播放器支持多种格式。

6.

➤ 试题详解

题号	出题类型	答案	解析
（1）	细节理解	A	题目：新闻为什么报道了爱德华学校？ **A** 这所学校的学生可能被迫去其他学校学习。 B 到了学校进行周年庆的时候了。 C 学校努力为运营成本筹集更多资金。 D 学校正在争取教育部门的批准。

续表

题号	出题类型	答案	解析
（1）	细节理解	A	由第一段中的 "which has recently been in the media"，即最近媒体对其进行了报道，可将答案定位至第一段。本段最后一句说到 "...the Department of Education is considering removing its financial support and moving all deaf education to the regular 'hearing' school system. （……教育部门正在考虑取消对聋人学校的财政支持，将所有的聋人教育转移到正常的"听力"学校系统。）"，这表明教育部门意在将聋人学校与普通学校合并，失聪儿童也要去普通学校学习，所以A选项正确。其余选项均未在文中提及，可排除。
（2）	观点态度	C	**题目：霍斯顿对唇读有什么看法？** A 聋人学校应该只教授唇读。 B 学习唇读的失聪儿童处在劣势中。 **C 唇读比手语更有用处。** D 唇读应该与手语一起使用。 根据题干中的 "Houstons" 可将答案定位至第二段。本段第三句提到 "Some, such as the Houstons, have taken this a step further: they are preventing their child from learning sign language. （有些人，比如霍斯顿夫妇，采取了进一步行动：他们阻止孩子学习手语。）"，这说明霍斯顿认为唇读比手语更有用，所以C选项正确。其余选项内容均未在文中提及，可排除。
（3）	细节理解	B	**题目：唐纳德·戴维斯认为失聪儿童在普通学校最大的挑战是什么？** A 对于大部分失聪学生来说，唇读很难。 **B 唇读有很多困难，是不可行的。** C 失聪儿童与普通学生交往时存在障碍。 D 失聪儿童比其他学生需要更多的语言输入。 由第三段第二句 "'Although lip reading is certainly a tough skill to learn, that is not the main problem here.' says Edward Principal Donald Davis. （"虽然唇读的确是一项很难学的技能，但这不是主要问题，"爱德华学校校长唐纳德·戴维斯说。）"，可将答案定位到第三段。并且根据本句可将A选项排除。选项及原文中虽然都提及了唇读是项比较难学的技能，但原文中又说到"这不是最大的问题"。其后的内容作者列举了唇读在使用中的多种问题，包括语言输入不足，使用场景受限等。第三段最后一句，作者指出 "In all these situations, a lip-reader would find communication difficult."（在这些情景下，使用唇读的人会发现交流困难。），作者罗列的种种问题是对自己观点的佐证，作者的观点是对以上情况的汇总，而不是所列举的某一种情况，所以B选项正确。 A选项内容未在唐纳德·戴维斯的看法中体现，可排除。C选项和D选项为作者列举的问题中的一个，带有片面性，并不是作者真正想要表达的观点，所以C选项和D选项错误。

续表

题号	出题类型	答案	解析
(4)	主旨大意	D	题目：第四段的主旨是什么？ A 相较于学业，聋人学校更注重社会交往。 B 失聪学生的学业成绩在主流学校中表现不佳。 C 聋人学校能在学业上给学生提供更多机会。 **D 失聪学生的社会需求在聋人学校能更好地得到满足。** 由题干可知，本题的设问针对的是第四段。通读第四段可知，第四段主要陈述了两个事实。一是"Fewer deaf children in mainstream schools are admitted to university than their hearing classmates, and many report feeling neglected in school."（在主流学校中，失聪儿童被大学录取的比例要少于他们的健全同学，许多失聪儿童感觉自己在学校被忽视了。）"。二是"there is the opportunity to use complex communication to develop deep friendships, something that deaf children often lack in mainstream schools.（这里有机会利用复杂的沟通来发展深厚的友谊，这是失聪儿童在主流学校经常缺乏的。）"。D选项可对本段内容进行概括，所以D选项正确。 由以上内容可知，A选项和C选项的内容在第四段均未提及，可排除。B选项虽在第四段中有所提及，但本段的主旨并不在此，属于以偏概全，所以也排除。
(5)	细节理解	C	题目：对于独立的聋人教育，作者的结论是什么？ A 聋人教育阻止失聪儿童释放自己的潜能。 B 聋人教育有不足之处，但我们无需关注。 **C 聋人教育应与主流教育相结合。** D 聋人教育可能适用某些人群，但却不是失聪儿童。 第五段最后一句说到"Perhaps combining residential schooling with periods in mainstream schools could provide the best of both worlds.（也许将聋人学校与主流学校相结合可以达到两全其美的效果。）"，这与C选项说法相符，所以C选项正确。 A选项和D选项在文中并未提及，可排除。通过最后一段首句"Of course, deaf schools face a dilemma, too.（当然，聋人学校也面临着困境。）"，可知聋人教育确实遇到了困境，但作者并未说到不需要关注这些问题，相反作者在为这一问题寻找解决方案。所以B选项错误。
(6)	主旨大意	A	题目：哪个标题最适合这篇文章？ **A 谁能最大程度地满足失聪学生的需求？** B 聋人学校能满足未来的需求吗？ C 爱德华：反对聋人学校的案例 D 主流学校准备接纳失聪学生

续表

题号	出题类型	答案	解析
(6)	主旨大意	A	本题考查对全文的总结归纳能力。解答本题可从全文各段落的主要内容入手。第一段作者指出了聋人学校的处境——要与健全人学校合并。第二段和第三段，作者比较了失聪学生学习的两种语言，手语和唇读。第四段作者比较了聋人学校相较于主流学校的优势所在。最后一段作者给出结论，即将聋人教育和健全人教育相结合。所以全文紧扣失聪学生的各种需要，所以A选项正确。 本篇文章的叙述都围绕聋人学校能否满足失聪学生的需求展开，并不是聋人学校是否满足未来的需求，所以B选项错误。C选项与原文主题相悖，文章并未反对聋人学校。D选项在原文中没有体现，可排除。

➤ 全文翻译

离上课还有几分钟。乍一看，操场上的活动似乎在任何小学里都能看见，充满活力的孩子们彼此亲密互动。但如果你期望在这里听见很多噪声，那你可能要失望了。操场上只有一片寂静，孩子们用流利的手语交流，手指、手臂和面部快速地做着动作。我现在在爱德华聋人教育中心和寄宿学校，学校成立于1905年，最近媒体对其进行了报道。一大群以前和现在的学生和家长正在为学校的未来而努力，尽管取得了巨大的成功，但教育部门正在考虑取消对聋人学校的财政支持，将所有的聋人教育转移到正常的"听力"学校系统。

失聪儿童的父母自然会对确保他们的孩子能够与更广泛的群体交流感到不安。他们中的大多数人认为，如果去普通正规学校，学习唇读，也就是跟着人们说话时嘴的动作，对于他们的孩子而言是最好的解决方案。有些人，比如霍斯顿夫妇，采取了进一步行动：他们阻止孩子学习手语。"我们这样做是为未来考虑，"霍斯顿太太说，"如果我们不想让凯茜脱离正常的生活，或者限制她的选择，那么她就需要学会流利阅读，接受良好的教育，尽管她有残疾。所以，我们把她送到了我们当地的学校。"

那些为拯救爱德华学校所付出的努力与霍斯顿的目标是一致的，但这些在使用手语的环境中会更好，因为这能提供更好的语言输入。"虽然唇读的确是一项很难学的技能，但这不是主要问题，"爱德华学校校长唐纳德·戴维斯说，"如果孩子不擅长唇读，讲话者必须面对他们，孩子才能理解。在普遍的、所谓的主流学校中，许多提供语言输入的情况无法提供这种支持。在普通学校的教室里，孩子们可能会四处走动，在教室后面大声喊出答案，或者隔着操场互相喊叫。在这些情景下，使用唇读的人会发现交流困难。"

戴维斯补充道虽然幸运的儿童会有一个全职助手，但大多数儿童只能得到有限的帮助。由于缺乏支持，最终他们错过了很多东西。研究也支持这一观点。在主流学校中，失聪儿童被大学录取的比例要少于他们的健全同学，许多失聪儿童感觉自己在学校被忽视了。此外，聋人学校除了提供学术机会外，还提供了更广泛的社交机会。最重要的是，这里有机会利用复杂的沟通来发展深厚的友谊，这是失聪儿童在主流学校经常缺乏的。

当然，聋人学校也面临着困境。他们的许多毕业生在聋人学校待了多年后，都在努力适应健全人世界的要求。毫无疑问，只使用手语是有局限性的。但彻底关闭学校似乎是对这些困难的过度反应。也许将聋人学校与主流学校相结合可以达到两全其美的效果。

➢ 词汇笔记

glance /glɑːns/ *v.* 乍一看；一瞥

                     n. 乍一看；一瞥

搭：at first glance 乍一看

例：She took her eyes off the road to glance at me.

    她把目光从马路移开，瞥了我一眼。

近：glimpse

elementary /ˌelɪˈmentri/ *adj.* 基本的；初级的；简单的

搭：elementary school 小学

例：My little brother is in the elementary school.

    我弟弟在读小学。

intimately /ˈɪntɪmətli/ *adv.* 亲密地；私下地

例：He did not feel he had got to know them intimately.

    他觉得自己不必和他们亲密熟悉。

strive /straɪv/ *v.* 努力；力争

搭：strive for 为……奋斗

例：You should strive for increasing your endurance and your strength.

    你应该努力提高你的耐力和力量。

近：struggle

lip /lɪp/ *n.* 嘴唇；开口；容器边缘

例：How did you split your lip?

    你怎么把嘴唇划破了？

enroll /ɪnˈrəʊl/ *v.* 登记；使加入

例：The university plans to enroll four doctoral students starting next year.

    大学计划从明年开始招收4名博士生。

派：enrollment *n.* 登记；入学

adept /əˈdept/ *adj.* 熟练的，擅长的

搭：be adept at 擅长……

例：The author is adept at depicting vast scenes.

作者很善于描写大的场面。

近：proficient

dilemma /dɪˈlemə/ *n.* 窘境；困境

搭：in a dilemma 进退两难

例：They try to find a way out of their dilemma.

他们试图摆脱困境。

近：plight

overreaction /ˌəʊvəriˈækʃn/ *n.* 过度反应

例：A result is a growing risk of overreaction and conflict.

结果就是，过度反应和冲突的风险不断增加。

7. 【答案】B

【出题类型】词义辨析

【解析】A选项意为"追求；追赶；执行"；B选项意为"练习；实践"；C选项意为"知道，了解"；D选项意为"培训，训练"。选项均为动词，结合空格后的"their skills in real-life situations"，所以B选项正确。句意为"实践课为学生提供在真实场景中实践技能的机会"。

8.

【答案】B

【材料类型】通知

【选项翻译】

A 人们可以背诵任何词汇作为参加背诵挑战的一部分。

B 只有特定的人可以参加背诵挑战。

C 所有参加背诵挑战的人都会获得奖项。

【解析】本则通知首句提到"Spring reciting challenge for library members aged 10~18.（10~18岁的图书馆会员可参加春季背诵挑战。）"，可知该挑战的参加者有特定的范围，所以B选项正确。

通知的第二句提到"Choose from the attached word list.（从后附的词汇表中选取单词。）"，可知背诵的词汇有特定的范围，所以A选项错误。通知第三句提到"You'll get a certificate for every 100 words you recite and a prize if you recite 500 words.（背诵100个单词会获得证书，背诵500个单词会获得奖品。）"，可知获得奖品需要背诵一定数目的单词，所以C选项错误。

9.

> **试题详解**

（1）【答案】C

【出题类型】词义辨析

【解析】A选项意为"修饰，美化"；B选项意为"美化"；C选项意为"改善，改良"；D选项意为"装修，装饰"。根据本句中的"environment-friendly"，可知本句表达的是让建筑的性能得以提高，C选项最符合语境，所以C选项正确。本句意为"他们也掌握着改善当前环境状态的权力"。

（2）【答案】B

【出题类型】内容理解

【解析】本句中的"environment-friendly"与空格处并列，A选项意为"可支持的"；B选项意为"可持续的"；C选项意为"柔韧的，易曲折的"；D选项意为"可弯曲的"。分析可知，B选项能够与"environment-friendly"并列，表示建筑优越的性能，所以B选项正确。本句意为"由于他们的技术和设计策略可以使建筑结构更加可持续、更具环境友好性"。

（3）【答案】A

【出题类型】词义辨析

【解析】A选项意为"奇迹，让人惊奇的事物或人"；B选项意为"感觉，意义"；C选项意为"器具"；D选项意为"责任，义务"。结合空格后出现的"monuments"（纪念碑），可知空格处内容应该与其并列，所以A选项正确。本句意为"一个地区的建筑奇观或纪念碑使其独一无二、易于辨识"。

（4）【答案】D

【出题类型】词义辨析

【解析】A选项意为"显著的；看得见的"；B选项意为"可察觉的"；C选项意为"可比较的"；D选项意为"可区分的"。空格前出现了"unique"（独一无二的），可知本处旨在强调建筑特征鲜明的性质，所以D选项正确。本句意为"一个地区的建筑奇观或纪念碑使其独一无二、易于辨识"。

（5）【答案】C

【出题类型】词义辨析

【解析】A选项为"sprint"的现在分词形式，意为"冲刺，疾速奔跑"；B选项是"limp"的现在分词形式，意为"跛行"；C选项为"gallop"的现在分词形式，意为"飞迅发展"；D选项是"propel"的现在分词形式，意为"推动"。空格处内容应该能与"urbanization"搭配，C选项与之搭配最为合理，表示城市化的迅速，所以C选项正确。本句意为"此外，建筑师可以尝试通过设计一个和谐的物体——空间环境来保护这个星球上剩下的任何东西，在这个环境中，建筑元素代表着为抵消过快的城市化带来的不利后果的努力"。

➢ 全文翻译

成为一名建筑师的意义

建筑师不只是设计结构；他们为用户和下一代创造了完整的体验。有人告诉他们，他们的设计可能对用户的心态和心理健康产生各种影响。由于他们的技术和设计策略可以使建筑结构更加可持续、更具环境友好性，他们也掌握着改善当前环境状态的权力。一个地区的建筑奇观或纪念碑使其独一无二、易于辨识。此外，建筑师可以尝试通过设计一个和谐的物体——空间环境来保护这个星球上剩下的任何东西，在这个环境中，建筑元素代表着为抵消过快的城市化带来的不利后果的努力。

➢ 词汇笔记

exert /ɪɡ'zɜːt/ *v.* 运用；施加

搭：exert oneself to 努力；尽力

例：In order to be successful he would have to exert himself.

为了成功，他必须努力。

派：exertion *n.* 努力；运用

mindset /'maɪndset/ *n.* 观念模式；思维倾向

例：People need develop a fixed mindset.

人们需要养成一种固定的思维模式。

近：mentality

monument /'mɒnjumənt/ *n.* 纪念碑；古迹

例：A monument was erected in the spuare.

一座纪念碑矗立在广场上。

派：monumental *adj.* 巨大的；不朽的

spatial /'speɪʃl/ *adj.* 空间的

例：They prefer to use more spatial language.

他们更喜欢使用更多的空间语言。

neutralize /ˈnjuːtrəlaɪz/ *v.* 抵消；中和；使中立

例：Acids neutralize alkalis and vice versa.

酸能使碱中和，碱亦能使酸中和。

派：neutralization *n.* 中和反应；中和作用

近：counteract

adverse /ˈædvɜːs/ *adj.* 不利的；相反的

搭：adverse effect 不利影响；副作用

例：If an adverse reaction to a drug is serious, consult your doctor at once.

如果对药物的不良反应严重，你就要立即咨询医生。

派：adversity *n.* 逆境；厄运

近：detrimental